THE BANKER LADIES

Vanguards of Solidarity Economics and Community-Based Banks

All over the world, Black and racialized women engage in the solidarity economy through what is known as mutual aid financing. Formally referred to as rotating savings and credit associations (ROSCAs), these institutions are purposefully informal to support the women's livelihoods and social needs, and they act to reject tiered forms of neo-liberal development. *The Banker Ladies* – a term coined by women in the Black diaspora – are individuals that voluntarily organize ROSCAs for self-sufficiency and are intentional in their politicized economic co-operation to counter business exclusion.

Caroline Shenaz Hossein reveals how Black women redefine the banking co-operative sector to be inclusive of informal institutions that are democratic and focused on group consensus, and which build an activist form of economic co-operation that is intent on making social profitability the norm. The book examines the ways in which diasporic Black women, who organize mutual aid, receive little to no attention.

Unapologetically biased towards a group of women who have been purposely sidelined and put down for what they do, *The Banker Ladies* highlights how, in order to educate oneself about their contributions to politics and economics, it is imperative to listen to the voices of hundreds of Black women in charge of financial services for their communities.

CAROLINE SHENAZ HOSSEIN is an associate professor of Global Development and Political Economy at the University of Toronto Scarborough; Canada Research Chair, Tier 2 of Africana Development and Feminist Political Economy; and Founder of the Diverse Solidarity Economies (DISE) Collective.

THE BANKER LADIES

Vanguards of Solidarity Economics and Community-Based Banks

Caroline Shenaz Hossein

UNIVERSITY OF TORONTO PRESS
Toronto Buffalo London

© University of Toronto Press 2024
Toronto Buffalo London
utorontopress.com
Printed and bound by CPI Group (UK) Ltd, Croydon, CR0 4YY

ISBN 978-1-4875-1783-0 (EPUB)
ISBN 978-1-4875-5703-4 (paper)
ISBN 978-1-4875-1782-3 (PDF)

Library and Archives Canada Cataloguing in Publication

Title: The banker ladies : vanguards of solidarity economics and community-based
   banks / Caroline Shenaz Hossein.
Names: Hossein, Caroline Shenaz, 1971–, author.
Description: Includes bibliographical references and index.
Identifiers: Canadiana (print) 20240338448 | Canadiana (ebook) 20240338464 |
   ISBN 9781487557034 (paper) | ISBN 9781487517823 (PDF) |
   ISBN 9781487517830 (EPUB)
Subjects: LCSH: Rotating credit associations – Social aspects. |
   LCSH: Rotating credit associations – Political aspects. |
   LCSH: Women, Black – Economic conditions.
Classification: LCC HG2035 .H67 2024 | DDC 334/.2 – dc23

Cover design: Lara Minja
Cover image: Mali Gabriela Souto Reiter

The Diverse Solidarity Economies (DISE) Collective is made up of feminist scholars
focused on excluded groups in the Global North and Global South who seek refuge
in the solidarity and social economy ecosystem because of systemic sexism, racism,
casteism, and other forms of business and financial exclusion. Members of the DISE
Collective provided support for this book. See more about the DISE Collective at
https://africanaeconomics.com/.

We wish to acknowledge the land on which the University of Toronto Press
operates. This land is the traditional territory of the Wendat, the Anishnaabeg, the
Haudenosaunee, the Métis, and the Mississaugas of the Credit First Nation.

This book has been published with the help of a grant from the Federation for the
Humanities and Social Sciences, through the Awards to Scholarly Publications Program,
using funds provided by the Social Sciences and Humanities Research Council of Canada.

The book also draws on research supported by the Social Sciences and Humanities
Research Council: SSHRC Insight Development Grant no. 430-2017-00691. This
research was undertaken, in part, thanks to funding from the Canada Research Chairs
Program: Canada Research Chair in Africana Development and Feminist Political
Economy (Tier 2).

University of Toronto Press acknowledges the financial support of the Government of
Canada, the Canada Council for the Arts, and the Ontario Arts Council, an agency of
the Government of Ontario, for its publishing activities.

Canada Council   Conseil des Arts
for the Arts   du Canada

ONTARIO ARTS COUNCIL
CONSEIL DES ARTS DE L'ONTARIO

an Ontario government agency
un organisme du gouvernement de l'Ontario

Funded by the   Financé par le
Government   gouvernement
of Canada   du Canada

This book is dedicated to the hundreds of Black women in Ethiopia, Benin, Brazil, Ghana, the United States, Ireland, Canada, and the Caribbean who taught me about the essence of mutual aid and business co-operation. These women co-operators made it clear to me that community-based banks such as ROSCAs are at the core of any people-led solidarity economy. And that there is theory making to be found in those very spaces will set us free. The work done by the Banker Ladies gave me the courage to continue pursuing this line of research, even when it was stressful to do so as an academic. It is to members of the Banker Ladies Council, who bravely chose to create a ROSCA Federation, that I dedicate this book to. Blessings to all women who give their labour to building ROSCAs – financial economies rooted in feminist virtues of mutuality, trust, and reciprocity – and who receive no just compensation for this contribution in economic development.

For Shayan and Amba, who make me happy every day.

Contents

Illustrations

Tables

Women's Empowerment through Wealth Creation

AFUA COOPER

Professor in the Departments of History and Sociology and Social Anthropology, Dalhousie University, Halifax, Nova Scotia, Canada

I grew up in East Central Kingston, Jamaica, with my aunt, Elfleda Campbell. She was a Banker Lady. Once a week, persons from near and far, mainly women, would come to our house to "throw their hand" for the Pardner that they and my aunt had established. These women trusted my aunt to keep their money safe. Because the banker was often in charge of large sums of money.

When the women would come to our house to pay their hand, my aunt would often invite them to eat, and they chit-chatted, gossiped, and spoke about their troubles and triumphs until it was time to go. A Pardner then was not only about the money; it was also a way to create community.

Eventually, one by one, each woman would receive her "draw," the sum of all the monies put in the "bank" by everyone who participated. And the Pardner would continue because it was a rotating system of credit and wealth creation. A Pardner draw could be used to purchase property, assist in constructing a church, help offset children's school fees, buy plane tickets, open a business, and help in the payment of wedding receptions, funerals, and fines.

There was a time when my aunt ceased being a Banker Lady and became one of the Pardners. At another time, she joined a Pardner where the Chief Banker Lady lived at the other end of the city, in a place called Cassia Park Road. Once a week, after school, my aunt gave me money for her hand. It was my job to deliver the money to the banker, which I did by taking two buses from my home and across the city. Once I delivered my aunt's hand, I would play with the banker's children until it started to get dark. It never occurred to me to ask my aunt why she chose a Pardner so far from our home in East Central Kingston. But that is not the point. The point is that my aunt was always in a Pardner whether as a banker or one of the hands. For women like her, that was a common thing. Everyone I knew, including the men in my family, belonged to a Pardner. Children, too, often had their own Pardner. At the primary school I attended, some of the students organized a Pardner; I had a hand in it, while another girl in my class was the banker. The weekly hand was something our pocket could afford, such as funds taken from our lunch monies. The draw was $5. I got my draw eventually and was very happy with it.

Pardner was my introduction to the world of money, and women and money – away from official banks and other financial institutions. Little did I realize that as a child involved in a Pardner in several ways, it would impact my consciousness with regards to gender and wealth creation, and money empowerment. I *saw* women controlling large sums of money and bettering their lives with this money – and empowering other women to do the same. Migrating to Canada, I also discovered that the practice travelled with Jamaican immigrants, performing similar monetary functions as in Jamaica. And like in Jamaica, its practitioners were mainly women.

Using a Black feminist and Caribbean framework, Caroline Shenaz Hossein in her book, *The Banker Ladies*, has shone the spotlight on Black and racialized women in Canada and the Caribbean actively participating in a Pardner (or Susu, or Boxhand, as it is called in some Caribbean communities). She has also given voice to the experiences of the women she has written about, and to women like my aunt and her Pardner collaborators.

With great care and deliberation, Hossein has told the story of the Rotating Savings and Credit Associations (ROSCAs), and delineated how women participants – as both bankers and pardners – have created an alternate economy based on respect, mutual regard, and in the case of financial independence, wealth creation in line with the fourth principle of *Kwanzaa* – Co-operative Economics. ROSCAs are important for Black/African descent women in Canada and beyond. Oftentimes, these women are unable to qualify for loans from mainstream banks and other financial institutions because they are not deemed "worthy." Instead of seeing their dreams die on the vine, ROSCA women take charge of them and their family's financial life by turning to the empowering money system they have known all their lives – Pardner, or Susu. In so doing, these women create "financial services for their communities" (4) and thereby defy the racist, exclusionary nature of financial institutions, such as banks.

Over the course of the past five centuries, Black women's work, labour, and intellectual capital have been stolen from them and pressed into the service of Europeans. If the wealth stolen from Black women during centuries of enslavement were to be quantified, it would run into trillions of dollars. The irony in all of this is that in 1834, for example, after British slavery was abolished and the enslaved gained emancipation, it was *slaveowners* who were given monetary compensation by the British government for the loss of their property. The British government, knowing that Black bondspeople were capital, made sure white enslavers received reimbursement – and to the tune of £45 million (the equivalent of £34 billion today).[1] The slaves themselves, who did all the work to make whites and Britain rich, received nothing. From the British point of view, their "freedom" was enough compensation.

Black families had to start a new life from scratch – and in post-slavery societies where they were (still) at the bottom of the socioeconomic ladder. To survive and "outthink and outflank" the owners of the world,[2] Black women turned to co-operative

---

1 The official story is that the British paid the slaveowners £20 million. But most of the enslaved, come 1 August 1834, had to work for free for another four years under the "Apprenticeship" system. The free labour they provided slaveowners during these four years amounted to a further £25 million.

2 This quote is from the 1930 address, "Education and Work," found in W.E.B. Du Bois (1973, 77).

economics. With their families, they established mutual aid societies, farming co-operatives, and ... Pardners (Susu). These former slaves turned to money traditions rooted in their African ancestral heritage to break the bonds of a capitalist system that has little regard for Black people.

Hossein's work is courageous. Facing legal threats and belittlement from academia and mainstream finance alike, she created, by focusing on ROSCAs, an epistemology of care, respect, and power. It is an epistemology grounded in the exigencies of the daily lives of women impacted by migration, racism, sexism, poverty, and linguistic discrimination. Hossein has placed Black women at the centre of an inquiry in which they themselves are the main knowledge creators.

In this era of capitalism gone mad with high and ever-rising inflation and interest rates, Caroline Shenaz Hossein and the women leading ROSCAs have given us a money model that works for women and working people. That this model comes from poor, Black/African and/or racialized women, speaks to the radical and liberatory praxis of ROSCAs. *The Banker Ladies* is destined to become the definitive text of an emancipatory feminist economics. And for this I thank Dr. Hossein.

Preface

This book has been many years in the making. I have been formally presenting on the topic of informal co-operative banks and rotating savings and credit associations (ROSCAs) since 2010. I devote my life's work to democratizing the economy and finance – because it is an important challenge for our world today. As an immigrant child, I have been thinking about localized money systems (called rotating savings and credit associations, or ROSCAs) all my life because I have seen how cultural financial goods passed on from generation to generation allows excluded people to achieve their livelihood needs. The women I know have always engaged in ROSCAs, usually the Caribbean form known as Boxhand or Susu. These ROSCAs are a well-known tradition. Migrating to the United States and Canada can be a struggle, and Black people who come here turn inwards to form ROSCAs to cope with livelihood needs and to build community along the way.

Business exclusion in a sexist and racist society can, in a peculiar way, bond people of the same race, gender, and/or socio-economic background to form their own banking co-operatives (Vélez-Ibáñez 1983). I have always felt personally connected to the Banker Ladies that I have been interviewing for over a decade because of my own life story.

What I now choose to share with the world is a family secret. My family remains broken in so many ways because of this pain. In 1984, when I was 13 years old, my father attempted suicide. His pain was the result of working in one of the six big banks in

Canada. I remember to this day what happened like it was yesterday and I still to this day carry this pain and shame. We were living at 19 Castle Rock Drive in Richmond Hill, a suburb north of Toronto. I opened the garage to put my bike away – only to find the place full of smoke and reeking of gasoline. My father was unconscious in his car. My mother called the ambulance, scolded me, and sent me to my room as they dealt with grown up matters. I remember visiting my father at the hospital. As a family we have never spoken about that incident. I believe it is this episode that has created a tension in the family that has endured to this very day. I buried this story for 40 years because of the shame, but for me letting go of the pain means telling this story as my story too. This personal story speaks to why my body of work on advancing economic justice matters so much to me.

After my father lost his job and needed time to recover, my mother became the breadwinner. Even with this support, the family was instantly thrown into a precarious financial state that lasted for quite some time. We eventually had to sell our house and move again. This time it was to Empringham Drive near McLevin Avenue in Malvern of Scarborough, the east end of Toronto. Growing up, I can recall living in eight or nine different places in the Greater Toronto Area, from Downsview to Richmond Hill to Malvern, then to Vaughan towards the end of my high school years when my parents bought a house in a new subdivision. This kind of moving around is typical for immigrant families and especially those who are unskilled with no university degrees. The one constant in my life was the cultural goods of self-help groups, and the social solidarity economy, which allowed us to meet our cash flow needs and build camaraderie with the community.

Collectivity is a form of business survival for many people, and it also works as an antidote to the societal exclusion endured by many people of colour. Political scientist Cedric Robinson's (1983) concept of racial capitalism explains why certain groups have felt so alienated by capital. The 2020 Black Lives Matter protests also remind us that these kinds of traumas are why informal institutions are so valuable to the African diaspora. Mohawk scholar and activist Patricia Monture (2010) points out that scholars who have experienced barriers should know that their own experiences can count as part of knowledge making. I am no longer ashamed of my lived experience; it is the reason I do what I do. My experience has emboldened me to find the diverse financial economies where Black and racialized people, hardened by a racist economy, are able to propose new economies that are truly diverse and inclusive.

Before turning to academia, I worked for 16 years as a practitioner in the field of international development to work on economic inequality issues, and the barriers to finance. I am still stunned that so many unqualified people – often young, rich, and white – masquerade as "experts" in this field though they are completely detached from what it means to be an immigrant or an excluded person in Canada, let alone in other parts of the world. Black and racialized women who have many years of community development expertise by ways of organizing ROSCAs are overlooked for what they do, even as they speak on behalf of marginalized women.

During my time as a practitioner, I was influenced most by an international non-governmental organization (NGO) out of Philadelphia called OIC International. It was led by African Americans and founded by the late Reverend Leon Sullivan, a civil rights activist (Sullivan 1969). What I learned from African Americans was how to do business equitably. At OIC International, they believed in co-opting the white man's money (also known as foreign aid) to help brothers and sisters in Africa. That is how we viewed development from a Black-led organization. This training made me mindful of the biased allocations that occur when monies are distributed. My personal journey of growing up in precarity, combined with this knowledge of how to co-opt goods for a new kind of co-operative economy, informs my research. My research is unapologetically biased toward the co-operative model, especially co-ops that are informal, since Black women co-operators undo the fixation on market fundamentalism to show there are other ways to do business. Yet they have been maligned for this collectivity.

For the past 11 years, I have been writing about Black people in both the Global South and the Global North – with a focus on women – who engage in "alternative" financial systems. I use quotations around the term "alternative" because these collaborative economic systems are not new but rather ancient systems rooted in reciprocity and mutual aid. Excluded people draw on collective economies for their own personal needs in order to survive. However, they also do so because these systems speak to belonging and caring for one another and addressing their traumas. I know, having lived through it as a child, the harms that business exclusion can cause a family. I saw firsthand how the system alienates people of colour who only want to improve their standard of living. After losing his job at the bank, one of my father's many business ventures was a haberdashery shop on Eglinton West, a well-known corridor back in the 1980s for Jamaican and Caribbean businesses. When I worked in his shop, I saw how small businesses struggled. I learned then that money pooling systems of Susu, Meeting Turn, and Partner save Caribbean people from debt and bankruptcy.

These experiences compelled me to tell a story about development, co-operatives, and mutual aid from a Black feminist economist perspective. Finding that voice has taken me a long time – mostly because what we say, as Black and Caribbean people, is scrutinized more closely than what others say. As an untenured academic (2012–16), writing on ROSCAs proved a harrowing experience. My work was undermined by many of those with whom I worked because it was viewed as "popular" or "not serious" academic work. I was denied the opportunity to teach a foundational introduction course on the "Social Economy" because some of the white men (who specialized in formal co-operatives) worried that my introduction of informal co-operative systems – and my nod to the contributions of Global South people to knowledge making in the solidarity economies – would unravel their life's work.

More threatening to some of these detractors was my ability to draw on Black feminist economic theorizing to understand the co-operative sector. White academics were not supportive; in order to understand informal institutions, the European theory they knew needed to be combined with local theory too. Difficulties arose when I chose intentionally to focus on the abundance of Black political economy theory (see Gordon Nembhard 2023 for a detailed analysis). Like so many Black feminist political economists, our work is often left uncited and ignored. The research on the Canadian Banker Ladies particularly troubled white scholars working in the field because it exposed discrimination against Black women in the social economy. Moreover, it blatantly revealed how the social economy turns a blind eye to informal co-operative users. Many anti-development scholars, blinkered by European Marxism, rejected my work because they were not willing to see that self-help groups led by Black women did not conform to bootstrap politics. My research pushed against the idea of self-help as a coping mechanism, situating self-help on one's own terms as a liberating practice. I was warned numerous times by social justice warrior-types that women using ROSCAs were usually engaged in "illegal" activities. Again, there was no understanding before the pandemic that the Banker Ladies would choose solidarity systems over subsidies and a charitable model. They failed to see how African-descended women, focused on self-reliance, could mobilize goods on their own terms.

For years some of my colleagues at York University made me feel like I was less than a scholar because I studied informal, member-owned institutions and purposefully used feminist economic theory that reflected the lived experience of the Black women co-operators whom I studied. Several white colleagues made it abundantly clear to me and my students that ROSCAs have no place in the co-operative sector. In fact, students were told that they would get a zero grade if they submitted papers on such a topic. During one fall course I taught, a male graduate student informed me that his mentors felt that my work did not examine "real" institutions because such institutions were informal. Even within critical development spaces there are blind spots when it comes to Black co-operators. In 2021, my community partner of Jamaican ancestry was vilified by my former employer with insinuations of fraud because she and her organization trained women on the Partner banking system. I had to intervene on her behalf to stop the harm.

These kinds of anecdotal experiences are an indictment of the design of a Black Social Economy. ROSCAs are ignored in development studies or treated as a sideshow; the scholars who work on these topics are sidelined and their work dismissed. Co-operative "fanatics" only count formalized co-operatives as useful; indeed, they write entire books about the global co-operative sector from this premise, silencing informal solidarity institutions.[1] I now understand that they viewed my work as subversive because it amplified the role of Black and African-descended women in finance and development.

Scholars, and particularly women scholars who want to work on informal institutions, should be aware of the grave risks involved for those of us who do this research within academe. After nearly a decade of fighting to do my research, I filed a provincial human rights complaint against my former university. I now know that my work on ROSCAs felt threatening to white faculty who wanted co-operative economics to be expressed in a certain way. It has been hard to deal with the amount of trolling I have experienced, and the hostile reactions to my public writings and comments on social media in defense of ROSCAs and mutual aid systems. Nevertheless, my experience as an academic concerned about ROSCAs and informal institutions has made me acutely aware that this body of research is needed.

Times are Changing

The COVID-19 lockdown, which exposed humanity's vulnerabilities, along with the Black Lives Matter protests, helped me clarify my message. In this era of ineffective commercial systems, mutual aid and informal collectives are assisting vulnerable people. Being in a lockdown during the pandemic confirmed for me (and for all of us) that we are indeed interconnected – something that women in the Black diaspora have always said. The Black Lives Matter movement has helped people to understand better anti-Black racism and why Black people have kept their co-operatives under

---

1 In this work, I use the term "social solidarity economy" and not "social economy" (which is widely used in Canada) because the former speaks to the liberatory fight for excluded people, which was carried out in the Global South.

wraps. Those once critical of ROSCAs and my concept of the Black Social Economy now invite me to give lectures at their associations and use this material in their courses.

There is growing understanding of mutual aid and informal co-operative economies, thanks in part to a global pandemic. Still, this research is not easy to carry out; so much of it is hidden from the public eye. Researching and writing about community-based ROSCAs takes time; the institutions are informal on purpose, while much of the academe continues to insist on formalized research. Being informal does not mean that there are no governance structures and accountability, and this book interrogates that understanding of informal institutions.

In 2023, the Bank of England Museum along with Museumand, the National Caribbean Heritage Museum launched a year-long exhibit about the value of community-based finance known as the Jamaican Partner to Caribbean immigrants – financial groups that offer a way to manage business exclusion and access credit. Going to see the *Pardner Hand* exhibit at the Bank of England in November 2023 was a crucial part of wrapping up this project, as it showed to me that these co-operative banking systems used by immigrants are being recognized by the country's major banker, which has never been done before. Since the 1940s, these ROSCA systems by the Windrush generation were forced to go underground because of a racially hostile environment. Partner and other like money pooling systems are being noted as helping newcomers to the UK to meet their daily needs.[2]

Canada has a lot to learn from Museumand, the National Caribbean Heritage Museum, and the Bank of England Museum about recognizing the role ROSCA systems have played in our economy. If one chooses to look at groups that rely on ROSCAs for their day-to-day livelihood needs, then one will learn quickly that these systems are protected – or hidden – from outsiders. ROSCA users are easier to find in the Caribbean because there is no fear involved in organizing these systems – unlike Canada,

---

2   See more about the story published in the *Guardian* newspaper at Sherwood (2023).

where Black women ROSCA organizers are justly fearful about disclosing information about what they do. This story is, first and foremost, about making known these collective mutual aid financial co-operatives among the Black diaspora, but my intent is also to use empirical research to influence public-policy thinking in Canada and beyond.

My Positionality

The reader will learn early on that my work falls outside of the mainstream, including the paradigms of the white Left and white feminism, both of which often ignore my line of research or get it wrong. I have taken on this work because I have been professionally victimized and marginalized. It is because of these experiences that I value what the Banker Ladies do. It is my own positionality and my life lived as a Black woman academic that connects me so deeply to the system of informal co-operatives led by Black and racialized women. I am a US-born woman of Black and Indo-Caribbean heritage who self-identifies as Black because few people in Toronto, Canada – where I was raised – know the meaning of a Dougla. My parents, who immigrated to Canada more than 50 years ago and had to struggle, found socio-cultural ties to be valuable. I name and shame white androcentric academic hubris and how these very academics produce knowledge on "alternatives" that seldom speaks to Black and racialized people's own lived experiences. This is why I do the work that I do.

This research has changed me. It has made me take note of my Grenadian-born maternal great-grandmother, Maude Gittens, who was a food vendor and well-respected Susu banker in Sangre Grande, Trinidad, for hundreds of women members. Her work as Chief Banker Lady was to create banking co-ops that met people's money needs; she cared about people in her community. This story was handed down to me as a child of the Caribbean diaspora. With this book, I am now telling the stories of the hundreds of women I interviewed, each of whom represents the many who came before them. All the women I meet who organize ROSCAs are admirable:

they are builders and they are co-operators. The Banker Ladies who organize ROSCAs are the vanguards of knowledge production in long-standing ideas such as mutual aid, self-help, and co-operation. They are growing the field of political economy for the African diaspora and feminists alike. We should be seeking out their wisdom and experience to bind and enrich society, and to help us think through how to transform exclusionary economic systems and make the world a better place for all people.

Acknowledgments

I am a Dougla. Few people in Canada know the meaning of this term, but Caribbean people do. It means that my bloodlines are both African and Indian. Some of my ancestors were enslaved and came from Africa (I do not know from where exactly) and some were indentured servants from India, possibly Bihar and Bengal. My ancestors laboured for colonizers under cruel conditions in various parts of the Caribbean – Guyana, Grenada, Trinidad, and St. Vincent. I choose to self-identify as a Black woman for many reasons, but mainly because of my mother, Jacqueline Pearline née Gittens (an Afro-Trinidadian-Vincentian-Grenadian), and my ties to the Caribbean community in Toronto.

So much credit goes to my mother and my father, Isaac Lorrington Hossein (an Indo-Guyanese Muslim). They have endured my questions about their mostly painful journey of migration, first to New York City in the 1960s, then on to Toronto more than 53 years ago. Much gratitude also goes to family members – especially my sister Annie, Jolanta, my family in NYC, and my in-laws, Anita Sen and Siddhartha Sen.

My husband Shayan and daughter Amba have travelled the world with me to support my research in the field. My girl would often play with the children of the women whom I was interviewing. It helped to humanize the work I do, and made a difference in the way people viewed me – I too was a mother. During my 2018–19 sabbatical year, my family came with me to Bahir Dar, Ethiopia; Thiruvananthapuram and Kolkata, India; and Bangkok, Thailand.

I travelled to these locations to share my work with scholars based in these regions and learn about what they do. It also gave me the quiet time I needed to write, to pore over hundreds of interviews, and to engage with scholars working on co-operatives, self-help, and mutual aid. For fieldwork, I travelled to many countries in the Caribbean, as well as Ghana and Ethiopia, and stayed in Montreal for long stints. My three-month sabbatical in Kuala Lumpur, Malaysia gave me the space to edit and revise a complete first draft. The process made me re-read my work in new ways, and allowed me time to contemplate other ways of being that are not focused on the Americas. Having my family wherever I go settles me. Their presence enables me to do my very best work.

I want to thank the hundreds of Chief Banker Ladies who trusted me to tell this story. These Banker Ladies are very special to me (and so many more not named): Mabinty, Laylah, Asha, Margot, Susan, Renée, Miss Betty, Gloria, Fardosa, Natla, Miss Paddy, Dragon, Ayesha, and Miss Charmaine. I am grateful for the brave women who joined the Banker Ladies Council in April 2022, and who are committed to building a ROSCA Federation. Professor Judith A. Teichman of the University of Toronto was right when she told me to put the ROSCA work to the side because there would be a time when I could write on the topic more fully, and people would be ready for it.

Doing work on informal institutions and those organized by Black women is doubly difficult in the fields of political science and economics, the two disciplines I straddle as a researcher and scholar. Feminist scholars have helped me more than they know in this political economy space and deserve a major vote of thanks: Sharon D. Wright Austin of the University of Florida; Lisa Aubrey of Arizona State University; Eudine Barriteau of the University of West Indies at Cave Hill; Bipasha Baruah of Western; Michelle Stack, UBC; Andy Paras, University of Guelph; Suzanne Bergeron at Dearborn; Bev Mullings of the University of Toronto; Naila Kabeer at LSE; Jessica Gordon Nembhard of the City University of New York (CUNY); Christabell P.J. of the University of Kerala; and Rebecca Sanders of Cincinnati University. Thank you for being my wonderful mentors and my sister-friends. Since my days in Jamaica, John Rapley, a fellow at Cambridge, has been an excellent sounding board for my ideas. I am also grateful to those outside of academe who keep me sane: Amina Ally, Nancy Nazer, Chello Rogers, Star Thurston, Khalid Ahmed, and Celine Cooper helped me during a very hard period. Members of the Diverse Solidarity Economies Collective (DISE), and the #GroupME anti-racist feminist group bravely pushed me and helped me build a space for support. Thanks to Mathew Forstater of the University of Missouri–Kansas City and Mike D. White of the College of Staten Island, CUNY, for making me see what I did was a paradigm shift. Nina Banks of Bucknell University and Jessica Gordon Nembhard of CUNY reminded me to own the concept of the Black Social Economy for which I am grateful. Fellow Caribbean sister Nia Evans of the Ujima Boston Co-operative, Tamela Block of NBCA/CLUSA, and Rickey Gard Diamond of An Economy of Our Own supported the Banker Ladies project from the get-go and welcomed this budding research into the co-operative sector.

The International Association of Feminist Economics (IAFEE) has been an amazing place to share ideas. Thank you IAFEE colleagues Lynda Pickbourn, Diane Elson, Nina Banks, Smriti Rao, Naila Kabeer, S. Charusheela, Ilene Grabel, Barbara Hopkins, Lyn Ossome, Lee Badgett, Alessandra Mezzadri, Rhonda V. Sharpe, Jackie Strenio, and so many others. I love these feminist economists! I would like to recognize colleagues from the National Conference of Black Political Scientists (NCOBPS), especially Sharon D. Wright Austin of the University of Florida, Tiffany Willoughby Herard, UCI, and Russell Benjamin of Northeastern Illinois University, who provided the support I needed at critical moments. I am thankful for my circle of friends who reviewed this manuscript early on: Haddy Njie of North Carolina State University (chapters 1–3), Christabell P.J. of the University of Kerala, Samuel Kwaku Bonsu (chapters 2 and 3), and Joshua Clarke Davis of the University of Baltimore. Thanks to members of the Community Economies Research Network (CERN) – Jenny Cameron, Katherine Gibson of Western Sydney University, and Kelly Dombroski of Massey University in New Zealand – for giving me a place to share my work early on when I was a new PhD.

Many people around the world assisted me in getting the interviews done. Thank you to my excellent research assistants over the past decade. In Kingston, Jamaica – Althea, Ackney, Wayne, Rasta Brian, Betty, and Mary; in St. George, Grenada – Belvine; in Port of Spain, Trinidad – Clayton and Panther; in Georgetown, Guyana – Shebeca; in Montreal, Canada – Amanda Whittaker, Amandine Guy, and Deborah Cherenfant; in Accra, Ghana – Kumiwaa Asante (in Makola market); in Toronto, Canada, a lot of wonderful souls, a mix of students and activists, made my work advance under tough circumstances – Celia McDougall, Maymun Abukar, Amber Aleman, Wesner Marcelin, Semhar Berhe, Arushi Dahiya, Amrith David, and Reena Shadaan. My then-PhD students carried out a careful literature review: Megan Pearson, Katherine Earnshaw, and Jane Lumumba from York University; James Patriquin from Carleton University; and Agnes Mochama, Serena Bahadur, Arushi Dahiya, and Adimu Mataru from the University of Toronto. Tatiane Reis, a MA student from Brazil at the time, translated *The Banker Ladies* film into Portuguese.

Ever since my graduate school days, Clive Y. Thomas of the Institute for Development Studies and Kadasi Ceres, Government Department at the University of Guyana, have shifted my thinking on local development. I thank all the activists in Guyana – many of whom I cannot name. I will always remember my friendship with the late political scientist Perry Mars, a true scholar of development politics in the Caribbean. In Haiti, Louis Herns Marcelin of the University of Miami, Wesner Marcelin (now in Toronto), and Suzy Castor of CRESFED advised me well; what I know about Haiti I credit to them. Samuel Kwaku Bonsu of the University of Ghana provided wonderful support during my research stay in the summer of 2017, and Susu expert professor Ellen Bortei-Doku Aryeetey was generous with her time. In Jamaica, Tony Harriott (now retired from the University of West Indies) always has time to read whatever I send his way, and continues to mentor me.

In my sabbatical year of 2018–19, I had time to rejuvenate my ideas among a vibrant group of academics in Bahir Dar, Ethiopia; Kolkata, Pune, and Thiruvananthapuram, India; and Bangkok, Thailand. In Ethiopia, I thank Abebe Zegeye of Woldia University and all my friends in Bahir Dar, as well as Fantu Cheru (now retired from American University) for daring to question things. Sajad Ibrahim at the University of Kerala and Arhendu Shekar Singh of Symbiosis University in Pune invited me to share my work in 2018. I am also grateful to Sanjukta Bhattacharya of Jadavpur University for inviting me to be a Visiting Fellow in Kolkata in 2018–19. In Bangkok, I was invited by my CERN colleague Istvan Rado to give a lecture on informal co-operative banks and community economies at Thammasat University in 2019.

In Montreal, I am grateful to Kari Polanyi Levitt and Ana Gomes for welcoming me to the Polanyi Institute for Political Economy during the summer of 2016. Dave McKenzie of Concordia's Molson Business School, and Anne Kettenbeil and Indu Krishnamurthy of Microcrédit Montréal (formerly ACME, a community-based credit association) were beacons of information, and helped link me to many people. Handwritten letters with newspaper clippings on Susu from Bajan-Canadian Margot Blackman, one of the most knowledgeable people on ROSCAs in Canada for the past 50+ years, were also helpful.

In Toronto, the women who make up the Banker Ladies Council – formed in spring 2022 – mean the world to me. Trevor Fortune, a community advocate for ROSCAs, has shared much useful material with me over the years. Many community practitioners deserve a vote of thanks for assisting me along the way: Esther Enyolu of Women's Multicultural Resource and Counselling Centre; Post Growth Institute; Omar Freilla of Collective Diaspora; good folks at the Ontario Co-operative Association; Sunder Singh of Elspeth Heyworth Centre for Women; Ginelle Skerritt, formerly of Warden Woods; and Paul Chamberlain of Toronto Enterprise Fund.

After joining the University of Toronto in 2021, and in the wake of launching a human rights complaint against my former employer in 2020, I was able to overcome the writer's block I had with this book. I am grateful for the care showed by former York colleagues while I was there: Anita Lam, Narda Razack, Meg Luxton, Aime Avolonto, Kamala Kempadoo, Carl James, Tokunbo Ojo, Leah Vosko, and the BUSO colleagues. I want to give special shoutouts to those always there for me at my new academic home: Notisha Massaquoi (sister-friend from way before UTSC), the "Bajan crew" also known as Beth Coleman and Kamari Clarke, Ito Peng, Bev Mullings, Judith A. Teichman, Anne-Emmanuelle Birn, Husseina Dinani, Alissa D. Trotz, Rafael Grohmann, Girish Daswani, Clelia Rodríguez, Wisdom Tettey, Kanta Murali, Leslie Chan, Paul Kingston, Irena Creed, Kevin Edmonds, and Joe Wong. A huge debt of gratitude to my new colleagues in the Department of Global Development Studies at UTSC, and the Graduate – Department of Political Science at the University of Toronto, St. George. As always, people in research services and the finance offices deserve so much thanks for their behind-the-scenes support: Viola Stylla, Francesca Andrade, Sue-Ann Hicks, Sharon George, Sarah Scott, Naomi Dachner, Carmen Sui, Andrea Hung, Joel Faber, and Amanda Pennington.

My gratitude to Professor Faye V. Harrison of the University of Illinois at Urbana-Champaign and Leonard Wantchekon of Princeton University for assisting me more than I can possibly thank them, and to Peggy Antrobus and her partner, Nan, for making room for what I do and seeing the value of Meeting Turn systems and co-ops during my trip to Barbados. I am deeply indebted to two scholars whom I admire, Afua Cooper of Dalhousie University and Eudine Barriteau of the University of the West Indies at Cave Hill (recently retired), who gave a special tribute situating this work in and outside of the Caribbean in a way that matters for Black diaspora women. Thanks also to Lakshmi Ramarajan and Robin Ely at the Harvard Business School for sharing research on ROSCAs at the 2023 symposium on Tools for Humanity.

I am indebted to the online groups (especially the "Binders Full of Black Women and Black Nonbinary People" on Facebook) and various podcasts that helped me think through my ideas, particularly during the pandemic when I felt lost: "Frontiers on Commoning" with David Bollier; "Everything Co-op" with Vernon Oakes; *The Dig* with Daniel Denvir; and "Hear to Slay" with Roxane Gay and Dr. Tressie McMillan Cottom. All have stretched me in new ways. At the Association of Social Economics, Mark D. White of Staten Island University and especially the late Cecilia Winters helped me to secure permission from Taylor & Francis to reprint sections of the article on Money Pools that appeared in the *Forum for Social Economics*. Canada's doyen of the social economy, the late Jack Quarter, made space for me in the Association of Non-profits and the Social Economy Research (ANSER) – our monthly lunches at the Beaches Cafe are cherished memories. I am thankful for the comradery of Derya Tarhan at the University of Guelph and Laurie Mook of Arizona State University for welcoming me to ANSER.

In the beginning, when I had no money for my work, I would self-finance my research. Eventually money did come in, and these funds enabled me to expand my scope of study and train students. I am grateful for the first seed money I received from the Association of Social Economics' Walter Grant, which gave me the means to carry out an early set of focus group discussions in Toronto and Montreal (2015–16). My 2017–20 SSHRC Insight Development Grant, titled *African Origins in the Social Economy*, funded my travel to research sites, paid for my assistants in the later years, and helped expand my work in Canada, Ghana, and Ethiopia. Thank you to the following funders: the Canada Research Chair program for my Canada Research Chair in Africana Development and Feminist Political Economy (Tier 2); the Government of Ontario for an Ontario Early Researcher Award; and the Co-operators Group for yearly research grants. Andria Barrett and members of the Banker Ladies Council and Jennifer Ross of the Ontario Co-operative Association have worked hard to advance Black women's co-operation in Canada.

My two-time editor at the University of Toronto Press, Jennifer DiDomenico, believed in my project and waited on me as I got this work done. The entire team at UTP was so thorough and a joy to work with, including Mary Lui, associate managing editor; Adebe DeRango-Adem, copy editor; Mylinh Hamlington, indexer; Ashley Bernicky, production coordinator; Lucille Miranda, marketing manager; Stephanie Mazza, product marketing specialist; Kristjan Buckingham, advertising and graphic design coordinator; and Jessica Carter, publishing assistant. I am indebted to four anonymous reviewers who gave me five rounds of reviews; I am humbled by the time they took during a pandemic to read this work, and this review process has made a substantial contribution to this work. My lawyer Morgan Sim made it possible for me to move on in a safe way and to be able to complete this manuscript. Jane Springer gave the manuscript a very good proofreading after the second round of reviews and Janet Friskney read the penultimate version of the manuscript for infelicities of style. I now have a piece of work that I am truly proud of because all these communities that I belonged to helped to sharpen my thinking. All errors in this book are mine alone and I am sorry for any oversights.

Abbreviations

AFIs	Alternative finance institutions
CERN	Community Economies Research Network
co-op or coop	co-operative
GIMPA	Ghana Institute for Management and Public Administration
ICA	International Cooperative Alliance
MMD	Mata Masu Dubara
NJM	New Jewel Movement (Grenada)
NGOs	non-governmental organizations
NPOs	non-profit organizations
ROSCAs	rotating savings and credit associations
UN	United Nations
UNDP	United Nations Development Programme
USAID	United States Agency for International Development
VSLAs	Village and Savings Loans Associations

THE BANKER LADIES

Valuing the Informal

Many scholars who write about "alternatives" are not ready for the pluriverse envisioned by Arturo Escobar (2020), nor willing to take note of what the African diaspora and Indigenous peoples have done collectively to lead effective and sustainable development efforts. Exceptions are Barker, Bergeron, and Feiner (2021), a group of feminist economists whose second edition of *Liberating Economics* argues that viable plural economies may indeed provide better outcomes for structurally disadvantaged groups. Western experts often impart their own "knowledge" without considering how the communities to which they travel have their own models for what their development should be. Local perspectives are not inferior (Hall 1992). The local innovations of local people are situated practice; it is what they feel they can do to respond to their daily needs (Amin 2009).

Some local innovations are informal institutions. They are known by vernacular terms that mean something to the members who create these institutions. Have you heard of Ajo, Osusu, Sandooq, Altin, Partner, Chit, or Arisan? These are the cultural names for member-owned institutions – or banking co-operatives – used by people around the world. Other institutional names include Ghana's Susu, the Chinese Hua, and Sri Lanka's Cheetu (Low 1995). These co-operative banks are known by academics as rotating savings and credit associations (ROSCAs). (I also use the terms money pools, self-help groups, co-operatives, and banking co-ops interchangeably with ROSCAs.) ROSCAs are hidden forms of co-operatives that Black/African descent women – and many diverse groups – practice in Canada, the United States, the Caribbean, and elsewhere in our world.

Many of the women I met while doing my research have engaged in ROSCAs their whole lives – indeed, ROSCAs are a tradition among African diasporic groups. Migrating to another country is a struggle; when people move, they turn inwards to form ROSCAs to address livelihood-related needs as well as to build friendships and form ties with people in their new lands. For this reason, ROSCAs are seen as a form of mutual aid: people can count on others for financial assistance as well as for social connections. The racism and exclusion immigrants encounter in their new countries can, in a peculiar way, bond them with people of the same race and socio-economic background (Vélez-Ibáñez 1983). The co-operative banks they form are made up of voluntary members who, together, decide on the rules and make regular contributions to a fund that is later given either in whole or in part to each member in turn. Ordinary people jointly create the rules according to the interests of their members.

Black women in charge of these financial services for their communities – known as the Banker Ladies – have much to teach us through their contributions to politics and economics. A long-standing saying in the Black Muslim community (among American Muslims especially) holds that "politics without economics is symbol without substance." This adage suggests that politics and voice is limited if people are struggling economically (Farrakhan 2019). The Banker Ladies are the vanguards, the keepers, and saviours of mutual aid and economic co-operation because they demonstrate the ability to build and mobilize capital from within society and achieve it from inside of a group. In *Reversed Realities*, development scholar Naila Kabeer (1994) explained three decades ago that "power within" is a vital concept for marginalized women because they are the ones who can band together to bring sustained changes in society. The Banker Ladies whom I have studied for years know full well that, without economic clout, little can be done to bring lasting change to their communities. The Banker Ladies are aware that any change to their position or status in society must work in tandem with internal collective organization.

The Banker Ladies are building financial solidarities for racially marginalized people using inherited business traditions – they know from the women who came before them that, to be free, you need a livelihood. In her work examining Jamaican partner banks in the United States using a Black feminist lens, Dianne Stewart (2007) notes that the Banker Ladies do not compete over how to make business inclusive; instead, they set out quietly and pragmatically to do the work as a group. They collect monies in their locales through networks of camaraderie, friendship, and trust, often in low- and middle-income communities. The ROSCA systems that the Banker Ladies organize are purposefully gendered. It is not the case that men do not organize ROSCAs; they do. My point is that ROSCAs are crucial to women and worthy of academic research. Caribbean feminist economist Eudine Barriteau (2003) argues that a feminist analysis must be applied to research focused on women's work. It is unfortunate when male scholars who write about ROSCAs fail to invoke feminist economic theorizing in investigating a phenomenon that is clearly led by women (Barton 2000).

For generations, Black and African descent women have taught one another how to save and lend to each other co-operatively and outside of formal institutions.[1] During the COVID-19 lockdown in April 2021, one of my community partners familiar with ROSCAs in Toronto's west end proposed we launch a Partner Savings (Jamaican name for a ROSCA) workshop for young women using my funding for social innovations within the Black Social Economy. Hiring Banker Ladies to offer training on a Partner Bank was a trying process because university financial personnel would scrutinize my projects and insinuate that my Banker Ladies were "frauds." I think it was viewed this way because the idea of Black

---

1 I use the terms "Black people," "African-descended people," and "people of the African diaspora" or "of African descent" interchangeably, to refer to people who consider themselves part of the African diaspora and who have a lineage to Africa. For usages of the word Black to refer to a group of people, the "B" is always capitalized (Coleman 2020).

women teaching others about money systems is "unknown" to most people. The perception that ROSCAs are a form of "fraud" is commonplace. Whether intentional or not, this negative framing reveals an example of systemic racism at work, one in which white (and typically cis-het male) people refuse to see the Banker Ladies as equipped to lead financial training sessions. Such responses from university administrators undermines my body of work acknowledging informal co-operatives of people of the Black/African diaspora.

This book, *The Banker Ladies*, will demonstrate that ROSCAs are indeed co-operatives – and anything but underdeveloped. Millions of people around the world are participating in the ROSCA system. In fact Grassroots Finance Action, using the World Bank's (2021) Findex21 report, estimates that there are at least 419 million ROSCA users in the Global South amassing between 50–100 billion in savings (Ashe 2023). That is a lot of people choosing to self-organize and to assist one another through informal co-operative banks. Given the deep-seated exclusion felt by certain groups, or people who do not trust commercial banks, ROSCAs must often function underground, as noted in the Canadian case in this book. Forming co-operative banks informally is one way to push back against an elitist Babylon (Jamaican word for establishment) and a racial capitalist system.

The Banker Ladies in Canada hide what they do because of systemic anti-Black racism and violence. Toronto Metropolitan University professor Akua Benjamin (2003) was one of the first people to apply the concept of systemic racism to explain the historical and lived experiences of Black people in Canada, and to address how colonial policies and education practices continue to penalize African-descended people. The concealment of the Banker Ladies in underdeveloped parts of the Global North creates a vacuum in the literature of solidarity economics. I cannot count the number of times people have asked me whether ROSCAs actually exist, and to provide names of the Banker Ladies as evidence. My answer is yes, they do exist. However, I am not obliged to reveal the identities of any Banker Lady; many are understandably afraid of being traumatized by outsiders.

Taking Time with Human Ethical Protocols

My goal as a researcher is to change society for the better; making ROSCA systems known comes with a degree of risk – or at least it used to when this work began in 2014 in the Canadian context. I have since been attuned to the possibility of legal issues, and that authorities may pressure me to give them my data; still, I have chosen anonymity and confidentiality in all instances. I have been careful with legal issues that may arise out of this work and changed the names of individuals afraid of reprisal. In recent years, a few of the Banker Ladies have chosen to be known and seen, and even refer to themselves as the Banker Ladies as a symbol of pride. In any case, I have erred on the side of caution and sought legal advice. This project went through an escalated ethical clearance process to ensure that no legal authority could contact any of my subjects because all materials have been destroyed at the time of production and the completed peer review process. My duty is to respect the ethical research guidelines under which I operate as a researcher.[2]

The foundation of the ROSCA system is based on community, sharing, and giving. Njeri Kinyanjui's (2012) work highlights that redistribution is critical to Kenyan Vyama groups since the sharing of funds is how this form of business financing works. The fact that these women save funds and share them with one another to help advance each other's life goals is compelling. It demonstrates how care for one another underpins these money pools, and reveals another way to organize the financial economy. ROSCA systems give time and attention to sharing funds while also undertaking the social work of repairing harms done against Black women.

---

2 Research for this volume occurred under a series of ethics certificates issued by the universities at which I have been based. The University of Toronto approved human ethics protocol no. 41957, which was re-issued on 12 June 2023 from a follow-up on March 2022. Previous approvals for this project included York University certificates under the project title "The Black Social Economy": no. 2014-319 (expired 5 November 2018) and no. e2019-172 (expired 25 November 2021).

ROSCAs create a safe space for folks to be heard, exert their citizenship, and access the goods they need.

How ROSCA Funds Help Women

The women I met in the Caribbean and Canada use ROSCAs for several reasons. The Banker Ladies I interviewed told me that they organize these groups because members choose to do their savings collectively with people they know and trust. Many of the women I met with often had a sideline business or were self-employed. Accessing a line of credit or business loan was often out of reach for them, while having access to a lump sum of cash could help develop their existing business or start a new one. Some of the common businesses I encountered were craft and sewing shops, "buy and sell" trading systems (selling household goods from markets to local communities), food and catering services, hair salons, and daycares.

To make sense of how ROSCAs help women, it is imperative to know how they use these funds. Jamaican higglers (small business traders) I interviewed told me that they used Partner funds to pay for their travel to Panama or Miami; they also used the Partner hand to buy consumer goods they could then to sell in Kingston's markets (see also Ulysse 2007). Fishmongers I met in Accra's Makola (in Ghana) in 2017 explained how Susu helped them purchase freezers to prevent spoilage. A Bajan entrepreneur based in Montreal recounted (2016) how she had drawn on Meeting Turn to start up her catering business; she continues to use ROSCA systems regularly to help expand her business. A Guyanese mobile hairstylist in Scarborough (Toronto's east end) confided in me (2017) that Boxhand money helped her purchase a second-hand car, which has allowed her to attend to more clients, including clients in areas of the city where public transportation is limited. The diamante poem below offers a quick glance at what a ROSCA represents and how it helps the women who use these community banks.

Rotating Savings and Credit Associations (ROSCAs)[3]

Money Pools
Ancestral   Democratic
Collect   Share   Listen
Money   Mutual Aid   Women   Community
Eat   Laugh   Invest
Transparent   Equitable
Co-op Banks

Money is fungible and ROSCA users can decide on how they want to use the funds. Some users will fund their children's education or pay for their own training. Women who find themselves in a bind employment-wise, or contending with a difficult home life, might organize an emergency ROSCA to assist them in the search for better work or safer lodgings. Some women relayed the important place ROSCA money had in commemorating important life cycle events (e.g., a birth, marriage, or burial). In some cultures, a newborn baby is reason for a major celebration; in other cultures, saying goodbye to a loved one is the most sacred event, where all take part in remembering that person's life.

Many of the women I interviewed identified themselves as casual employees or self-employed, lacking in benefits they may require on short notice. Many do not have extended health care benefits and need money for dental visits, injury care, and counselling. There are times when a group will organize a ROSCA to help member who has just lost a loved one to gun violence, and these funds are raised as a gift to the grieving family, or to help with funeral costs. Some women reported using the money for travels to visit family, conduct home renovations, and engage in other activities in the name of joy.

---

3 Inspired by my daughter's (online) third-grade class, which was learning diamante poems from English teacher Denise Wales (St. Cyril School, Toronto, Canada, 7 March 2021). The assortment of words in this poem helped me to capture the essence of what a ROSCA is.

The Black women who lead ROSCAs are not the only ones involved in this financial self-help model. They are the ones, however, whose contributions to inclusive financial economies are ignored – even stigmatized – when alternatives to exclusion are being discussed. Or men will take to the platform to analyse and assess what is very clearly feminist, and clearly women's, work. ROSCAs are an example of the Black Social Economy in action,[4] where members tap into good will, mutual aid, and reciprocity to confront violence and exclusion (Hossein 2018b).

Collective organization can be threatening to those who want certain groups managed and contained. The very idea that Black women – often not schooled in corporate finance due to systemic barriers – are able to communalize money systems to do good and assist in economic development exposes the elitism within commercial economic systems. By emphasizing collective financial action by the oppressed, Black Social Economy Theory looks to the possibilities of politicized co-operation where people choose to come together to pursue a business activity. Black Social Economy Theory asserts that the Banker Ladies deliberately take up space in the informal arenas by organizing ROSCAs to counter various forms of social exclusion. By doing this work largely out of sight, The Banker Ladies expose the lies, hubris, and deeply embedded exclusion – largely a result of colonialism and the vestiges of white supremacy – that lurk in development and solidarity economics, a field built to ignore the presence and potential of community-focused economies.

Informal Co-operatives Matter

Studies about mutual aid, self-help groups, or ROSCAs are largely absent from academic literature. Du Bois's (1907) research examined collective forms of African business, a historical grounding that inspired the Black diaspora beyond the African continent. A

---

4 See the video defining the term at *Black Social Economy* (2022).

few years ago, an exhibit titled *Free Black North* at the Art Gallery of Ontario (AGO) documents Black refugees fleeing the United States into Canada, and notes that upon arrival the immigrants relied on "True Bands" – co-operative, mutual aid groups – to help them settle and adjust (AGO 2017). Abolitionists worked through an intricate network of economic co-operation to help thousands of slaves escape the United States and resettle in Buxton and the Niagara region of present-day southern Ontario.

Mutual aid and people informally co-operating has thus been an integral part of societal formation in the Americas while ideas of peer-to-peer banking have adapted to the cultural milieux in which Black people now live (Hossein 2018b). The Underground Railroad is one example. Bryan Prince (2004, 44), a Canadian historian and founder of the Buxton Museum in southwestern Ontario, describes the Underground Railroad as a

> secret network of good-hearted people, black and white, who risked their safety and their lives to help fugitives find their way to Canada. Over thirty thousand people are estimated to have found safety and a new home in Canada prior to the American Civil War, and the constitutional amendment of 1865, which finally put an end to slavery in the United States.

The Underground Railroad was, without a doubt, a co-operative. It relied on the pooling of economic resources and good will to help enslaved Black people escape poverty. This form of co-operation had to be hidden because of the dangers of moving people towards freedom, which included the risk of death. When Africans settled in Canada – in towns like Buxton – True Bands were created to help people receive the goods they needed to live.

The historical context for the development of Black co-operatives must consider these precursors of formal co-operatives developed by free Black people who settled in Canada. Gordon Nembhard (2014a, 34) describes self-sustaining communal Black farms and communes operating in Wilberforce, Upper Canada (later Ontario), as early as 1831 – a finding that predates the Desjardins and Antigonish movements (Murphy 2009; Alexander 1997). Lia Haro and Romand

Coles (2019, 658) argue that True Bands by Black immigrants had to operate underground because they would be seen as illegal and could endanger the newly arrived Black refugees. In documenting some of the earliest first-hand accounts of co-operatives and Black folks who escaped slavery, Benjamin Drew (1856, 220) defines True Bands as co-operatives at heart: "A True Band is composed of coloured persons of both sexes, associated for their own improvement. Its objects are manifold: mainly these: the members are to take a general interest in each other's welfare; to pursue such plans and objects as may be for their mutual advantage."

The legacy of True Bands has often been obscured, treated as a footnote in history texts; but these ROSCA-type systems – and that they had to be partially hidden – were essential in Black people's efforts to get, and remain, free. Historian Michael Hembree (1991) emphasizes how important True Bands were in these communities for the integration of Black people, many of whom refused to be dependent on handouts or charity. In 1853, a Black convention held at Amherstburgh in Essex County, Canada West (later Ontario) established vigilance committees in eight communities to coordinate relief for Black refugees. The first True Band society was funded by its own members in Maiden in 1854; by 1856, Black people had organized 14 similar societies (Hembree 1991). Shirley Yee (1994, 62) highlights the critical role True Bands played in the 1800s in the organizational networks that sustained Black communities, noting that the goal of these "benevolent organizations" was "to foster independence by raising money to improve schools, providing temporary assistance to needy Black families, and caring for the sick."

A back issue of the *Montreal Community Contact*, a Caribbean diaspora newspaper circulated in Quebec, documented the work of Antiguan Canadian Daisy Tonge (Blackman 2016). Known as the "Susu Lady," she ran a ROSCA in Montreal for 47 years. During the past three decades, African immigrants from places like Somalia and Nigeria have brought their own versions of ROSCAs to Canada. Yet no research explores the ways in which African Canadians, both immigrant and Canadian-born, organize money collectively as a way to adjust to their new countries or deal with business exclusion.

Always Co-operating

While people around the world have engaged in co-operative, commoning, and communal economics for centuries, especially in the Global South, these activities have been largely ignored (Federici 2019; Ostrom 2009; Annisette 2006). The Habesha people of Ethiopia and the Ashanti people of Ghana with whom I met during my research could not provide a precise date for when these practices began (Baradaran 2015; Bortei-Doku Aryeetey and Aryeetey 1996). Indigenous writer Leanne Betasamosake Simpson (2020) has shown that individualized forms of business-making run contrary to community well-being, unity, and co-operation among the Nishnaabeg people. The collective business traditions practised by African and Indigenous Peoples have passed down to them by way of their ancestors. Lack of a clear start date does not mean that these informal co-operative systems do not exist.

Several scholars have documented what they believe to be the origins of ROSCAs to Nigeria, West Africa (Annisette 2006; Falola 1995; Bascom 1952). Others cite Ethiopia in eastern Africa (Begashaw 1978). When the West "invents" new economic programs around the notion of "financial inclusion," it omits the fact that people have always had their own banking co-op systems. Scholar Mojalefa Lehlohonolo Koenane (2019) reminds us that "Stokvels" in rural South Africa helped Black people living under apartheid. Irrespective of location, excluded people continue to do what they have always done: engage in informal co-ops, mutual aid groups, and ROSCAs.

Nobel Prize winner Muhammed Yunus (2007) was influenced by the Chit (or Samity) systems (names for ROSCAs) of Bangladeshi women. Aware of group financial systems, he modelled his Grameen Bank on these local systems of collectivity. CARE International, which received significant USAID donor funds for its world-famous Village and Savings Loans Associations (VSLAs), takes credit for the Mata Masu Dubara (MMD) movement in Niger. I lived there from 2003 to 2004, and it is well known that the MMD movement was locally inspired. Grant and Allen (2002), who are white and hail from a Euro-Western tradition, characterize the MMD movement as the invention of CARE, which was in turn able to capture significant donor funds to "teach" Nigerien women about solidarity economics. However, Nigerien women always knew about saving and borrowing from each other using local banking groups called *caisses informelles*.[5] Local people credit the original thinking behind the village micro-banking concept to Madam Réki Djermakoye, who had to endure complications with the MMD movement when formalized aspects of it were seized by the state (Niamey Soir 2019; *Actuniger* 2018).[6] The most-cited publication on the MMD movement in the *Journal of Microfinance* (Grant and Allen 2002) fails even to name any of the women who were the actual founders and inspiration behind the movement.

Development finance experts are not the originators of group financial services; ROSCA systems predate formal co-operatives, credit unions, and group-based microfinancing. Many microfinance experts have simply copied what local people already know and do. When I lived in Athieme, Benin (1997–9), many local women simply called these banks "*les caisses.*" These *caisses informelles*, as they were known in the local vernacular, were neither derived nor created by Europeans. The term "Tontines," commonly used by development finance experts, is of Italian or otherwise European origin.[7] *Caisses informelles* exist all over the Sahel region in Africa. When I worked for the Global Hunger Project in the early 2000s, I visited dozens of *caisses informelles* throughout the region – in Burkina Faso, Togo, Guinea, Côte d'Ivoire, Niger, and Senegal. Senegalese *caisses* are revered for being some of the continent's

---

5 When speaking to foreigners, some ROSCA users will use the term Tontines (under the assumption that foreigners are likely more familiar with European, as opposed to local/African, systems and terms (e.g., Susu).

6 In March 2022, Halima Therese Gbaguidi, a Nigerien national and then-PhD student at Penn State University, provided me with the newspaper clippings on the state takeover of the formalized aspects of the MMD movement.

7 Many academics wrongly credit Europeans for inventing/coining the ROSCA phenomenon and insist on using the term European term "Tontines." For example, American business school professors have a 2024 conference call for "Tontines and Retirement" without any acknowledgment of the contributions of Tontines to Africa and the Global South.

largest. Kenyan development scholar Njeri Kinyanjui (2012, 2019) has been writing boldly about the Kenyan people's Chama (plural: Vyama), which is based on the African philosophy of Ubuntu. "Ubuntu" loosely translates to "I am because you are," a designation meant to remind people about their shared humanity and interconnectedness. This body of thinking negates capitalist and usury systems in favour of co-operative and people-centred development, one in which the motive should not be profit, but rather working together on common goals. ROSCA systems are focused on people-to-people interactions.

Black People and Co-operating

Black people, and particularly Black women, have always needed to co-operate and pool resources to survive. Women in Canada, the Caribbean, the United States, and Brazil have had (and continue) to turn to each other to meet their basic needs (Mitchell-Walthour 2023). Embedded in their African origins, ROSCAs have been remade by those living in the Americas (Mayoukou 1994). Yet much of the Western (white) narratives about co-operativism do not acknowledge ROSCAs as co-operatives. In white-dominated places, ROSCAs are seemingly unknown or have "never [been] heard of." Yet the Raiffeisen banks, or Rochdale weavers active in the latter part of the 1800s (Fairbairn 1994; Guinnane 2001), or Quebec's Desjardins of the 1900s are repeatedly cited (Mendell 2009; Shragge and Fontan 2000). All of these co-operatives began informally. The Banker Ladies, or people involved in organizing ROSCAs, are seldom mentioned or cited. In 2012, McKnight and Block's *The Abundant Community* emphasized early white settlers to America as pioneers who "made everything they used" and helped each other out, while omitting any mention of enslaved people. Black people's co-operatives and self-help initiatives, created under circumstances of duress, were erased from history.

Ethiopian scholar Mamo Tirfe (1999) holds that "Equub" is an indigenous co-op banking system practised by Ethiopians for centuries. It would be preposterous not to know about these systems, whether they are written down or not. In *Vyama: Institutions of Hope*, Njeri Kinyanjui (2012) has exposed the fact that informal co-operatives known as Vyama (pluralized term for Chama) are the local inventions of Kenyans, and not Western imports. More than a century ago, Du Bois (1907) made the point that co-operatives inside and outside of Africa are the business model of African-descended people.

In this study, I examine ROSCAs organized by women in five Caribbean countries and two cities in Canada. Finding the Banker Ladies who organize ROSCAs, meeting with them, building their trust, and understanding their issues takes a lot of time. Much of the work done by the Banker Ladies is undertaken out of sight – in their homes, churches, shops, and community centres. ROSCAs are born out of crisis and established in communities facing stigma and inequality. They are created by the very women who are overlooked for their community development efforts. For these reasons, these institutions are left out of academic literature. The toughest part for me as a researcher was asking *why*: "Why do you create these banking co-op systems?" The women responded that they participate in these systems to help people who are "thrown away" and ignored. The women explained to me that they feel their ROSCAs are "under-rated," "misunderstood," and "not valued" by others. These perceptions were difficult enough to absorb, but hearing the Canadian Banker Ladies admit that they work in fear and hide their ROSCAs because they do not want them to be seen as "illegal" crushed me.

Some kinds of research must occur underground. For the Banker Ladies, it took courage to speak to a researcher because it required letting me into their privately held financial groups. I knew that the stories they relayed, and which I would eventually share, could not be rushed. In the academy, and especially in the co-operative sector, people were not ready to listen to what I knew needed to be asserted: that ROSCAs are at the core of the co-operative sector. ROSCAs are the precise antidote needed to counter racial capitalism. The Banker Ladies show us that, for co-operatives to be culturally diverse, ROSCAs must be a central part of the story. We are finally getting to a place where a few of the Banker Ladies themselves are now talking publicly about why ROSCAs are vital to our financial economies. But it has taken a decade of this work to finally get to this place and so much advocacy is still needed.

Giving Credit Where Due

People doing business *on their own terms* – to enhance their lives and the lives of their community members using a collective/shared profit model – is the very essence of co-operativism. ROSCAs are a widely studied phenomenon in the context of the Global South (Collins et al. 2009). More than two decades ago, Shirley Ardener and Sandra Burman's (1996) *Money-Go-Rounds* detailed ROSCAs as grassroots co-op banks used to address women's exclusion from banking. Yet, the origins of co-operatives seldom acknowledge the role of ROSCAs in co-operative finance. It suits some scholars to start the story from what they deem "formal" co-operatives.

A deep examination of ROSCAs remains conspicuously missing from Western economics; scholars and community leaders have barely cited these systems, let alone exhibited appreciation for the lessons ROSCAs offer on managing economic development. Instead, the fixation for the last four decades has been on *microfinance* – a system involving mainly (white, male) foreigners going to southern locales to help Black and Brown women have "access to finance." When I researched microfinance as a type of development finance in five Caribbean countries in 2007 for my book, *Politicized Microfinance* (Hossein 2016c), I interviewed over 500 people.[8] It was then that I became convinced that professionalized financial systems concerned about alleviating poverty were limited in what they could do.

Euro-Western academics who examine microfinance in "foreign" lands give little recognition to the community-based financial economies in which women take part all over the world. This lack of acknowledgment occurs even though Carlos G. Vélez-Ibáñez

---

8 View a short, one-minute video ("Politicized Microfinance" 2022) about the meaning of politicized finance.

(1983) has been writing about the Tandas of Mexicans and Chicanos for decades, conveying how these systems are about *confianza* (trust), or what he refers to as bonds of mutual trust. The concept of trust between ROSCA users is rooted in a reciprocal exchange between people who share a similar class experience and want to help one another (11). Stuart Rutherford (2000) has also written extensively about ROSCAs, emphasizing the importance of savings, and building wealth from within. ROSCAs are useful in moving communities from a debt culture towards one of savings.

That money exists locally is important to remember. Kenyan scholar Kinyanjui (2012) reminds us that African co-operatives, especially Vyama and SACCOs, predate Western notions of how to organize finance and run a business. During the COVID-19 pandemic (2020–3), the University of Kerala, India, organized online conferences on solidarity economics and various forms of membership institutions, with the intent of showing how these co-operative lenders address financial exclusion. Indian scholars discussed self-help groups, the Kudumbashree movement, Sanghas, and Chits, highlighting them as various forms of co-operative institutions, and emphasizing as matter of fact the indigeneity of these systems. In South Africa, Koenane (2019) argues that African people have always had their own co-operative systems called Stokvels, which amplified the value of one's own savings by sharing them with a group. Co-operative scholar and political economist Jessica Gordon Nembhard (2014a) reveals that, for hundreds of years, African Americans created informal and formal co-operatives to survive racist violence – a story that has been buried for too long. Knowledge-making beyond Eurocentric canons shows that informal banking co-ops – ROSCAs – count as part of the global co-operative sector.

ROSCAs are defined as voluntary co-operative institutions made up of people, usually women, who decide, through a consultative process, on fixed monetary contributions for specific cycles (Hossein 2020; Ardener and Burman 1996; Vélez-Ibáñez 1983). In researching the Mexican Tandas, Professor Carlos Vélez-Ibáñez (1983) found that fixity and regulations around these systems are decided by members, thereby advancing ideas of democracy in decision-making. But the "fixity" is about maintaining transparency: fixed,

Table 0.1. Inventory of Some of the Names of ROSCAs across Africa and Its Diaspora

Names	Countries
San	Dominican Republic
Susu	Ghana, Trinidad and Tobago, Grenada, St. Vincent
Adeshi	Northern Ghana
Esusu, Ajo	Nigeria
Asousou, Esu	Bahamas
Gbeh, Eso Jojo	Benin
Boxhand	Guyana
Moziki	Democratic Republic of Congo
Asousou	Niger
Monee	Côte d'Ivoire
Osusu	Gambia, Sierra Leone, Liberia
Ngangi, Chama, Itega	Kenya
Meeting Turn	Barbados
Lodge	St. Lucia
Tandas, Cundina, Ronda	Mexico
Juntas	Peru
Caja	Ecuador
Pandero	Panama
Gameeyaa	Egypt
Partner/Pardna	Jamaica
Sol, Sabotaye	Haiti
Stokvel	South Africa
Hagbad, Shalongo, Ayuuto	Somalia
Equub	Ethiopia/Eritrea
Caixinha	Brazil
Sandooq	Sudan, Iran
Rounds	Zimbabwe

regularized payments help to build strong bonds of trust. ROSCAs have been studied extensively in the Global South, but less so in the Global North. ROSCAs go by many names, and it is how they are known in the local vernacular that matters to users (Low 1995). Table 0.1 lists the local names for ROSCAs used by African-descended people around the world.[9]

9 Alaine Low (1995) provides an excellent bibliographic reference list of scholars from around the world who are studying ROSCAs. There are local names for this phenomenon around the globe. I have added to this list, focusing on the names used by people of African descent who choose to call these systems simply "Susu" or "caisses" or "co-op" or "money pool."

Who Comprises the African Diaspora?

A study that focuses solely on women co-operators of the African diaspora is viewed as disruptive when taken into the academic arena. Yet these women, whose imperative is to push beyond boundaries to make life more livable, are engaging in a continuum; it is work they have always done. Feminist scholar Sylvia Federici's (2019) work reminds us that people have been commoning and sharing goods for thousands of years

For more than two decades, we have been discussing what comes after development. Arturo Escobar (2020) maintains that we should be moving towards the "pluriversal" form of development – that is, multiple forms of economic development driven by local people who know what is best. The African diaspora is defined as persons who self-identify as African-descended people but who live outside of the continent of Africa. I draw mainly on African feminist Amina Mama's (2005) definition of women of the African diaspora: Black women living outside of Africa, who have had to endure legacies of colonialism, enslavement, and exclusion across different spaces while holding on to a sense of African identity. University of the West Indies professor Rhoda Reddock's (2007) work locates the African diaspora as part of the African diaspora as cited by the African Union in 2003. In addition, Reddock also gives attention to the struggle and contributions of Black women born outside of the continent to the feminist movement in the Americas.

The ties between African-descended women inside of Africa, and African-descended women in the Caribbean and Canada, are very much key to this project. Black/African women have a shared past of many things and the enslavement of women is one of those things. Figure 0.1 documents the transatlantic slave trade that resulted in African people being displaced from Africa to other parts of the world.[10] The map was produced by Emory University's (n.d.) Slave Voyages 2.0 project, which examines mostly women of the African diaspora who share a common history of

---

10 See the database and learn more about the inter-American slave trade online at
    Emory University (n.d.).

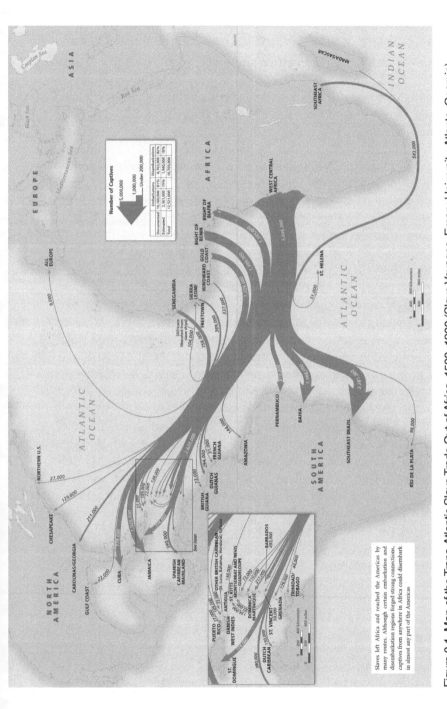

Figure 0.1. Map of the Trans-Atlantic Slave Trade Out of Africa, 1500–1900 (Slave Voyages, Emory University, Atlanta, Georgia). Reproduced with the permission of Yale University Press.

Source: Eltis and Richardson (2010).

systemic exclusion. In the Canadian context, not all Black women who are immigrants from Africa share or identify with transatlantic slave trade history.

Understanding how knowledge is produced in the social sciences reveals why the study of ROSCAs and the role of Black/African women has taken the better part of a decade to produce. Social science, and theorizing about "economic alternatives" specifically, is about preserving whiteness. While those on the inside want to be the ones to define the field of co-operation, social science – and knowledge-making as a whole – must be reflective of other worlds.

This book, *The Banker Ladies*, addresses a notable absence in the literature by discussing co-operative institutions built and maintained by women, on their own terms, to deal with social and economic inequalities that exist along the axes of gender, race, and class. This book drills down into the ideas of women of the African diaspora who organize ROSCAs, even when modern banks exist all around them in their urban capitals. Many of these women, and especially those in Canada, I've found, take risks when they decide to co-operate. Stories from Canada and the Caribbean, while equally important, are strikingly different in terms of context and how their respective systems developed.

As the Banker Ladies move, or travel, they enlighten us about ROSCAs as a respected tradition. The Banker Ladies are the chief architects, remaking co-operative banking practices in the places they live. These initiatives have an impact on the many lives intertwined with theirs, including those of their children and partners. Whether living in the Global South or Global North, Canada or the Caribbean, Black women are engaging in politics and economics in powerful ways, consciously undoing the idea that individualized forms of banking are the only model. They are also demonstrating something of profound significance: the work in which these Black women engage is co-operativism and should be supported.

A Legacy of Mutual Aid

Mutual aid and coming together are, in my view, antidotes to the structural racism endured by Black women in society and in business. Economist Jerry Buckland's (2012) work on fringe banking has found that many low-income, racialized people feel uncomfortable, and even outwardly mistreated, when they walk into commercial banks. So why wouldn't any logical person engage in informal co-ops to avoid business exclusion? The COVID-19 pandemic and subsequent lockdown revealed the value of informally assisting one another through collectives and mutual aid groups.

While mutual aid groups experienced a resurgence during the pandemic, the idea of coming together has always been a part of our world. In *Re-enchanting the World*, feminist theorist Sylvia Federici (2019) describes the commons as something that is shared. Its point is to bring people together as a collective, and to engage in a coming together of "social relations," and not of things. According to Federici (2019), the idea of the commons is long-standing and will continue to endure, especially among the Indigenous peoples of Africa, Asia, and South America because it is a way of being. However, much of the development thinking in the West clings to the fiction that humans seek modernity – and with it, commercial capital.

In *Governing the Commons*, Nobel Prize-winning political scientist Elinor Ostrom (2009) argues that while people can make the "rational" decision to work together and share common goods, academics (particularly those in political science) have written off collective action because of the idea of "free riders" – that is, people who will not meet their responsibilities and instead take advantage of the system (Olson 1965). Many active in the solidarity and commoning worlds view this dismissal as one that conveniently upholds private enterprise and the politics of individuality (Bollier 2014). It is also a view, some critics argue, that does not disrupt structural problems, question the bias of the Western Left, or offer tangible proposals to sustain the commons (Obeng-Odoom 2020; Bollier 2014). On the matter of these deliberations, I find the need for co-operation – integral to the activities of the Banker Ladies – aligns with Ostrom's (2012) ideas of a sense of duty and the commons-pool resource. The Banker Ladies focus on access to financial goods, social well-being, and camaraderie for themselves as well as for the communities to which they belong.

Ideas of co-operation are long-standing and not unique to members of the African diaspora. Indigenous Peoples have always had systems of collectivity because it was a sensible way to live. In *Braiding Sweetgrass*, scientist Robin Wall Kimmerer (2015) reveals the story of Skywoman to be one about co-operative economies and advocates engaging with goods from a perspective of abundance. This view of living with abundance, however, and figuring out ways to gift one another, has been erased from the human story about how to live well (Wall Kimmerer 2015).

The legacy of mutual aid has been silenced. It has been put down for decades, its efficacy denied in order to move along the modernity project focused on returns and profiteering. When these modern systems alienate people, the alienated may opt instead to organize and collaborate with one another. Still, the decision of some to embrace alternatives is seldom acknowledged – likely because the logic of co-operation is the antidote to individualistic corporate mindsets. The Banker Ladies of the diaspora enabled me to recognize and better understand this phenomenon by advising me to connect with ROSCA users in countries where ROSCAs have their origin. At first, I did not see the link because Caribbean people have always used these systems of money pooling to cope as well as connect with one another. However, my research in Ghana and Ethiopia taught me important things about the roots of mutual aid originated by African people. I learned that the practice of mutual aid and ROSCAs in Ethiopia and Ghana – known, respectively, as Equub and Susu – is common knowledge. The system is respected for its richness and abundance, and invested with a meaning that goes beyond a financial transaction. This understanding of a sharing economy, along with the principles of Ubuntu, have deeply enriched my research agenda on co-operativism.

ROSCAs: Part of the Economy

I travelled to the Amhara region of Ethiopia in spring 2017. My plan was to learn about various forms of economic co-operation, such as Idir, Wenfel, and Equub. Ethiopians had let me know that anyone who studies co-operative institutions should start in Ethiopia since Ethiopians are the inventors of this way of life and business. After years of doing this work, I am very much inclined to agree with this assessment. Ethiopia is one of many places across Africa advancing the ideas of collective or group economics (see also Du Bois's early work on this topic). During my first trip to Ethiopia, I was struck by how many people referred to Equub simply as "co-operatives," or used the two terms interchangeably. During this trip, I learned from the Ethiopians that Equub is a co-operative, and that informal co-operative finance is a choice. That informality adds to the richness of Equub, which should not be viewed as less than or inferior. On a longer, three-month sojourn in 2018, I learned from Ethiopian scholars and people that much about everyday life is reciprocal and involves sharing – especially in politically strained times. Ethiopia's use of Equub transcends ethnicities; people of various ethnic backgrounds have used these informal collective money systems for thousands of years.

Equub continues to be the first choice for banking for most people. It can be easily hidden. It is informal on purpose, and deliberately designed to assist people who are excluded, or dealing with crises and inequality (Tadesse 2020; Bekerie, n.d.; Mequanent 1996; Begashaw 1978). Ethiopians are proud of Equub and all classes of society engage in this system. Ethiopia's many varieties of co-operatives include formal co-operatives, but also encompass Idir, Wenfel, and Equub because the act of coming together to support one another in life is a significant part of economic and social development (Tadesse 2020; Aredo 2004). The Ethiopian people with whom I interacted did not identify any conflict between formal and informal forms of co-operatives. Nor did they privilege one type over another.

In Ghana, co-operatives, Susu, and ROSCAs all have a role in the economy. Development's fixation on modernity is old news. Ghanaians themselves are thinking about development through various forms of co-operative institutions. Ghana is the birthplace of Susu. For the African diaspora, Susu has evolved in the Americas. The same name is used in Grenada, Trinidad, and Tobago, as well as with immigrant groups in Canada and the United States. These systems remain informal and rooted in kinship, much like when Herskovits and Herskovits (1947) first documented them (see also Levin 1975 and Maynard 1996).

With economic liberalization, Ghanaians have been thinking about how to make Susu part of the economy. Since the 1990s, they have been formalizing a segment of the Susu system as part of the regulated financial system (Bortei-Doku Aryeetey and Aryeetey 1996; Steel and Aryeetey 1994). None of the scholars with whom I spoke in Ghana thought of Susu as a communal tradition out of step with modernity. The country reorganized its national economy to make room for formal Susu collectors. In the summer of 2017, my colleague Samuel Bonsu (then dean of the Ghana Institute for Management and Public Administration [GIMPA]) and I worked on understanding the relevance of the Susu system within the growing field of community economics. For the study Hossein and Bonsu (2023), we carried out interviews with traders in the cities of Tema (see figure 0.2), Kumasi, Cape Coast, and Makola (Accra's largest market).

Ghana's leading development economist, Ernest Aryeetey, has carried out extensive research on ROSCAs and Susus in the country, underlining the value of the ROSCA system. Professor Aryeetey has primarily examined informal aspects of ROSCAs. His highly regarded work is considered essential research since more than 80 per cent of adults join a Susu at some point in their lives. Impressed by the Susu sector's move to formalize (i.e., become part of the formal economy), the Banker Ladies in Scarborough (Toronto's east end) invited the head of the Ghana Co-operative Susu Collectors Association (GCSCA) to speak at a community meeting in March 2018. Although they admired the African legacy of co-operativism, the idea of formality was not well received by all of the Banker Ladies in the Canadian context.

India has also made major strides in acknowledging the relevance of ROSCAs to society. In South India, the states of Tamil Nadu and Kerala regulate ROSCAs known as Chit funds. During my meetings with Indian academics at the University of Kerala in November 2018, I learned that citizens wanted this protection from the state. This finding stayed with me because the Banker Ladies of Canada did not trust their own state leaders to create policy sufficiently flexible to include both the informal and formal. Regulation in South India came about because people agitated for the Central Bank to protect users against fraud. This action required people to trust that their leaders would do what was demanded of them. Chit funds in India have thus joined banks and other

Figure 0.2. Photo of a Regulated Susu Enterprise Called Humility
Enterprises in Tema, Ghana

financial institutions in being recognized as legitimate financial retailers (Christabell, interview and meetings, 29 November 2018, Trivandrum).[11] However, as is the case through most of the world, people in India still typically engage in these informal co-operative systems through networks of friends and family operating outside the scope of government regulation.

Political scientist Fantu Cheru (2016) points out that countries of the Global South rebel against Western prescriptions of how to modernize. Instead, people are doing what makes sense to them, thus asserting their self-determination. Development economist C.Y. Thomas (1974) makes a similar argument with his theory of convergence, arguing for people to produce what they need locally so they do not lose their way of life and become part of an extractive economic system that uses their labour to endow colonizing countries. Despite efforts and pressures to modernize, people in

---

11 In my meeting with Christabell P.J. of the University of Kerala, she identified the *Travancore Chitties Act* of 1945, the Kerala Chitties Bill of 1972, and the *Tamil Nadu Chit Fund Act* of 1961 as legislation created to regulate ROSCAs.

Figure 0.3. The Banker Ladies Council (2023)
Source: Luke Willms, mbuntu Media.

Ghana, India, and other countries where ROSCAs form part of their financial ecosystems defy neo-liberal rules, and instead converge towards co-operative economies. In the diaspora, and the Global North specifically, people also use informal co-operative banks to meet their needs, even though they may live in financial centres and in places with a developed welfare system. People find the ROSCA system useful in developed locations (North America, Europe) all the same. In my work with the Banker Ladies Council in Canada since 2022, I have encountered citizens who are now finding their voice, and holding open discussions about ROSCAs and informal co-operatives, systems they traditionally held secret (the Banker Ladies Council meeting notes, 2022–3). This was never done before because of the fear and trauma these women were holding when they were tackling social and financial inequalities. A voluntary group, the Banker Ladies Council (figure 0.3) came together to advocate for ROSCAs as life-preserving systems and to educate the Canadian public about them.

Expanding Our Co-operativist Knowledge

Many countries in the world have a rich legacy of co-operatives with that heritage demonstrating variance across locations (Develtere 1993). Canada, the country where I live, has an especially important history of co-operativism. Mennonites in Canada, and elsewhere, have an important attachment to mutual aid financial systems because they help people to be economically independent and free them to contribute to their faith. Joseph Winfield Fretz ([1947] 2020) has described how early Mennonite settlers, moving from Lancaster, Pennsylvania, in the United States to Waterloo, Ontario, in Canada, relied on financial assistance from Mennonites in the United States to help them pay off the costs of resettlement through a money collection. Winfield Fretz (1947) makes no reference to harms against Mennonites for relying on money pooling systems. Similarly, in Levis, Quebec in the early 1900s, the *caisses populaires* started off informally, created in a moment of crisis by francophone Catholics who felt excluded by anglophone Protestants. This institution is now known around the globe as Desjardins. These francophone Catholics neither experienced violence nor were the funds of these informally organized financial collectives confiscated. In fact, the Desjardins origin story is revered as a model for those in the solidarity economy and alternative spaces to follow (Radio-Canada 2016; Lévesque 2013; Mendell 2009).

As an undergraduate student at Saint Mary's University in Halifax, I also learned about the Antigonish Movement. Like the *caisses populaires*, this movement began informally. Fisherfolk gathered around kitchen tables to imagine a world of co-operativism to counter the spread of commercialized fishing (Murphy 2009). Today, St. Francis Xavier University is an important site for learning about Canadian co-operatives. International visitors come yearly to hear about this legacy. Despite this apparent reverence for co-operatives in Canadian history and society, Canadian institutions do not teach the world about the Banker Ladies of Canada, or about ROSCAs organized by people of the Global South. Acknowledgment of the many and varied forms of co-operativism, mutual aid, self-help groups, and ROSCAs is long overdue. It is imperative we recognize their critical place in building up civic life in Canada and around the world.

The global pandemic has brought about a better general understanding of systemic inequities and anti-Black racism. We know the right language and we want to do more. However, we continue to ignore co-operatives, especially those in the informal sector. We say nothing and do nothing to expand the co-operative field to include non-white people, particularly in the West. In her lecture "The Challenge of Achieving Racial Equity in Co-ops," given at the Fourth annual Co-op Impact conference of the National Co-operative Business Association (NCBA), economist Jessica Gordon Nembhard (2020) explained that Black people have been alienated by acts of erasure and manifestations of white privilege within the co-operative sector. I would take Gordon Nembhard's assertion one step further. I would expand the definition of what we mean by being a co-operator to include co-ops that are not formally registered, but instead purposefully organized informally. Opening up what counts as a co-operator would help to decolonize the co-operative sector, moving it away from its fixation on the formal.

Informal Collectives and Legal Status

"Informal" financial structures are often stigmatized as "bad" and "criminal." Women who engage in self-help may be fearful. If they use their own savings to help each other, will their actions be deemed illegal? These women save money they make from their legal work as cashiers, or personal support workers, or other low-paying jobs. This money, which has already been taxed, represents hard-earned savings, but they choose to share it with each other in order to help each other. In the context of ROSCAs, the informal pooling and sharing of funds is far from illegal. Yet, the women who participate in ROSCAs still worry that their activities will be viewed as illegal or construed as a form of tax evasion.

Informal financial co-operation is an arena in which oppressed people can participate without fear of reprisals as they seek to repair the harms of anti-Black racism. Many of the women I interviewed are engaged in small catering businesses, others are school bus drivers, cleaners, retail clerks, and grocery store employees. We call these women "essential workers," but we do not pay them properly for the hazardous work they do. We refuse to see the work they do, and do not hire them for their community-building expertise.

Caribbean feminist Peggy Antrobus (2004) has been saying for decades that local women have to be the ones to set goals because they actually know what poverty is.[12] In *Women's Movements in the Global Era*, Amrita Basu (2010) warns that local women can take charge and bring about relevant development, but there is a risk of elite women laying claim to their successes. Decades later, we need reminding about these truths: that differences exist between community women, and some are only there to take credit for being the "first" or only one. Women around the world who draw on ROSCA systems are in it for what it represents as a collective – the opposite of individualized concepts of only one. We ignore this labour rooted in collective organizing and don't remunerate them for the economic and community building they do. In some cases, we even stigmatize them for contributing to economic development. In response to such erasure and hostility, the Banker Ladies involved in this work deliberately choose to organize informally, bestowing their collected resources in lump sums to group members in turn.

ROSCAs teach us that solidarity matters. They teach us not to rely solely on a charitable model. Formal voluntary non-profits (or NPOs) around the world are characterized by a colonizing history (Davies 2018). Development scholars Nicola Banks, David Hulme, and Michael Edwards (2015) insist that membership organizations may be the ones positioned to challenge the status quo and to push for social justice change. Well-financed NPOs, often predominantly led by white people in the north or south, are completely

---

12 See the interview with Antrobus by Professor Rhoda Reddock (2006) in *Development and Change*.

detached from the lived experience of the very people they claim to help. We need to invest in Black feminist-minded co-operators who understand trust, mutual aid, and reciprocity – concepts that are fundamental to rebuilding equitable economies.

Making This Work Known

The academy undervaluing or neglecting knowledge about informal institutions, like mutual aid groups and ROSCAs, shows blatant bias. It means erasure of an essential area of the social solidarity economy, one in which Black, Indigenous, and racialized people are active (Laforest 2009; McMurtry 2010). The social economy in Canada is typically studied from a Eurocentric perspective. I cannot tell you how many times I have made a presentation about the Banker Ladies only to be "corrected" with the information that white people engaged in mutual aid before Black people and other minorities. Work by feminist economists writing on this topic, especially Naila Kabeer's (1994) *Reversed Realities*, has been key to my own understanding of how collectivity is a form of rethinking power dynamics. As was Kabeer, Sudarshan, and Milward's (2013) study, *Organizing Women Workers in the Informal Economy*, which showed how women in India, Burma, and Brazil confronted patriarchy and elite politics by bringing in bottom-up economic systems to counter those of the mainstream. During my career, I have called out many times the sheer audacity of academics, many of them male and white, who write books on solidarity, collectives, and co-operatives from around the world without mentioning the informal institutions in which millions of racialized women engage in co-operative building.

In this book, *The Banker Ladies*, I am vested in citational justice. I want recognition for what these works bring to the table in terms of knowledge making, and I want to expose their history of erasure. The literature in Black political economy is vast. I cannot cite everything that I have read, but I try to cite as many of the works as I can, especially those on economic co-operation. Like the recent work, "Black Political Economy, Solidarity Economics, and

Liberation" by Jessica Gordon Nembhard (2023), I am also on the side of citing the abundance of what we have in the community and this includes an abundance of scholarship by Black and feminist political economists. Rama Salla Dieng of Senegal and Lyn Ossome of Kenya (forthcoming) cite a variety of feminist scholars writing about the economies of African-descended people; it is a conversation between two African feminist scholars noting the growing body of literature. I realize that my commitment to the breadth of coverage will result in losses in terms of sharing the depth and details found in these writings. I hope that readers will make time to excavate these works about people of colour in solidarity economics and so come to appreciate, as I have, what these studies bring to the field of community development in terms of theorizing and practice. If we only read works that exclude discussion of minorities in the solidarity economy, including what those minorities have to say, the story we learn will be limited indeed.

Thankfully, many exceptional works exist that include discussions of ROSCAs and mutual aid groups in the solidarity economy, or third sector. Members of the African diaspora have made major contributions to co-operative development, ROSCAs, and mutual aid – often in secret – for as long as they have been coming to the Americas. ROSCAs are very much part of the solidarity economy because they are focused on lifting up excluded groups (Hossein 2016d, 2018b).[13] Credit unions, which are European in orientation, are often praised without the work of ROSCAs being recognized.

In Canada, the foremost thinker on the social economy is the late Jack Quarter (1992), who affirmed mutual aid associations as belonging to part of the third sector. He firmly believed that more study needed to be done, but that these groups were too hard to pin down. In the second edition of *Understanding the Canadian Social Economy*, Jack Quarter, Laurie Mook, and Ann Armstrong

---

13 In Canada, the United States, and parts of Europe, the term used to explain the third sector is "social economy," but I am using solidarity economy as it reflects the work that the African diaspora are doing, and it is aligned with the movement in the Global South.

(2018) give a nod to the Black Social Economy. They acknowledge that ROSCAs operating among racialized people are the very core of the Black Social Economy because of their informal way of addressing exclusion.

ROSCAs speak to the functionality of an historically oppressed group getting things done through perseverance and the determination to push against racial and class exclusion. The established story of Canada's social economy often begins in the mid-nineteenth century, with reference made to the German Raiffeisen banks and the Rochdale weavers in Northern England (Fairbairn 1994; Guinnane 2001). Narratives by others make note of the pioneering efforts of Desjardins's *caisses populaires* of the early 1900s, which were expressly designed to make banking inclusive. But these co-operative histories are only part of the story. Recognizing the ROSCA experience in Canada is one way to decolonize the Canadian take on the co-operative story.

Publishers tend to welcome studies about the Banker Ladies in the Caribbean and their use of ROSCAs to overcome business exclusion, but resist work on the Black Canadian ROSCA experience. It was 2017 before I published my first standalone scholarly paper on Black Canadian ROSCAs because so many journals refused the work (Hossein 2017c). Much of my research on ROSCAs has been self-funded. In time, I received federal funds to examine the politicized co-operative actions by the Canadian Banker Ladies. Then, in February 2018, I met "Esther," a highly educated business professional who was a member of a Janjui (Cameroonian ROSCA) operating virtually out of Ottawa with more than 1,000 members. By then, I knew that the ROSCA system was entrenched among the African diaspora in Canada, much more so than I had initially imagined. Moreover, it was active for people of varying class levels. Despite the sheer number of Black people involved in ROSCAs in the Canadian context, resistance to learning about these co-operatives remains.

Many works written outside the West, dating back to the early 1900s or even earlier, insist on the social and economic value of ROSCAs. However, the politicized aspect of ROSCAs and the role of women of the African diaspora is missing from them. Even though millions of people use ROSCAs, few edited collections about ROSCAs or special issues of a journal are devoted to them. Few books tell the story of women pooling monies as part of the co-operative model. Even fewer studies analyse ROSCAs as a deliberate political act to contest business exclusion. Some works that have counted informal ROSCAs as co-operatives worthy of study include: Katzin (1959); Geertz (1962); Ardener (1964) and Ardener and Burman (1996); Bortei-Doku Aryeetey and Aryeetey (1996); Gibson-Graham (1996, 2006); Harrison (1988); Ulysse (2007); and Gordon Nembhard (2014a). Hossein and Christabell (2022) published an edited book detailing ROSCA systems across the world through case study analysis. The Community Economies Research Network (CERN) is made up of academics and practitioners focused on decolonizing political economies, writing, and sharing ideas. Elements of CERN's efforts have influenced my take on mutual aid, making it possible for me to build on the work this collective already does.

Racialized people and/or groups confronting systemic racism have turned inwards to redo business and economic development. The DISE Collective (The Diverse Solidarity Economies Collective), which I founded, is inspired by the Combahee River Collective (1977), which was created by Black feminists to outline their list of demands for emancipation and rights. The DISE Collective takes its cues from communities that have always worked on economic development issues. Part of doing the work of archiving and documenting involves citing the publications of African diaspora, Indigenous, and racialized women scholars who write about women's lives and use their theories to inform empirical work. The women in the DISE Collective should be cited – use the hashtag #CITEBLACKWOMEN. The work they do is different from the work done by men who parachute into women's lives to "discover" women-led financial economies. The DISE Collective's ambition is to give informal co-operatives their rightful place and due in economics and politics. The study of informal institutions pushes traditional fields of study to diversify their understanding of knowledge making. Many women working on co-operative and solidarity economies are pushing for a corrective script on mutual aid and co-operative work, one that illustrates how to do business humanely.

In January 2020, an interdisciplinary group of scholars whose work focused on informal banks, digital currencies, and Bitcoin met for the first time in Umeå, Sweden. Historians and social scientists came together to discuss modern-day, peer-to-peer banking (e.g., digital money platforms) rooted in banks with no intermediaries. This recognition of ROSCAs signalled a major change, one highlighted through my keynote address about Black women co-operators and their use of ROSCAs as part of the origin story of modern financial technologies (fintech). Until then, these events ignored the genealogical role that ROSCAs have played in fintech.[14]

I am excited by the wave of fresh work being done by many feminist students and emerging scholars writing on various forms of co-operative economies: Silvane Silva, Pontifícia Universidade Católica de São Paulo, Brazil; Kia Melchor Hall, Wellesley College, United States; Agnes Rinrin Haryani, University of Canterbury, New Zealand; Haddy Njie, North Carolina State University, United States; Salewa Olawoye, Nga Dao, and Megan Pearson, all at York University, Canada; Atyeh Ashtari, University of Memphis, United States; LaDonna Redmond, Saint Mary's University, Halifax; Stephanie Jones, University of California, Irvine, United States; Renee Hatcher, University of Illinois Chicago School of Law, United States; Priscilla Ferreira, Rutgers University, United States; and Halima Therese Gbaguidi, University of Rochester, United States. These scholars, by retelling stories about economic alternatives, and concentrating on self-help and co-ops by women, are opening the floodgates to the literature on the social and solidarity economy, posing new questions for human development.

The women scholars I noted above draw on local theories to inform their studies. I am no longer alone in this work. Far from it. Much of the writing now exists on community economies and

---

14 This invitation came at a time when academic work on fintech typically did not mention the genealogy of the indigenous ROSCA system.

"commoning," as attested by CERN and its founder, feminist scholar J.K. Gibson-Graham. Scholars are finally beginning to explore race and identity politics in relation to solidarity economics. In 2018, I established the DISE Collective to counteract erasure of Black and racialized feminist political economists.

From a Social Economy to a Solidarity Economy

Throughout history, people have gravitated to groups they know and trust. This is human nature. Russian philosopher Peter Kropotkin was one of the first to speak of living creatures grouping together to live and thrive. Kropotkin's ([1902] 1976) well-known essay collection, *Mutual Aid*, holds that animals, including humans, have always lived in groups, tribes, or clans. He spent many years studying various types of animals in Eastern Siberia and Northern Manchuria, examining their interdependence and how they rely on mutual aid to survive and flourish. Kropotkin concluded that most species live in societies in association, rather than in isolation, as a way of dealing with difficulties attributed to living; those who chose not to associate with others reduced their chances of survival. Kropotkin further argued that the values of love, sympathy, and self-sacrifice craft a way of being in a community that makes people happy.

Humans have engaged in various forms of collectivity to build up their societies. Harvard's Henry Louis Gates Jr. (2017) curated *Africa's Great Civilizations*, a six-hour series on the American Public Broadcasting Service to show community and business development in Africa as antithetical to stereotypes of people of African descent. The series documents the kingdoms of Ethiopia and Dahomey (today Benin) to show how people of the African diaspora created and built up their societies. My own travels to Lalibela, whose rock-sewn churches carved out of stones are a UNESCO World Heritage Site, testified to development in other places. For centuries the Ghanaian Susu system has helped people finance their needs and build their communities. Reverence for aspects of indigenous finance has been incorporated into Ghana's formal banking sector (Steel and Aryeetey 1994). Like many others, economist Frits Bouman (1995) argues that it is impossible to know the origins of these ancient rotating savings systems. What we do know is that Ethiopia, the Land of Origins, may be correct in claiming itself as a pioneer in this field of co-operativism.

Certainly, it is difficult to locate the exact beginnings of the solidarity economy across the African diaspora. As far back as the early to mid-1800s, when people migrated within North America using the Underground Railroad, they brought with them their co-op systems, including the True Bands. African Americans began with mutual aid associations before building formal, community-focused credit unions (Prieto et al. 2021; Rothschild 2009; Haynes and Gordon Nembhard 1999; Stewart 1984). The *Guardian* documented that the Windrush generation of the 1940s brought Pardner banks to the United Kingdom (Sherwood 2023). The Hornsey Co-operative Credit Union in England, formally registered by West Indian immigrants in 1962, later merged with the London Capital Credit Union in 2013 (Greaves, n.d.; O'Connell 2009). The social economy is defined as formal institutions that are not state or private-sector institutions (Amin 2009). The social economy assumes that groups in this part of the economy can "interact" or "bridge" with the state and the private sector (Quarter and Mook 2010).

Those who presuppose that the social economy can "interact" with the state and the private sector ignore the struggles of minorities. Black people have had to engage with co-operativism – either informally, or in a contentious way – to bring about change. In the context of helping Black people, the term "social economy" should encompass entities like co-operatives, mutual aid organizations, and ROSCAs, all of "whose activity is driven by values of solidarity, the primacy of people over capital, and democratic and participative governance" (OECD, n.d.). However, the established understanding of the social economy has limited usefulness because it does not work to change social relations. There are many reasons why some people would not "interact" with formal sectors. The Black Social Economy makes room for people who deliberately choose to engage in informal institutions. I add the term "solidarity" to the social economy to refer to how Black, Indigenous, and racialized people may not be able to engage with governments and the private sector, and there is no expectation that they should feel that need.[15]

The social economy must go beyond simply mapping out an "interactive sector," or bridging various organizations towards for-profit firms and state agencies (Quarter, Mook, and Armstrong 2018; Quarter and Mook 2010). In naming the actors in the social and solidarity economy sector, we conceptualize who the actors are, but fail to discuss the role that identities play within the solidarity economy. Some actors and people in the social economy do not interact with the state and private sector: their involvement with mutual aid and ROSCAs demonstrate that. Black people join the third sector as a form of solidarity with other people who endure the same forms of exclusion. Being part of a collective helps to push against "norms" that are typically synonymous with exclusion. The social economy cannot address these inequities when it simply engages in a mapping exercise.

The question is *how* to transform our economic systems (Loxley 2008; Thomas 1974). Ethan Miller (2010) attributes the concept of *economía solidaria* to people's movements in Latin America, specifically Peru, Chile, and Brazil, as well as sites where Black and Indigenous peoples have protested inequalities they have experienced in relation to white colonizers. The point is that "solidarity" is a term of meaning for people in the Global South and especially the African diaspora. As it now stands, the social economy sector is a catch-all sector for many things, rendering it conceptually less useful. The solidarity economy is a global effort to transform the current economic and political system. It is not merely an effort to reform, or work within, existing models.

For this reason, it is time to move towards a solidarity economy. Solidarity provides a space for Black and racially excluded peoples to meet their livelihood needs, as well as a place for people to socialize when they find themselves shut out by the mainstream. In this social economic sector, Black people can contribute in meaningful ways to society and the economy. Black people take these

---

15 See Hossein and Pearson (2023), "Black Feminists on the Third Sector."

solidarity spaces seriously; they create co-operative economies that build up communities and nurture their members. The dedicated role played by Black people in social and solidarity economics is largely absent from the discourse on voluntary and social services; and, when it is included, it is typically analysed using Eurocentric frameworks and theory. Black people find themselves in the social and solidarity economy because of deep forms of racism and exclusion. The social and solidarity economy is a place they can seek refuge. Knowing this circumstance supports the argument for theorizing that comes from within the community.

Not all is perfect in the social and solidarity economy. The Black women co-operators with whom I met over the years are endeavouring to make the solidarity economy more inclusive. Black people are engaging with the business sector in diverse ways, and flooding the social economy with inspiring ways of living. The Black Social Economy is energized, and most definitely politicized, in how it responds to the inequities built into the lives of Black people. The congregation of Black women in the social and solidarity economy has grown, and the academic literature must reflect on the large numbers of racialized people who earn a living from within the Black Social Economy. More stories need to be shared so we can move away from one-dimensional understandings of racialized people's role in the solidarity economy.

It is not enough for people of colour to congregate in the social and solidarity economy for help: Black and racialized leaders must assess the resources if the allocation of monies to development is to be fair and just. The Banker Ladies are doing exactly that: they are capturing resources and then redistributing monies to help people improve their lives. In their efforts to mobilize cash from people who are often seen as "poor," they are showing the world that they can organize financial goods and that they do not need to rely on charitable hand-outs. This act of mobilizing funds from within the group can be viewed as a political act in that it advances members' sense of agency. Folks on the Left and Right often do not see this aspect, or underestimate the power of local women to marshal their own resources (Kabeer 1994). Their ROSCAs are well-embedded institutions. Their members purposefully choose not to interact with state or private sector actors, opting to help those outside of these formal arenas instead.

Methods and Interviews

My research has involved an enormous amount of reading, including primary texts, policy reports, and critical analyses of current events. It has also been documented through multiple interviews and focus groups. Interviewing Black women, especially marginalized ones who are usually outside of research and knowledge production, has been a tricky process. Margaret Kovach (2005), an Indigenous scholar, has taught me the importance of making my research emancipatory, and made me aware that giving up control is part of sharing the process. Focus groups sometimes seemed "hijacked" by the women, who would quarrel with one another about racism, or digress when I wanted to focus on co-operative banking. These focus groups, however, were about sharing the research process with them, and making them feel included (Kovach 2005).

Taking the time to listen, and diverting my research agenda at times, has meant that producing this book has been an intensive, long-term engagement. While the duration of time taken to do this work was stressful, it also allowed time for material to sink in. I could digest it in a way that was fair, and experiment with new methods and forms of documenting (Maxwell 2012). I started interviewing and speaking to the Banker Ladies during my doctoral field work between 2006 and 2011. I began in Haiti (2007, 2008, 2011, 2013), then turned my focus to Jamaica (2007, 2009–10) and Guyana (2008, 2010, 2011), using the methods of storytelling and interviewing. I answered questions about my own life as part of a friendly exchange. This sharing aspect of the research process was something I had to learn as an academic interested in emancipatory research. It proved so effective that I continued to use this method in other locales.

Hundreds of Black women in the Caribbean countries – Haiti, Jamaica, Guyana, and later Trinidad, Tobago, and Grenada – as

Figure 0.4. Scene from the film *The Banker Ladies*
Source: Mondesir (2021).

well as dozens of the Banker Ladies in Toronto and Montreal, helped me to understand better the ways they co-opt money systems. My trips to Ethiopia (2017, 2018) and Ghana (2017) also provided a vital African context for ROSCAs, explaining the reality for women in the diaspora. I wanted photos to be part of the experience of this book. As an amateur photographer, I am experimenting with the use of photos to document my stories, using visuals as part of record-keeping. For ethical reasons, I did not take photos of the Banker Ladies, highly attentive to the reality that ROSCAs are viewed with hostility in some societies.

The Caribbean and Canadian cases allowed me to follow up with the same (and new) Banker Ladies over a period of 11 years. I also met with ex-Banker Ladies to learn about the pitfalls and risks they encountered; I wanted to be careful not to glorify ROSCAs. The material I collected is rich. It was helpful to meet with the women again and again, and to present findings to the Banker Ladies; they helped to set me on the right path with the research. Some women even called my work into question because it was not accessible enough for them. They asked me to make my work into a film to reach those who would never read academic papers. I agreed.

Their request for a film created a slight setback for my writing process. I found it difficult to think through how to share my work about ROSCAs in a creative way. In 2017, I secured the resources to hire a filmmaker ready to go deep into Toronto's communities in the east and west ends to shoot the Banker Ladies' story. Making a community-based documentary consumes energy and time, as I learned from documentary filmmaker Esery Mondesir. This film depicts the Banker Ladies as they want to be seen (see figure 0.4). *The Banker Ladies* (Mondesir 2021), which is open access in the collection Films for Action, is intent on changing mindsets, letting people know about Black women co-operators, and stopping harm from happening to informal co-operatives.

The Cases

It is not immediately obvious what the Banker Ladies do. To interview the Banker Ladies, a researcher must spend time getting to know people and integrate oneself into communities. The Banker Ladies are rooted in place and community, so they are unlikely to respond to outsiders asking questions. In each community where I wanted to conduct research, I hired a team of locally based research assistants, mostly women. These assistants, trusted by locals, were able to introduce me to the Banker Ladies.

To get to know the women better, I spent many days socializing. I hung out in their homes, watching soaps, eating their food, going to the markets, going to the bars and churches, running random errands, and visiting their community centres. In Trinidad, I hired taxi drivers who came from the Beetham, Sea Lots, or Laventille to take me into the communities. The Banker Ladies watched me carefully from the start. In Toronto and Montreal, I hired research assistants who were familiar with the streets and local places.

Living locally and knowing the place are key to working with the Banker Ladies, especially in certain locales where they keep what they do quiet. This research method was undertaken by careful design. In some cases, I also relied on local grassroots activists and non-profit leaders to guide me. In the Downsview area (west Toronto), I had my own community contacts as my father had run his business at Dufferin and Finch for more than 40 years. This network was valuable. Usually, meeting one Banker Lady would snowball into meeting more. I also made contacts with community activists who pointed me to other Banker Ladies – in addition to the ones known to my research assistants, local non-profit leaders, and taxi drivers.

Caribbean Fieldwork

Getting access to the "inner cities" (some say shantytowns) of the Caribbean can be politically difficult, especially if the focus is on independent segments of the community like the Banker Ladies. Monied elites worry about what these women will say about them and local politics, so they hover around when research is being carried out. Amrita Basu's (2010) *Women's Movements in the Global Era* helped me to see through biases within communities and demonstrated how to be mindful of exclusions quietly taking place. As a result, I watched people carefully, noting how they engaged with one another before I even started any interviews.

The Banker Ladies whom I interviewed were all of African descent and self-identified as Black. I used ethnography as a method for observing behaviour, as well as a variety of other qualitative methods (see Harrison 2008 and Schatz 2009 on ethnography that exposes political dynamics). Professor Faye V. Harrison's (2008) story of structural adjustment, and her description of how Miss Beluah Brown had to cope, stayed with me over the years because of the care with which it was written. Guided by Harrison's approach, I slowly collected data through several sources: (1) secondary materials (e.g., newspapers, such as Jamaica's national papers, *The Gleaner* and the *Jamaican Observer*; Haiti's *Le Nouvelliste*, and Guyana's private newspapers, *Kaieteur News* and *Stabroek News*); (2) interviews (both semi-structured and in-depth) with lenders, borrowers, and other actors; (3) focus groups; (4) surveys; and (5) textual analyses of reports and internal documents.

My two main cases were in Jamaica and Haiti. The Jamaican case is substantially larger because I lived in the country for a year, having received significant funding from Fulbright and Inter-American Development Bank. I carried out several short trips to Haiti, a total of about five to eight weeks over five years (2007–12). From 2011 to 2013, I secured some consulting work from the United National Development Programme (UNDP) and United States Agency for International Development (USAID), which allowed me to live in the country for a longer period, and to carry out my work in cities outside of Port-au-Prince, such as Les Cayes and Cap-Haïtien.

In 2007, my first set of interviews was with the Banker Ladies in a Sol (a ROSCA). The interviews occurred during my first trip to Haiti to work with a local microfinance organization called Fonkoze. This trip was also the one where I found myself thinking my life was over as I hid from gunfire in the organization's offices in Martissant. To this day, the manager who kept me safe, Marcelle St. Gilles, is one of my dearest friends. In Haiti, I met with dozens of the Banker Ladies who had micro-loans from targeted programs and were members of co-operatives, while also running Sols. The same year, I visited Kingston, Jamaica, where I met with a number of community leaders and activists engaged in financial inclusion, who shared details with me about Partner banks. But it was not until 2008, while carrying out doctoral work on microfinance institutions, that I interviewed the Banker Ladies in several of the downtown garrisons.

For the three cases of Guyana, Grenada, and Trinidad, I received less funding, which limited the time I was able to spend in each country. My Guyana field work was conducted during two extended trips in 2010 and 2011. I did research primarily in the Tiger Bay and Albouystown areas in Georgetown. I have family in Tiger Bay, so I was able to move around quite easily, and they helped with my transport needs. I usually travelled on foot, except if it was late at night. I carried out the Grenada and Trinidad field trips in the summer of 2013, spending one month in each location.

Table 0.2. Interviews with the Banker Ladies in the Caribbean and Canada (2007–22)

Method	Jamaica	Guyana	Grenada	Haiti	Trinidad	Canada	Total
Focus groups with ROSCA members, 2–3 hours	57	5	0	74	0	104	240
Individual interviews, average 60 minutes	89	14	17	19	23	41	203
Total	146	19	17	93	23	145	443*

Notes: Author's data collected from 2007 to 2022, with the Caribbean interviews completed in 2015. No in-person interviews were carried out during the pandemic years 2020 and 2021.
* Interviews and focus groups in Ghana (2017) and Ethiopia (2017, 2018) are not included in this table. Neither are the dozens of the Banker Ladies who engaged in special events and workshops. But I draw insights from all of these interviews and meetings.

Because the sample sizes are limited, I count these two cases simply as reflections. I do not think development studies scholars can learn a great deal about a place through short stays, so I am cautious in my references to these locations (even though these are places I know because my family is from both countries). Grenada is by far the smallest island in the sample, with a population of 100,000. Trinidad is an oil-rich, industrialized, middle-income country, which helped expand the comparative analysis. I narrowed my interviews to Laventille, the Beetham, and Sea Lots. In all three locations, I was also able to speak to several experts, activists, and professionals. I subsequently published detailed case studies for each country.

In 2013, I published my first paper about the Banker Ladies, with a focus on the Caribbean experience. It appeared in *Annals for Public and Cooperative Economics* (Hossein 2013). During this study, I acquired a lot of the context for my interviews by speaking to those who are not Banker Ladies. However, in this book I am focused on what the Banker Ladies had to say. It should be noted that this story is the result of hearing from thousands of Black women in the Americas. Even though table 0.2 itemizes 443 interviews with the Chief Banker Ladies located across five Caribbean countries and two cities in Canada, each Banker Lady interviewed represents dozens more women who are participating in ROSCAs. A ROSCA group may include 10 to 80 members. Therefore, if 25 members are associated with each of the 443 Banker Ladies interviewed, that would mean roughly 11,000 women involved in ROSCAs.

Fieldwork in Canada

My Canadian fieldwork arose out of the work I did in the Caribbean. I learned very quickly how transnational the Banker Ladies are. I found that Jamaicans in New York or Haitians in Montreal would take part in ROSCAs in their home countries. But when the Banker Ladies in Kingston, Jamaica, could name streets in Toronto without ever having visited because they had members who had a "hand" in a Partner is when it became clear to me that I had to expand my study to include Black Canadians and learn more about these banks in my own city.

During 2014, towards the end of my Caribbean-based work, I became preoccupied with expanding my research to include Canada. I went through intense grant writing to develop a new research agenda on co-operatives, mutual aid, and the Banker Ladies. During this period, I learned what an affront doing work on ROSCAs represented to the academy, as well as to those who study and work in formal co-operative institutions. In the early days, I had to self-fund my project, so my initial interviews were in communities with which I was familiar – first, the west end of Toronto, with subsequent expansion into the city's east end.

I was not prepared for the sheer numbers who would come to my sessions. It soon became clear that the Banker Ladies were deeply committed to the project; many of them stayed in touch to follow up on my work. To this day, the Banker Ladies write letters to me, send pictures to me, or leave voice messages for me via WhatsApp. This situation is every researcher's dream: to have more than an expected number turn out to sessions and for people to be engaged in the work. However, this substantial interest also required more sessions since a manageable number of 20 participants makes for an effective focus group – though, at times, this number would stretch to 26.

The women in Toronto were also not shy about telling me when I messed up. They told me when I should "try again," corrected me, and made me repeat and revise my questions until I sounded like a "normal person" and less like a teacher. I remember some of the Banker Ladies in Toronto laughed at me when I came back to share my findings with copies of my published academic papers. Some told me they were "not going to do homework," although others said they liked that I made the effort to come back and share what I had found. Those who made negative comments admitted writing books can be useful to a few. But they pointed out that policy changes were not going to happen if those engaged in policy did not read what I wrote. I needed to ensure that my research would reach the public – as well as policymakers – to educate them about the critical work the Banker Ladies do. In 2017, the Toronto Banker Ladies recommended we make a documentary to this end. The Banker Ladies assigned to me the work of just writing – work that would change mindsets. The film was launched during the pandemic in 2021; events were later screened to a Zoom audience during Black History Month in 2023. The group would come together to form a Council concerned about advancing the ROSCA system in the same year. On 22 April 2022, a group of the Banker Ladies, as well as grassroots activist women and students, met in my home in Downsview to hold the first meeting of the Banker Ladies Council. Our mandate was to discuss how to build a ROSCA federation and the group continues to meet on a quarterly basis, as they work to operationalize a ROSCA Federation for Canada.

On Being Tough

The Banker Ladies with whom I met are typically tough people. They have had to be, having endured so many hardships. Meeting with these women requires a thick skin: they won't give you an easy pass because you are a researcher. Many of my students over the years could not work long stints because they found the women difficult and critical of the work. As a researcher you must be ready for constant critiques. The Banker Ladies I met asked questions about why I was doing what I was doing, and they made suggestions about what I should be doing instead. I am also tough and scrappy too and I know why these women are tough; my Caribbean grandmothers were the same way. Women – especially immigrant women who struggled in their new home countries – have had to develop a tough exterior to cope with everyday slights, harms, and violence. They have figured out how to cope and to live within these new communities – often alone. Once you are part of a Banker Ladies group, they explained, you are with friends and have found a group for life. These women have taught me important lessons: it is good work that matters, no matter what adversity I endure in pursuing it; and to keep on doing the work because, most assuredly, I am on the right path.

My research about the Banker Ladies was not easy in the beginning – but my pressures did not stem from them alone, it came from within the academe. Their pushing helped me to continue along this line of work when scholars undermined the work that I was doing. With time, the research built special relationships and I have found myself passionate with the work that I do. I know meeting the Banker Ladies has changed me to look for engaged citizenry and to build a system that values this labour. They motivate me to be the kind of scholar who brings about social change through the work that I do.

Working in Toronto and Montreal

When one discovers the Banker Ladies, it is like winning a lottery. The dynamism in my sessions with them made me feel like I was doing the right work. The interest these women showed when participating in my sessions on ROSCAs was new to me. They were unlike microfinance clients, who usually require a great deal of cajoling and incentives to do interviews because they are accustomed to donor funds. In Toronto, I interviewed a total of 102 Banker Ladies in the east and west ends of the city. The Banker Ladies would spend hours with me, and I would order whatever the hosts felt was a good meal. For example, the Caribbean women wanted jerk, curries, and goat rotis with juice boxes while the Somalis would organize fish samosas, rice, and spicy tea.

Local development experts rooted in the communities indicated that offering a $30 Shoppers Drug Mart gift card would be appreciated. As researchers we take too much from individuals whom we interview. A nominal gesture like a gift card is a modest way of saying thank you for their valuable time and expertise. During ethical protocols, I went through numerous rounds to justify this expense. Offering at least modest compensation is unequivocally the right thing to do: the individuals we interview are the experts, and the least I can do is give a small gift that may be useful to them. My sample size of 102 does not account for the number of the Banker Ladies I met repeatedly through special workshops – an additional 26 women whom I met in July 2017. I gained additional insights, again from a financial workshop in March 2018 where more than 40 Banker Ladies participated in the event, including Cameroonian Canadians who travelled in from Ottawa and Gatineau.

Quebec is revered for "bringing" co-operativism to North America. In the early 1900s, the Desjardins's *caisses populaires* system, influenced by co-operative banks in Europe, "pioneered" informal co-operative banks in Canada. I wanted to visit Quebec to do a comparison because of the province's world-renowned *économie sociale*. So, in 2016, I started a six-week stay in Montreal, meeting women in the neighbourhoods of Little Burgundy, Côte-des-Neiges, Notre-Dame-de-Grâce, and Jean-Talon. My emphasis was initially on the English-speaking community because of my own contacts, but this sample soon expanded into a research trip that included Haitian Montrealers and other francophones from Burundi, Benin, Congo, and Martinique. During the summer of 2017, and again in 2018, I hired a research assistant to support further study of Haitians and francophone Africans from DR Congo, Cameroon, Senegal, and Benin who resided in the Montreal neighbourhoods of Papineau, Saint-Michel, and Jean-Talon.

The Montreal case, about half the size of the one in Toronto, involved 43 interviews. What I learned during my time in Montreal is that, even though co-operative institutions and the social economy are active in the province, the Banker Ladies in Quebec remain invisible. In this progressively-minded province, with its long-standing heritage of co-operatives, there is little to no knowledge about ROSCAs among Black people. Research in Quebec requires far more work in the Black communities located in Montreal, as well as the rest of the province.

The Banker Ladies of Canada disregard the fact that there are no resources in their midst. Nor are they intimidated by educational prerequisites. Instead, they keep their eye on the prize: to make money accessible to each other. They manage to make this happen in ways that defy conventional thinking. They apply an intuitive moral compass, which they use to share resources to help each other realize goals and projects. They think not only about what they need to live well, but also about what their neighbours need. They do this work in the face of much criticism, but carry on nonetheless, working pragmatically and quietly in pursuit of their ends. The Canadian Banker Ladies often hide themselves because they feel it is necessary to do so in order to continue their mutual aid work. Yet these Banker Ladies are heavily involved in social innovations, tightening social bonds and networks, and creating meaningful ethical business models. As Canadians, we miss learning from them because the hostile context in which they are forced to operate to avoid persecution drives the Banker Ladies to hide their good work.

Outline of the Book

This book on ROSCAs has involved a decade-long process of interviews, meeting ROSCA users, and speaking with the women who manage these banking co-operatives. This book should serve as a reference point for what ROSCAs mean, in the present day, for the people of the African diaspora. *The Banker Ladies* builds on previous work I have done that asserts that Black women make pragmatic decisions to form economic collectives, doing so as a response to social and economic exclusion, and to help one another (Hossein 2017c, 2018b). They are doing much more than just coping. We need to get past viewing these women as if they are operating in survival mode, and recognize instead that they choose these collective systems because of the moral implications embedded within them. For this precise reason, I use the term the "Banker Ladies." The women I met with called themselves the Banker Ladies, and it is my goal to respect how they self-identify. Theirs is an honourable title; despite the odds and the systemic exclusion they encounter, these women are building up society.

Both of my parents worked in formal banks for a good part of their lives. I learned a lot from them about banking. What I learned from them motivated me to spend a decade working in microfinance, banking for low-income people. Terms like "risk," "collateral," and "fiduciary responsibility" are used by bankers when they manage money. Formal bankers simply do not talk about the ethical treatment of racialized and marginalized borrowers who want access to monies. The Banker Ladies are the ones who get it right because they are, first and foremost, concerned about people who need access to funds. They focus on their members – human beings with needs and wants – and not this thing called money. The Banker Ladies emphasize managing money from the ethical stance of caring about one another (Gibson-Graham 2003; Dombroski and Healy 2018; Gibson-Graham, Cameron, and Healy 2013). These women meet and see each other as they are, and try to make life livable for one another.

My thesis is that ROSCAs are co-operative systems used by the women of the African diaspora as a form of deliberate, politicized economic activity, one that allows conscientious economic development to take place. Recognizing that women of the African diaspora who organize ROSCAs in the Caribbean and Canada are doing this work to address issues around equity is vital to understanding the struggle to bringing cultural diversity to the solidarity sector.

The structure and methods through which Black women organize ROSCAs are different in every context. The work of the Banker Ladies unfolds differently in the Global North than in the Global South. The Banker Ladies are activist bankers. They decide on what they can openly say and do. In the Caribbean (as well as in Ghana and Ethiopia), the Banker Ladies can boast about and promote

ROSCAs. By contrast, the Canadian Banker Ladies cannot because they fear reprisal. The Banker Ladies in both locations, however, demonstrate that they are leading banking on people's own terms.

This book is organized into seven chapters. Each speaks to the theory that is needed to understand collective business systems and draws on detailed case studies of ROSCA systems carried out by the Banker Ladies in the Caribbean and Canada. Chapter 1, "Disrupting Economics by Taking Stock of What We Know," shows how the Banker Ladies are ignored both by traditional economists and by co-operators, as well as by progressive interpretations of economics and politics. The first chapter asserts that, while the Banker Ladies have a rich legacy of co-operating and generating knowledge, their insights have been erased even within progressive circles. Through their economic practice of co-operation, the Banker Ladies can influence how we redo business to make it ethical and accessible to everyone. In chapter 2, "The Black Social Economy: Provoking an Africana Feminist Political Economy Epistemology for the World," I establish that we need to use Black political economy theories to understand business exclusion, as well as the alternatives that are available. This chapter draws on an abundance of literature by Black political economists and theorists. It is intended to be the go-to chapter for understanding a large body of theorizing called the Black Social Economy, which explains the politicized capturing of financial goods that Black and racialized people do, both in the economy and in the solidarity economy. For too long, progressives have silenced the contributions of Black/African thinkers who, using their own personal experience, are writing about the ways African peoples participate in business and society. This chapter grabs hold of the very best thinking and ties it to the conversation on the Black Social Economy. Knowledge of solidarity economics needs to be built into radical economics.

Nothing new is to be gained by listing the forms of racism and trauma that Black people endure. Plenty of Black suffering is already on display. Chapter 3, "ROSCAs: An Antidote to Business Exclusion," reconfigures the narrative to show how Black/African women are leading co-op businesses to stymie exclusion. The West has benefited historically from slave labour and the conquest of Indigenous peoples. It continues to privilege whiteness in the development enterprise by chasing neo-liberal business models. This chapter focuses on the ingenuity of ROSCAs fixed in co-operative and equitable economies, making individualized capital matter less in the lives of people. It also discusses the global appeal of ROSCAs. The Banker Ladies featured in this study insist on using ROSCAs alongside modern commercial banking. When they opt for informal co-operative banking, they are saying to the world: "We are taking back some semblance of humanity in business by engaging in co-operative financial economies." In a short piece called "Surviving Well Together," Dombroski and Healy (2018) argue that living sustainably means rethinking Western-imposed norms and sharing ideas across borders. The ROSCAs that Black women organize are rooted in community economies that try to make business sustainable for a historically oppressed people. It is community that matters first and foremost.

The next three chapters contain specific case studies. Chapter 4, "Acknowledging the Caribbean Banker Ladies as Co-operators," discusses case studies from five countries in relation to the Black women who organize ROSCAs in a specific cultural context. Stories from the Caribbean Banker Ladies show that banking co-ops contribute to their development and create opportunities for themselves and others (Sen 1999). Women are free to speak about the work they do and can put their co-ops on full display. There is pride and respect for these ancient African systems. People in the region see them as a benefit to everyone. Unlike this Caribbean case, the next two chapters, which examine the Canadian cases of Toronto and Montreal, diverge in terms of the perception of the Banker Ladies and the value they bring to economic development in the country.

A very different story unfolds in chapter 5, "Canada's Hidden Co-operatives: The Legacy of the Banker Ladies in Toronto and Montreal." This chapter presents my empirical work on the two major cities in Canada with the largest African diaspora populations. It addresses a gaping hole on research about financial exclusion in Canada as well as ROSCAs in the context of a developed country. A multitude of immigrants from all over Africa and the Caribbean bring ROSCA systems when they migrate. African-descended people who have been in Canada for generations engage in informal co-operative systems. But the Banker Ladies in Canada engage in their banking co-op systems out of sight; in Toronto and Montreal, the Banker Ladies hide what they do for a number of reasons.

The legacy of ROSCAs is unknown in Canada. Documenting and "knowing" more about ROSCAs are the point of chapter 5: we need to start seeing the economic value that the Banker Ladies bring to society. When I went to Montreal to explore the place known for its inclusive *économie sociale*, I discovered that Black Canadians in Montreal are also marginalized. Canadian scholar Amal Madibbo (2012) refers to the experience of Black people who speak French in a largely English environment (e.g., Black Quebeckers) as a "minority within a minority." Madibbo's description aptly explains their extreme forms of exclusion. This situation is exacerbated, to some extent, for anglophone Black people who live in Quebec. Black women – in both Toronto and Montreal – who organize mutual aid are viewed with suspicion and treated as if they engage in illicit activities.

More troubling is the empirical work captured in chapter 6, "Black Muslim Women Counter Business Exclusion." My work shows that citizens in Toronto – Canada's largest city – are labelled as terrorists and money launderers for organizing banking co-ops when, in fact, they are bringing cohesion to civil society. The Somali case was the catalyst behind my decision to make a documentary about the harassment Black women encounter when creating banking co-ops. In general, the Banker Ladies in Canada experience business exclusion, with the mutual aid they undertake rejected and viewed with contempt. Somalis participated in all my focus groups, but they also wanted their own separate focus group to address issues of ethnicity and Islamophobia – specifically the prejudice faced by Black Muslim women when they organize informal institutions such as Sandooq or Hagbad. The Somali case deserves a stand-alone chapter because of the social ostracization and hostile racism faced by the Canadian Somali women, who are both Black/African and Muslim.

Black women in the Caribbean and Canada experience intense forms of business and social exclusion, making even more remarkable the quiet, determined organizing they have done for decades, if not centuries. Chapter 7, "The Future of Co-operation:

Acknowledging the Black Feminist Economics in Public Policy," is instructive for understanding how Black women co-operators rely on mutual aid and collective financial systems to counteract social and financial inequalities. Without doubt, this work should be taken up in public policy. This chapter introduces Black self-help as the key ingredient to living well.

In *From Head Shops to Whole Foods*, historian Joshua Clarke Davis (2017) examines African American business owners of the 1960s and 1970s who were activist entrepreneurs – that is, businesspeople committed to the cause of ensuring racial equality. The Banker Ladies in Canada and the Caribbean are also activist bankers: their intention is to organize money through a group model to address issues of inequality in a pragmatic way. Korstenbroek and Smets (2019) refer to some social entrepreneurs as "antagonistic organizers." The Banker Ladies are indeed antagonistic social entrepreneurs because of their co-operative attachment, which represents a complete rejection of the corporate banking system. The Banker Ladies are both activist bankers and antagonistic organizers because they recognize group membership as a way to effect positive social change. They rebuild and contribute to solidarity economies as a group to push against systemic business exclusion.

Yet, the Banker Ladies are not being remunerated, in any context, for the work they do for civil society. While presumably the case in other Western countries, the drive of the African, Caribbean, and Canadian Banker Ladies for co-operative business is unquestionable, and one accompanied by compassion and a sense of community building. It is their quiet, take-charge attitude that is most impressive given they do this work primarily because they know it is the right thing to do. Member-focused forms of business undermine commercial designs.

It is past time to remunerate the Banker Ladies for the labour they contribute to addressing inequity and lack of diversity in banking systems in the countries where they reside. The funding model for development through charities and non-profits is long overdue for change. Funds need to be moved through co-operative economies, mutual aid groups, and ROSCA systems, all of which are led by bottom-up solutions.

chapter one

Disrupting Economics by Taking Stock of What We Know

To truly grasp economic co-operation, we need to learn from people outside of our own privileged spaces. Indian activist Ela Bhatt (2005), founder of the Self-Employed Women's Association (SEWA), finds it troubling to write stories about co-operation that will probably never be read by the women about whom she writes. Bhatt makes the poignant point that those who claim to be "progressive" seldom venture into a lexicon that articulates where members of self-help groups are going in relation to imagining financial systems. A lexicon that might speak to the forms of solidarity, social economist Walter Waters (1988) held as possible, through the remaking of our world, will take effort on all our parts. What does remaking the world in this way truly mean? Those activists and change makers invested in radical change must work as co-operators who believe their actions will bring about economic changes for the better, in spite of risks that may be involved.

Bhatt (2005) struggles with how, without being aware of it, women in the informal economy are making an impact on how we all think. This circumstance also troubles me. For years, I have been listening closely to the Banker Ladies and their struggles, noting how much they do to make things right in our economic systems despite experiencing harm. They continue to care for each other, build community spirit, and never ask for anything in return. Yet they remain unaware that the work they do is contributing to new knowledge-making. My own narrative of what it means to *do* economic development as a researcher has undergone a paradigm shift: it now embraces engaged citizenship, and values the ways in which women go about changing the world around them, on their own terms.

The women I study call themselves the Banker Ladies, and they are taking charge of the narrative on co-operativism whether we see them or not. They are disrupting social economics and exposing the ineptitude of those who only tinker with reforms and remain content to work within an exclusionary business system. The Banker Ladies have responded to the United Nations's (2011) declaration of the International Decade for People of African Descent (2015–24) by accounting for their trauma and identifying the ways in which women of the African diaspora are making an economic difference. This study of women of the African diaspora living in Canada and the Caribbean contributes to these efforts to recognize Black women who are writing the script of what it means to be a co-operator.

I receive calls almost monthly from people who have come across ROSCAs, or are piloting them and want to learn more. It seems that mutual aid work done by the Banker Ladies is having a profound impact on the societies in which they live, whether we credit their efforts or not – so much so that some women who organize these ROSCAs have formed the Banker Ladies Council.[1] Ordinary people of various backgrounds are frustrated by the greed of bankers. In *Economic Crisis*, economist Irene Van Staveren (2015) points out that the 2008 banking crisis heightened people's awareness that big banks are not infallible and indeed fail. In the face of that realization, regular people are reverting to community options when it comes to managing their hard-earned money. For instance, take the case of the 2015 Grexit, which saw Greeks instituting self-help groups to deal with the financial crash (North 2016).

It is usually economic crisis and/or business exclusion that leads people to form co-operative institutions. The Banker Ladies discussed in this book are resetting economies that have become

---

1   Visit the DISE Collective's (n.d.) website for information on inauguration of the Banker Ladies Council of Canada.

commercialized, individualized, and exclusionary to all types of people. These women organize a form of co-operative known as rotating savings and credit associations (ROSCAs) to build solidarity economies. Many people who find they cannot access monies from a bank for a variety of reasons come to rely on ROSCAs for their banking, using them as their main financial device because of business exclusion prevailing in their societies. In England, citizens have also created a network called "peer-to-peer lending." Advocates of this system are pushing for legislation to recognize non-bank lending (Jones 2014). Muslims, and Muslim women particularly, have drawn on collective money systems for as long as they have engaged in migrating because commercial banks tend to charge interest rates, something which is not respectful of Islam's religious rules.

The women of the Black diaspora featured in this study draw on centuries-old co-operatives to react against the harms they endure. They refuse to accept one-way development from external "experts" because they too have life teachings and cultural systems to share. Their quiet rebellion counters mainstream models, helping those who have been harmed. Resisting corporate financialization in the name of collective finance and mutual aid, it is perhaps not surprising that the history of ROSCAs has been suppressed. These informal institutions are solidarity economies, rooted in giving people, particularly the disenfranchised, new ways to think about banking.

Women Choosing Informal Co-Operation

ROSCAs – characterized as group, peer-to-peer lending – are a highly gendered phenomenon (Chiteji 2002; Ardener 1964; Ardener and Burman 1996). Women have led these co-operative institutions for as long as humans have been concerned about survival. In Frog City, an area within Maxfield Park in Kingston, Jamaica, I interviewed a 53-year-old mother and businesswoman "Joy," who told me: "We [the Banker Ladies] are addicted to Partner. It's, like, WOW" (interview, June 2009). This adoration of Partner banks helps women throughout the Caribbean and across Canada build businesses and meet livelihood needs. Black women do not need outside groups to teach them about "alternatives"; they know how to take care of each other and solve conflicts without having to negotiate (and compromise) with the state.

The informality of ROSCAs is what makes these women-led banks accessible to excluded people. For many Black people, the informal nature of this space makes it safe: people can organize their work away from the scrutiny of their oppressors. In essence, the informal nature of the social economy makes it a true civil society because the people within it do not have to broker any deals with the mainstream. Informality does not mean that these institutions do not have processes and governance. These institutions are highly structured and centred around what Marcus Mosiah Garvey, a Jamaican-born social entrepreneur and a powerful Black liberation theorist, introduced as a philosophy of racial self-reliance in business to counter mainstream business practices (K'adamwe, Bernard, and Dixon 2011).[2]

One fact is clear: women of the African diaspora who build co-operative economies have been ignored. As the world grapples with post-development, there is a pressing need to recognize local, community-based innovations. In *Pluriversal Politics*, development theorist and member of the Global Tapestry of Alternatives Arturo Escobar (2020) has formed his own theory drawing on the ideas of Black diaspora people – especially Black feminists – who have focused on local development when modernity has excluded their ideas. Black feminist and political scientist Tiffany Willoughby-Herard (2015, 167), who spent years examining global whiteness, identifies the powers that outlaw certain forms

---

2 I presented a paper on Garvey as a social entrepreneur at the Global Garveyism Symposium held in Richmond, Virginia, on 23 April 2016, on a panel with Michael O. West of the University of Pennsylvania (Hossein 2017b). He offered me many comments which I incorporated into this chapter.

of knowledge-making with the intent of keeping Black people contained:

> A racial attack on Black people sits at the heart of global affairs and the emergence of social science; this attack has used analytics that disavow racial suffering and allegedly provide analytics for understanding its costs.

Willoughby-Herard's (2015) point is that the research process, conducted in certain ways through corporate foundations and philanthropy, advances global whiteness. The Banker Ladies know this truth of being undermined and ignored for their contributions. Many of us are now rethinking the social sciences, considering ways to spotlight the harms and suffering of Black people, and specifically Black women. The new social science work of Gladys L. Mitchell-Walthour (2023) examines how African American and Brazilian women draw on welfare subsidies in different ways. What they have in common is their communion with one another. The spaces in which they connect to engage in self-help are usually informal institutions created by themselves to address the biases and exclusions taking place. American philosopher Olúfẹ́mi O. Táíwò (2020a) hammers home the point that the seemingly progressive guidance to "listen to the most affected" is misused by elites to decide which people to help. The Banker Ladies do not wait for those with power to invite them into the room of powerful elites; instead, they create their own room where they distribute social and economic provisions.

The co-operative work undertaken by the Banker Ladies combines care, strategic rage, and radical economics. These co-operators operate against the grain, taking risks in pursuit of efficacious alternatives to the status quo. Their very beings point to how we can address human development issues because they decide how to tell the stories of their trauma. To reach those who are excluded, they approach things from the grassroots, and operate informally and collectively. bell hooks (1999, 237) counsels that "no matter how hard or terrible our lot in life, to choose against lovelessness – to choose love." These women's pragmatic solutions come from a place of love and community. Their knowledge is localized and assumes that those who are excluded know self-development. The focus on the collective is certainly left-leaning in orientation since its intent is to upset the status quo regarding its assumptions about authoritative financial services. Even so, this same collective can also be viewed as aligned with the conservative right because it emphasizes self-help, or doing things for oneself. In her foundational reader, *Women, Race, and Class*, Professor Angela Davis (1983) explains that Black women like Claudia Jones (1915–64),[3] a Trinidadian-American, always stayed left and true to a cause, even when racism among the "progressives" was rife. The Banker Ladies counter the politics that negate their own human development by holding onto African ideas of collectivity, swaying left, and choosing love (hooks 1999).

But there is also pain and rage that is being used to assist these women in building new economies. Philosopher Myisha Cherry (2021) has made the case for "Lordean rage" – based on the work of the Black feminist poet Audre Lorde (1984) – as a way to fight inequality and make way for a new way of being as a co-operator. The Banker Ladies do this work out of love of community, but there is a lot of rage – and anger – in their lives, as they work through traumas and fear.

Knowing the Difference Between ROSCAs and Targeted (Micro)finance[4]

ROSCAs are completely different from targeted, professionalized microfinance institutions. The idea of solidarity circles in banking grew rapidly in the 1980s, a consequence of development programming focused on financialization programs like microfinance. The notion of group banking was revived in Bangladesh

---

3 See Carole Boyce Davies's (2008) story of Claudia Jones in *Left of Marx*.
4 This section draws, to some extent, on my chapter (Hossein 2020) in *The Handbook of Diverse Economies*, edited by J.K. Gibson-Graham and Kelly Dombroski (2020).

during the 1990s, a period of economic liberalization, because of interest in the local ROSCA systems of Bengali women known as Chit or Samity. Aided by his students, Professor Mohammed Yunus (2010) carried out formalized micro-banking experiments in Bangladesh. He revived the concept of micro-lending through a group model which involved making a personal loan of $27 (856 taka) to a group composed of 42 women stool makers. His intent was to test whether, by making credit available to them, the women could earn more money. The Grameen Bank model, an innovation of the Global South, stressed solidarity finance for women (Christabell 2009, 2016; Sengupta and Aubuchon 2008; Yunus 2007; Wahid 1994). Through this microfinance "revolution," civil society organizations overturned conventional banking norms and decolonized the impoverished world's existing ideas of business. Over the past three decades, microfinance has developed into a $70-billion industry. In 2006, Yunus and Grameen Bank were awarded the Nobel Peace Prize for providing loans to millions of women. This form of alternative banking was made possible by the cultural practice of mutual aid – ROSCAs.

While ROSCAs have informed the current practice of professionalized microfinance, they are far more sustainable and diverse in the ways they conduct business. This sustainability and diversity arise from the fact that these ancient money pooling systems are run and owned by people of the same socio-economic class as those who use this alternative financing. Microfinance institutions, on the other hand, are professionalized and run by educated elites interested in reforming commercial banks, but not in changing them. In *Money with a Mission*, James Copestake et al. (2005) show that microfinance banks which emphasize savings have a wider social impact than those focused on profits and financial viability. Microfinance banks managed by "experts" are vastly different from ROSCAs organized by women typically of the same socio-economic class as their members; the latter focuses on savings than debt or credit. Kim Wilson (2001), who worked in formal microfinance programs for American NGOs (non-governmental organizations), has referred to self-help groups in India as a "best-kept" secret because of their bottom-up form of development through

localized saving groups. Professionalized microfinance institutions, often driven by elites, can create various burdens for people.
Indeed, I have documented one such case of people of African
descent in the Americas being hurt (Hossein 2016b, 2016c). The
Banker Ladies, well aware of this bias within managed poverty
financial programs, have chosen to maintain their own parallel
co-operative and development systems separately.

The Banker Ladies Means Correcting Bias

No group knows more about freedom and human development
than the Banker Ladies. Yet "radical" and "progressive" thinkers
continue to overlook the informal arenas of the Banker Ladies,
engaged in "redoing" development with a focus on the person.
Self-help is not simply about boot-strap development; it also allows
people who have skills and expertise to pursue what they want
to do. I often tell my leftist "allies" who are sceptical about Black
women in co-op business that these women are the most radical of
progressives because they are not beholden to ideologues. When
I read the work of development scholar Franklin Obeng-Odoom
(2020), I am reminded that the Western Left is often unclear about
what it means by growth and short on meaningful proposals.
Political economist Jennifer Cohen (2018) rightly brings in feminist
scholarship to the table, which emphasizes social reproduction –
a concern overlooked in masculinist concepts of radical economics. What remains absent are the academic works of Black/African
feminist scholars.[5]

The Banker Ladies are Black women who speak about how they
practice economic development. These women are not trying to
fit into any one ideological stream; they simply want to get things
done. Many of them want to be recognized and/or appreciated

---

5 Jennifer Cohen (2018) cites an interview with bell hooks but not her prolific body
   of work. Cohen also does not cite other Black feminist political economists whose
   work can readily be found in the *Review of Black Political Economy*.

for their labour in contributing to equitable financial economies. Many progressives – mostly Left, white, and privileged – have a hard time understanding or dealing with the fact that some people do manipulate and co-opt traditional business practice(s) for their own sake. Black, Indigenous, and other racialized people faced with exclusionary environments have had to figure out how to do business differently – and on their peoples' own terms. Liberals also do not see that Black and non-white people have a long history of collectively organizing; they don't need to be taught about collectivity (Williams 2007). Those who have faced financial ruin know the power business has to carve out one's own freedom. Black minorities, like the Banker Ladies, are designing business in ways that allow them to endure exclusion and take charge of their own destinies.

Scholars critical of neo-liberal economics miss an opportunity to draw on theories that show how co-operative business forms resist oppression. For example, in *Banking on a Revolution*, social work professor Terri Friedline (2021) highlights how microfinance is politicized, but misses an opportunity to feature ROSCAs as viable financial devices, even though they are used frequently by American newcomers. Many scholars who critique neo-liberalism ignore Black political economy scholarship, despite it clearly being a way to understand what is going on in "alternative" economics. Many scholars neither read nor cite the Black Radical Tradition. They do not draw on any of the political economy research published in the *Journal of Black Studies*, *National Review of Black Politics*, or *Review of Black Political Economy*. Leftist sympathizers who cheerlead for the social and solidarity economy sector, identifying it as a place for transformation, often ignore the fact that much of it is elitist and harbours anti-Black racism.

The Banker Ladies featured in this book organize co-operative banks in innovative ways that others are not thinking about. Yet, when their stories are revealed, rather than being celebrated, they are rebuked – even silenced. Many scholars view the pooling of goods as nothing more than a coping mechanism, arguing that these women do very little to improve their quality of life. The Banker Ladies counter that they are living life. While what they do appears to be social, their activities are about remaking business and finance in an ethical way. They are co-operating, teaching self-reliance, and creating a forum for consciousness as it relates to Black women's lives.[6] For radical economics to speak effectively to those without power, it is important to *see* the Banker Ladies as innovators in community development.

Redefining Radical Economics for Humanity

The Banker Ladies are radically altering economics as we know it because they are concerned with wiping out exclusionary systems. In doing this work, they draw on ancestral knowledge of finance and self-development. A group of activists and scholars formed the Black Social Economy hub in 2015. I edited *The Black Social Economy in the Americas* (Hossein 2018b), a collection to which many members of the hub contributed, and which documented the economies of Black diaspora people. The work defines the Black Social Economy as a practice and theory that prioritizes the various forms of informal co-operation in which people of the African diaspora engage. It is a politicized economy, fixated on people standing up together to fight inequities. Part of making theory for Black women means reaching out to those who have already laid down theory, and then drawing on it to enable our communities to move forward.

Much of the literature of the mainstream political economy has missed out on the contributions of Black people. Business school professor Marcia Annisette (2006) notes that the practice of Esusu is not considered in any business or accounting literature, and she boldly questions this absence. In his writing, Senegalese scholar Cheikh Anta Diop (1974) works to correct erasures from human history, arguing that everything we know and do as a human race – including business – has roots in Egypt and Black Africa. Yet,

---

6 Clealand (2017) argues that organizations fail to see racism as an issue in the Cuban political project. As a result, Afro-Cubans have developed a group consciousness to react against systemic racism embedded into the country's institutions.

knowledge produced in these regions of the world has been side-lined. Professor Maulana Karenga (1993), who founded Kwanzaa, has said for many years that the experience of colonization wiped out knowledge of Indigenous co-operative development that came out of Africa and the Global South.

Stories told about co-operativism in the Global South are limited. When they are told, they are cast in a negative light, often suggesting that colonizers brought a dysfunctional form of co-operative development (Develtere 1993). However, this reading of co-operative development is neither complete nor accurate. While the version of co-operativism brought to the Global South was certainly top-down and elitist, many places already had their own indigenous systems of co-operation and collectivity, ones with a deep understanding of Ubuntu, as noted in the work of Kenyan scholar Mary Njeri Kinyanjui (2019). These African systems have sustained the diaspora through generations as they lived in enslavement and under racial capitalism.

Not all scholars buy into the neo-liberal dependency binaries of understanding world economies. Many scholars concerned about politics, the economy, and Black people have revived the Black political economy and use intersectional and feminist perspectives that may or may not be wedded to a political ideology. These scholars particularly include contemporary Black women researchers working in the field of political economy. Their work has informed mine. Let me note specifically: Nina Banks, Beverley Mullings, Sharon D. Wright Austin, Gina Ulysse, Mary Njeri Kinyanjui, Patricia Hill Collins, Jessica Gordon Nembhard, and Tiffany Willoughby-Herard (figure 1.1). These scholars are making it abundantly clear that solidarity within oppressed groups is not going away. Collective organization is an established part of the self-development of Black people.

Many works by scholars of the Black political economy are absent from the so-called canons of development, economics, and political science because these publications are not viewed as "fitting in" with the conversations taking place in these disciplines. In fact, these disciplines are too narrow for the interdisciplinary writing being done by Black political economy scholars as we rethink politics and economics. Our work argues that co-operatives, community economies, mutual aid, self-help groups, and ROSCAs are

Figure 1.1. Jessica Gordon Nembhard, Leading Scholar on Co-operatives in the United States
Source: Gordon Nembhard (2014b).

all important traditions of African-descended peoples. Many of us also choose to write together, or alone, to keep true to what we do. Political science, economics, and global development studies are slowly moving towards an opening up of their canons, but those of us writing on Black and feminist economics still take on risks for the work we do.

We form our own groups because we are not invited into edited collections – and dare not write with many white colleagues in our field because it just does not make sense. Many of us never actually get hired in the disciplines for which we trained, so we decide to work from a new place of learning. It is worth noting that political economy is often absent even within Black Studies, an issue that has been discussed for a long time (Stewart 1984).

Acknowledging that Other Worlds Have Co-operative Expertise

Privileged white scholars who study co-operative economics do not acknowledge, or simply do not know about, ancient Black civilizations such as Axum, Lalibela, and Gondar in Ethiopia – civilizations that have produced big builders, grand philosophers, theologians, and economists who have cultivated ideas about business and society since humanity began. During my sabbatical stay at Bahir Dar University in the Amhara Region of Ethiopia, I found that once people learned I study co-operatives and ROSCAs, they made sure I understood that the Habesha people invented Idir, Wenfel, and Equub, as well as other indigenous forms of co-operatives, all of which have been around for thousands of years.

Massive developments in humankind were achieved through various forms of local co-operation (Karenga 1993; Obenga 1992). India, too, has a long-standing tradition of co-operatives, especially in the south – a practice and expertise that underlines the expanse of co-operative economics far beyond that of the European experience (Christabell 2009; Datta 2000; Sethi 1996). In fact, most of the world's co-operators are in India, and it is from these roots that the co-op sector can grow and flourish if we start to recognize the strength of these well-established practices in our economic system (Williams 2007).

Kerala, in South India, is renowned for co-operativism. There we find various types of co-operatives, including "Sanghas" (collectives), other types of formal and informal associations, credit unions, and the state program of Kudumbashree (Devika and Thampi 2007). The Kudumbashree system is successful because the state advances local women's Sanghas and ensures they feed into development plans (Kerala, n.d.; Agarwal 2020; Christabell 2013). During "Cooperative, Mutual Aid and Solidarity Economies" (2021), a web conference held at the University of Kerala, scholars and students underlined Kerala's expertise in co-operative development, and the fact that these systems are indigenous.

Many countries have a deep understanding of co-operative development. The international co-operative sector tends to locate its beginnings in the Rochdale Pioneers story, but this can be limiting and erase other people's contributions to co-operative development (Gordon Nembhard 2020, 2023). A timeline that begins in the nineteenth century – with the German Raiffeisen's co-operative banks, Owenism/New Lanark – is equally problematic (Guinnane 2001; Quarter 2000; Fairbairn 1994). Africa and Asia have far older histories of co-operative development. In the Americas, Brazil's Quilombolas and Haiti's Kombit systems (informal collectives) were born out of crisis and pain, and the fight for humanity and freedoms (Bohn and Kreiger Grossi 2018; Smith 2016; Kelley 2002). In Brazil in the mid-1500s, Africans and their descendants escaping slavery set up Quilombola communities in remote areas far from plantations (Silva 2023). They were helped by Indigenous groups and their communities, and they are still there today.

African women, and women of the African diaspora, choose the practice of money pooling, which involves dividends being shared by members, and members consulting each other about any special projects in which they want to invest.[7] Even while enslaved, members of the African diaspora held on to collective systems because they imagined a day when they would be free and able to buy their own land. In *Freedom Dreams*, Robin D.G. Kelley (2002) reminds us that Black people who fled plantations were viewed as renegades. They built maroon societies, which were basically co-operatives shared by Black and Indigenous peoples who refused enslavement. As Guyanese feminist and activist Andaiye (2020, 18) explains, "We need first to identify the world we want to build, not in the old language of 'isms' but in a new language that has clarity and purpose." Many people around the world, and especially those being harmed, have been thinking through ideas of inclusive world economies.

It is insufficient and misguided to regard European experiences as the only ones to have formulated co-operatives in the right way. Yes, the Quebecois couple Alfonse and Dorimene Desjardins started the *caisses populaires* in the 1900s to reach excluded French Canadians. Many scholars recall this story but fail to note co-operative traditions among Black Canadians (Bouchard 2013;

---

7 Njie's (2022) early work examined this concept of collectivity among Gambian women, who used it to pay for their children's schooling.

Mendell 2009; Shragge and Fontan 2000). The Underground Railroad was the culmination of that hidden form of collectivity, made up of a network of informal co-op institutions created to free human beings. To focus on the white, French Canadian experience erases the co-operative economics of African people who have also contributed to Canada's co-operative sector.

It is time to broaden what we know about co-operativism, and to cite and include those many stories. The stories we now communicate about alternative economic systems need to be revised, drawing on that wider history. This means looking into a past that predates the West's efforts to (under)develop non-Western societies (Rodney 1982; Escobar [1995] 2012; Mohanty 1991). Sociology professor Oyèrónkẹ́ Oyěwùmí (1997, 122) in *The Invention of Women* exposed how in the case of Nigeria, the histories of both the colonized and the colonizer have been written from a male point of view, and that women have suffered from double colonization.

If one applies a Black diaspora and feminist and liberation theory to the political economy, it becomes increasingly obvious that other worlds exist – a view to which many anti-racist scholars and feminist economists also subscribe (Banks 2020; Gordon Nembhard 2014a; Asante 2007; Gibson-Graham 2006; Karenga 1997, 1972; Diop 1974; Du Bois 1907). Feminist scholars Gibson-Graham (1996, 2006) have been saying for decades that ideological arguments about markets miss seeing what is going on inside communities, and that people in other places are – and always have been – making economies humane.

What Are Varieties of Co-operativism?

Informal co-op institutions are not defective or underdeveloped co-operatives. As others have argued before me, I hold that ROSCAs, rooted in localized systems of collectivity, should be considered co-operative institutions (see Jain 1929; Ardener 1964; Harrison 1988; van den Brink and Chavas 1997). We need to expand what we mean by a co-operative by including institutions that are informally organized. The term "varieties of co-operativism" was influenced by the concept of varieties of capitalism (Hall and

Soskice 2001), which maintains that capitalism does not have a single form, but rather varies from place to place. The concept of varieties of co-operativism also does not follow a single model; rather, understandings of co-operativism should encompass informal and formal institutions, and not condemn informal ones to obscurity.

For far too long, the co-operative sector has been dominated by white experts preoccupied with formal co-op institutions, which has left informal ones largely unaccounted for. Such privileging relegates informal types of co-ops to the sidelines – co-ops that are, notably, run primarily by marginalized and in most cases racialized women. Many books, underpinned by Marxist (read: European) theory, have been written by white scholars on global co-ops without ever mentioning ROSCAs or other informal co-ops set up by Black/African descent people living under duress. Erasing informal institutions formed by non-white peoples of the world does not constitute radical or honest research. On the contrary, it shrinks knowledge production about the multiplicity of co-operative businesses around the globe.

By introducing the concept of "varieties of co-operativism," and by asking people to use the term co-operativism, I urge everyone to widen the scope of the co-operative sector to capture what Black, Indigenous, and racialized people do in and for the co-operative sector. Inventorying other people's labour in co-operative economics is how we achieve a better understanding of why people choose member-owned firms (Gordon Nembhard 2014a). I first read about the term "co-operativism" in the work of economist Curtis Haynes Jr. (2018), who, in his decades-long work on Du Bois, used it to explain the meaning of co-ops for African Americans. Haynes Jr.'s work showed how Black people together organized politically and economically, and much of it was not public knowledge.

Varieties of co-operativism is defined as member-owned institutions focused on the collective, which prioritizes the well-being of community. These institutions include: self-help groups, informal co-operatives, community associations, collectives, money pools, mutual aid, and ROSCAs, as well as other formal co-operatives. Valuing informal institutions within varieties of co-operativism means moving away from the big-C co-operative, meaning those co-ops that are legally registered and formalized. Small-c co-operatives subscribe to the same co-operative principles and values as the big-C co-operative: rooted in democracy, they value voting, voices for members, community well-being, and dividend sharing for the greater good. Small-c co-operatives recognize that co-operatives can adopt a range of structures. The term varieties of co-operativism should be used as part of the co-operative sector to ensure that the various models of co-operating are included.

Black Diaspora Theorizing in Solidarity Economics

Understanding the Black Social Economy and solidarity economics means using literature written by and for the African diaspora that speaks to the collective economic projects developed by Black/African-descended people. African, Caribbean, and diasporic African scholars have written extensively on social-purpose businesses that prioritize human well-being.

W.E.B. Du Bois (1907), an African American writer of Haitian heritage, advocated for Black-run co-operative enterprises through his academic works and the journal *Crisis*. He was a leading founder of the National Association for the Advancement of Colored People (NAACP), a civil rights organization that advances Black people's voices (Haynes Jr. 2018). Another important influence is Madam C.J. Walker, a businesswoman of humble beginnings who became a millionaire by developing a line of hair products. She supported numerous human rights efforts (Bundles 2001).

Ardener and Burman's (1996) *Money-Go-Rounds* reports on a dozen case studies of ROSCAs in Kenya, Ghana, and India, as well as the Somali diaspora in the United Kingdom, Korea, and Japan. However, the authors do not discuss systemic racism. The cases of ROSCAs described by them reveal how women are excluded from formal finance based on gender, and they demonstrate how members then intentionally redesign co-operatives with an emphasis placed on women's well-being. Women in ROSCAs need these all-female spaces to share ideas, gossip, discuss politics, and plot out how to improve their social situations.

ROSCAs formed by women of the Black diaspora are also mindful of the African values of Ubuntu, which are wedded to ideas of democracy, co-operation, and collective values (Kinyanjui 2019; Molefe 2019; Nussbaum 2003). In response to her Nairobi-based research with women traders, Mary Njeri Kinyanjui (2012) explains that Vyama depends on group cohesion and community values, and that those norms and values are not informalized where none of these systems exist.

Gambian scholar Haddy Njie (2022) similarly notes that Osusu banks are embedded in community. She draws on the East African theory of Ubuntu – "I am because you are" – to document, through her interviews, how Gambian women refuse to accept conventional business practice as the norm. Instead, these women choose their Osusu system because it is rooted in trust, care, and reciprocity, where the sharing of goods is the norm. Despite such scholarly exceptions, the social economy literature seldom discusses ROSCAs as actors that run counter to neo-liberal economics. It is usually marginalized women who take the risk of proposing new forms of economic organization. In addition, male bias has always figured in the design of development programs, which do not consider the lives of women, and miss entirely how their reproductive labour contributes to making humanity what it is today (Barker, Bergeron, and Feiner 2021; Elson 1995). Development designers, rooted in their own elitism, have much to learn from these women, many of whom have years of experience tackling gender, class, and racial discrimination.

ROSCAs, through a practice of co-operative building, can also be viewed as entities that tend to be theory making because they refuse to accept Babylon's (the establishment's) project of modernity and individualism. Using theories embedded in the lived experience of African women is key to understanding the work of the Banker Ladies.

ROSCAs Born in the Americas

Black, Indigenous, and racialized people, especially women, have engaged in co-operatives for as long as they have lived in the Western hemisphere. This chapter reinforces the research that shows

Figure 1.2. Sole Window at the Door of No Return at Elmina, Ghana
Note: Photo taken during my field work on the Susu system (July 2017).

that community-based banks, rooted in mutual aid, are aligned with African cultural and business traditions (Kinyanjui 2012; Dunford 2009). Further, Kinyanjui argues that "markets cannot perform without the social and the social cannot perform without the market" (2012, 36). She does so to make her point that the Vyama (ROSCAs in Kenya) blur any divide between economic and social life because the two connect in various contexts. These are the lessons of business, collective and co-operative, and being mindful of the everyday social living that African people value and hold on to.

In *Capitalism and Slavery*, Eric Williams ([1944] 2004) depicts a slave voyage carried out by Europeans. The depiction takes us back to the white-painted, concrete walls of the slave forts at Cape Coast, Ghana, where we see people being forced off the ledge at the

Door of No Return, bound for a life of enslavement. (Figure 1.2 is my photo of the sole window at the Door of No Return at Elmina, Ghana, taken during my field work on the Susu system [July 2017]). In their struggle to hold on to dear life, African people cherished things that made them whole. As a result, the people they are today in the Americas claim as their own certain foodways, music, dances, faiths, and money systems. We often forget that for people of the African diaspora, managing their own financial economies, and thinking through their journey to freedom, was part of the quest for survival (St. Pierre 1999).

Despite the evils of plantation life, slaves in Santo Domingo (known today as Haiti) retained Kombit (an informal collective) and Gwoupmans (associations) as a means of saving so they could one day buy their freedom (Heinel and Heinel 2005). Historian Maurice St. Pierre (1999) has documented the Boxhand and saving clubs of African Guyanese, who, upon emancipation, collectively organized to buy, systematically, plots of land. Their concept of solidarity as African people was sustained by the knowledge that, one day, their children would be free. In the Haitian constitution, there is a section recognizing co-operation as a sacred value of the Haitian people. The film *Poto Mitan* (Bergan and Schuller 2009), as well as Hossein's (2014b) work, have documented the importance of co-operativism in Haiti.

For too long, ROSCAs have been studied as practices designed to "cope" with exclusion and finite resources. ROSCAs are much more than that: they are politicized co-operatives for Black people. Arturo Escobar (2020) and the Global Tapestry of Alternatives, a group of Global South activists and intellectuals, are interested in proposals (from the Global South as well as from local communities) intent on showing how to reconstruct the world.[8] The concept of "pluriversal" encompasses the process of being attentive to non-Western locales in terms of what they are doing. This includes: first, asserting that the Global South no longer needs to be provided with external expertise; and, second, affirming that people can be part of their own development process. Black feminist Patricia Hill Collins (2000a) has offered much instruction on situational knowledge production, demonstrated that Black women have

---

8   See more about the Global Tapestry Alternative (n.d.) online.

always had to work, and shown that their own lived experience is what has enabled Black women to contribute to the intersection of race in the field of political economy (Hill Collins 2000b).

The African diaspora experience in banker co-ops is indigenous to Africa in its origins, and it was carried to the Americas by African people centuries ago (Katzin 1959). As first made clear by Du Bois (1907) – and later reiterated by Nyerere (1968), Karenga (1993), and Gordon Nembhard (2014a) – nobody needs to teach Black people about co-operative economics; the knowledge is ancestral. African American activist Karenga (1993) reveals that, while much has been written about alternative political economies, the focus is always on the European version. It is as if Black people had never engaged in any organizational or business activities. Others find that Black Americans are discussed in a one-dimensional way, with focus placed on the use of their labour in exploitative ways (Marable [1983] 2015).

The Banker Ladies, whether located in the Global South or in the Global North, are organizing mutual aid groups and rotating funds among groups of people of the same social class who want to share goods equitably and collectively. During the COVID-19 pandemic, we have seen many acts of mutual aid, with people helping each other every day. When formal systems get shut down, people find ways to support each other co-operatively. This is radical economics – stepping in with alternative ways to help people when mainstream banks fail to do so.

People need each other. That is the very essence of ROSCAs, which are steeped in mutual aid. *Mutual Aid* by legal scholar Dean Spade (2020a) establishes there is nothing new about mutual aid. Spade (2020a) illustrates how African Americans became vested in mutual aid groups because it was the option open to them; they refused to be part of managed and subsidized charities. Excluded, racialized minorities, immigrants, and LGBTIQ people have drawn on mutual aid for a very long time because it is internally funded – and safe. Mutual aid is rooted in the collective. It is about trust and reciprocity. Stigmatized groups find it is better to organize aid with those they know and trust. Spade (2020b) argues that solidarity is not charity because the grassroots collectives organized by people are not dependent on external aid; rather, it is the people themselves who must seek out resources and bring about social change.

Knowing When to Converge

Black women who organize ROSCAs value and preserve concepts of smallness and group economics. They essentially work against individualized business systems. Economist E.F. Schumacher (1973), in his best-known work *Small Is Beautiful*, tells us that the constant push for economies of scale associated with modern economics is not sensible for all people on the planet. Working on a small scale is a better model. While ROSCAs and mutual aid may be viewed by some as "underdeveloped" forms of doing business, the Banker Ladies have always disagreed, and we can see that they were right. Women of the Black diaspora who live in countries in the Global South and Global North are leading mutual aid-driven banking co-ops because formal finance has alienated them. Instead, they choose – deliberately and unapologetically – to lend money using systems modelled on consensus and democratic principles.

The benefits of small-scale economies are also upheld by Guyanese economist C.Y. Thomas, who is not well known outside of the Caribbean. Thomas wrote many papers and major works, including *The Poor and the Powerless* (1988), in which he examines world systems and the Caribbean's racially tiered, class pyramid system – the result of enslavement and colonization. An earlier work by Thomas (1974), *Dependency and Transformation*, pushed for "de-growth" (or "small is beautiful") in light of his dissection of the capitalist world system, which he argued it blocked countries like Guyana from becoming fully independent and developing sustainably. Thomas notes how Guyana and other countries have become dependent on imports, and filling gaps to meet international demand, rather than focusing on what was in the best interest of local communities. His idea of turning inwards and thinking about community is key. Thomas (1974) refers to "divergence" as a negative outcome, referring to instances of countries working against their own interests to feed into a world system, generating products that would not help Black people. By contrast, Thomas's convergence theory advocates for people coming together in carefully meditated ways to pool resources and produce what they themselves need. Convergence is about local economic development, with residents concerned about their own consumption needs and local reinvestment.

The Banker Ladies engage in convergence to prioritize local needs. They do not want to be a cog in a commercial wheel. These women set aside time to pool their funds with the objective of making financial goods available to those left out of formal systems. Professor C.Y. Thomas's convergence theory, conceived in the Caribbean, subsequently travelled to Canada, where it was used in the work of the late John Loxley (2008). Thomas's theory of producing goods locally in order to stymie the World System's extractive economics influenced the development of the Neechi principles, a set of values that assist Canadians in economic development (Hossein and Ceres 2022). "Neechi," for which the principles of economic development were originally derived, was an Indigenous worker co-operative out of north Winnipeg in Manitoba (Rebel Sky Media 2018).[9] The Neechi principles for community economic development align precisely with the work of the Banker Ladies because they place local people in charge of deciding what goods are needed and how they should be shared.

Black women have engaged in self-help and mutual aid precisely because of the values of duty, compassion, and love. They also hold on to rage as a way to resist and build membership organizations that can reach those being left out of formal finance. This rage aligns with the kind Cherry (2021) describes as a necessary part of the community-building process. These values converge to prioritize helping each other first. In the introductory chapter to *All About Love*, the late bell hooks (1999) asserts that love is how we can grow and flourish, and that it is radical to use love to fight against the exclusions so pervasive in society.

In *The Terms of Order*, political scientist Cedric Robinson ([1980] 2016) argues that associations of people are the consciousness of the people. Such entities bring people together of their own volition to discuss ideas and concepts, thus ensuring elites do not control the process. In writing about mutual aid, philosopher Peter Kropotkin ([1902] 1976) explains that group support is a requirement of all animal species, especially for those inhabiting complex

---

9 To learn more about economic development in Manitoba and work carried out by the Neechi worker co-operative, the open-access documentary can be viewed at Rebel Sky Media (2018).

environments. Pooling resources has been fundamental to living as a Black person in the Americas because of the suffering experienced by individuals and communities. Organizing in this manner was deliberately hidden to give an oppressed people a sense of refuge (Hossein 2018a; Gordon Nembhard 2014a; Karenga 1993; Stewart 1984; Ofari 1970). My interviews with the Banker Ladies revealed two key points: first, ROSCAs helped them to meet their needs; and, second, being members of these groups allowed them to show kindness and caring for others, which in turn provided happiness and satisfaction. This emphasis on well-being is very much what feminist economists would count as economic success (Power 2004).

The Banker Ladies film is a powerful record of development solutions built on the foundation of experiences of those women who know it best. Black women will do what they feel they must do – under the radar if necessary – to establish equitable co-operatives. Those looking for alternatives and speaking to diverse community economies should prioritize the work of the Banker Ladies. In their societies, these women battle intense forms of racial discrimination, sexism, and hostility. Even so, they seek refuge, engage in self-love, and cultivate vibrant community economies for themselves and their communities. It is insufficient to talk about radicalizing development if the solutions we look to are not indigenous, or fail to arise from the lived experience of the people who know how to correct these wrongs (Mullings 2021). We need to listen to their stories about co-op systems like ROSCAs. We need to learn how they have managed, in quiet and unassuming ways, to make economies equitable. Bringing together the very best of the Black political economy is the project of the Black Social Economy, which prioritizes learning grounded in practice and lived experience.

chapter two

The Black Social Economy: Provoking an Africana Feminist Political Economy Epistemology for the World

The Black Social Economy underscores what we mean by radicalizing, changing up, and making the economy more inclusive. Drawing on a body of literature that speaks to the experiences of 200 million people of African descent living in the Americas – where violence, racism, and discrimination against Black people are well-known – is a prerequisite for understanding their standing in business and society (Mbembe 2017; Taylor 2016).[1] Empirical and survey research carried out by political scientist Sharon D. Wright Austin (2007) in the Mississippi Delta, one of the poorest places in the United States, demonstrated that wealth resided with white people and not Black people. No matter how much things changed legislatively, economic and political power remained with a few white families while Black people continued to be alienated and mistreated. When she later surveyed hundreds of Black Americans of Caribbean heritage about how they vote on political issues, Wright Austin (2018) found that many voted with African Americans on issues due to the societal oppression they faced. Black people will come together strategically when they are being denied basic rights (see also Forstater 2007). Systemic racial exclusion is one of the main reasons why ROSCAs exist in developed countries.

Scholars can no longer force "generic" (i.e., assuming no racial bias) canons that are ignorant of the Black experience to explain

---

1 See more in Alamenciak (2014), "Banking While Black," and Morgan (2016), "Why Canada Needs Black Lives Matter."

business exclusion. There needs to be intentional citation of works rooted in Black liberation, especially for the solidarity economy, the citizen's sector. This chapter will assist primarily political economists, political scientists, and economists – faculty and students alike – to rethink the theories they use. A scholar cannot claim to be progressive for studying the racialized experience if that same scholar continues to draw exclusively on certain white thinkers when articulating their own work. As noted by philosopher Achille Mbembe, "Returning to the literature of political science and development economics, it becomes clear these disciplines have undermined the very possibility of understanding African economic and political facts" (2001, 7).

Mbembe (2001) nailed it when he said that the academy, media, and others have shown themselves unable to speak rationally about Africa. Development scholar Kalpana Wilson (2012) also pinpoints racism and "race" to be at the core of international development programs, which view African people as either victims who need saving, or corrupt titans. We do not read about the innovations of the Banker Ladies, nor about their accomplishments in reaching those who are excluded because of the inherent bias within development studies. Sociologist Oyèrónké Oyěwùmí (1997) has explained the phenomenon as the complete inferiorization of African women, which renders those working in development studies unable to see the Banker Ladies as people engaged in remaking economics. Knowledge-making on solidarity economies has minimized the contributions of Black people, and erased their role in economic co-operation. I have studied, read, and used these "standard" works in my own teaching and scholarship, and I am very much aware of their limits.

In a time when people are conscious of anti-Black racism, it is no longer acceptable to write books and spread knowledge about co-operative and solidarity economies without documenting, or at least being mindful of, the experiences of Black scholars. "Foundational" works – like Jonathan Michie, Joseph R. Blasi, and Carlo Borzaga's (2017) *The Oxford Handbook of Mutual, Co-operative, and Co-owned Business*, Peter Uttig's (2010) *Social and Solidarity Economy*, and Keith Hart, Jean-Louis Laville, and Antonio Cattani's (2010) *The Human Economy* – simply ignore the contributions of Black women. An exception is *Banking on a Revolution* (Friedline 2021), whose author, social work professor Terri Friedline, makes a point of drawing on the work of Gordon Nembhard to understand fully the corporatized, capital-focused American economy and its impact on racialized people in the United States and around the world. Few scholarly works by political economists cite the abundance of Black political economy literature and it is important to see African political economists Dieng and Ossome (forthcoming) talking about land, colonization and political economy from a feminist perspective. In "Black Political Economy, Solidarity Economics, and Liberation," Gordon Nembhard (2023) demonstrates that co-operative economics are at the root of a caring economy, and that the Black diaspora has much to offer on the topic. Scholars who fail to read (and cite) literature that reflects the lived experience they are studying cannot capture what is really going on, in business and society, for Black people or other excluded racial minorities.

J.K. Gibson-Graham's (1996) *The End of Capitalism (as We Knew It)* has resonated with many of us working on financial economies of the Global South. This study notes that most market activities going on in our world are hidden from plain view. This finding is very much a truism for peoples of the South. Gibson-Graham (1996, 2006) likens this reality to an iceberg, with only formal markets (or the tip of the iceberg) visible because they are on the surface (figure 2.1). The living economy, the place where most people interact with one another, is submerged below water (the massive body of the iceberg). The iceberg analogy developed by Gibson-Graham and the Community Economies Collective (2014) provides a compelling mental picture because it pushes us to let go of the myth that there is only one form of doing business – in reality, there are all kinds of business exchanges outside of formal capitalist systems. While this understanding of informal and hidden activities assists us in rethinking "alternatives," it is void of addressing power dynamics, and the relegation of Black, Indigenous, and racialized women to the sidelines.

In this chapter, I start by pointing out why ROSCAs can be viewed as an antidote to exclusion. Next, I discuss the social economy, and why terms like "bridging" and "interactive" do little to help Black

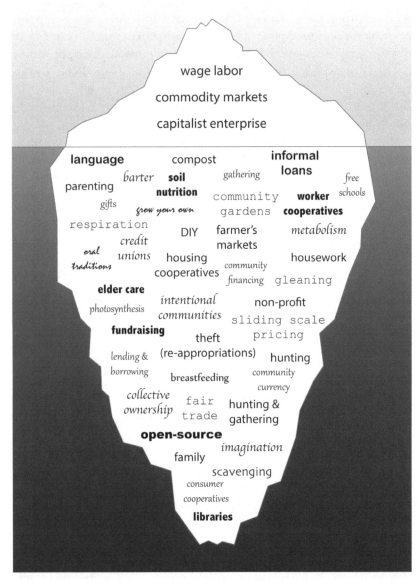

Figure 2.1. Iceberg Analogy to Outline Community Economies (Gibson-Graham)
Source: Community Economies Collective (2014). This image is licensed under the CC BY-SA 4.0 licence.

people. In chapter 1, I made it clear that I deliberately choose to use the word "solidarity" rather than "social" for people of the Black diaspora in the field of social economics. I use the word "Black" in front of the concept of the social economy to make explicit my focus on a specific group of people who have experienced extreme forms of abuse and hostility in business and society. The choice of "solidarity" is highly intentional. Presenting a theory of the Black Social Economy is a way to provoke the solidarity sector to see how much members of the African diaspora struggle and fight just to be in this world, especially those whose history includes enslavement. The section that follows is about invoking Black feminist thinkers in the diaspora with the intent of widening what we know about the Black Radical Tradition. I take note of what Black women scholars know, and why ordinary women choose to organize co-ops. I highlight the erasure of their experience as scholars and practitioners in the fields of politics and economics. As the final section reveals, there is no shortage of knowledge-making by scholars of the Black diaspora. Their scholarship demonstrates just how tied capital is to race; yet these ideas are still absent from progressive analyses, even in progressive feminist spaces.

There is certainly a place for formally registered co-operatives and non-profits. However, the institutions (mutual aid organizations, self-help, and grassroots organizations) towards which Black and racialized people tend to gravitate are frequently labelled as "unofficial," "primitive," "crooked," "illegal," or "inferior." In her foundational work mentioned earlier, *The Inventions of Women*, sociologist Oyèrónkẹ́ Oyěwùmí (2017) lays out plainly the ways in which the European colonizing project was both racist and masculinist. Its objective was to denigrate and destroy the knowledge of African peoples, especially knowledge held by African women. Developing a Black and feminist epistemology for co-operative economics is important because it will explain why Black women, regardless of location, go underground with their banking co-ops. When their very beings are under attack, and when the systems they choose to use are deemed inferior, Black women are poised to hide what they do. It is a form of survival, especially for those living in predominantly white/ened societies.

Why Is the "Bridging" Idea Limited to Black People?

No scholar examining the lives of Black and racialized people can understand their experience – and especially those of Black women – without drawing on theories from thinkers who also happen to be African/Black. Applying Eurocentric theories to explain underdevelopment for racially marginalized people simply does not work (Rodríguez 2018).

More than two decades ago, the Canadian social scientist Vijay Agnew's (1996) *Resisting Discrimination* documented extensive work with Asian, South Asian, African, and Caribbean women in Toronto. Agnew (1996) found that several women felt more at ease working for community-based organizations than they did for formal corporate workplaces where discrimination was common. Scholars should examine their own locations first. Even though my work has involved travelling to my cultural origins of the Caribbean, I also learned that it was vital for me to examine the local economies of where I am currently situated, and to learn about financial exclusion from groups of the Caribbean women to which I belong.

Crisscrossing the globe to critique other locations without looking at where we ourselves are located is problematic too because business exclusion also occurs where we live. All over the world, Black women are making proposals for banking co-operatives, but this work is unseen. Writing from our own locations is where we should all begin. Nishnaabeg writer Leanne Betasamosake Simpson (2020), author of *As We Have Always Done*, reminds people to remember what came before, and to see that Elder wisdom casts light on how to care for each other and the planet in ways that do not subscribe to Western patriarchal systems. Remembering in this way requires doing your homework, and reading those "start where you are from" philosophies. *Decolonizing Academia*, by feminist scholar Clelia O. Rodríguez (2018), challenges scholars to unlearn what they believe to be "radical" thinking, and to read and then re-read works by people – especially women and non-binary folks – who have the lived experience, and therefore vital insight, into how to rebuild an inclusive economic world.

Black people are vulnerable to police brutality and killings, so we need to move away from literature that does not reflect this lived experience, especially if we want to think effectively about new economies (Táíwò and Mbembe 2021; Morgan 2016; Peck 2017; Taylor 2016). Ta-Nehisi Coates's (2015) award-winning book, *Between the World and Me*, reminds readers that many young Black men are killed in the United States by state officials – the police. How does a group of people recover from this kind of constant violence?

Fear of a Nation, by Canadian author David Austin (2013), warns of deeply embedded racism in Canada, and cites the fallout from a two-week occupation of the computer lab at Sir George Williams University (now Concordia University). The protest was sparked by the university's disregard for Black students' allegations of racism against a biology professor. It ended with police storming the building, where they made 87 arrests (with 37 Black people separated from 50 white people). The event heightened fear that Montreal was becoming a hub of Black radical politics. The white supremacist rally in Charlottesville, Virginia, and confrontations with La Meute in Quebec in August 2017, similarly unleashed a racist platform against minorities and racialized people (Astor, Caron, and Victor 2017). Racial tension has since increased. The awakening of the Black Lives Matter movement, a phenomenon in both the United States and Canada, makes it abundantly clear that the lives of Black citizens are threatened (Harriot 2017).

In *Marvellous Grounds*, scholars Jin Haritaworn, Ghaida Moussa, and Syrus Marcus (2018) document the various ways in which Black/racialized queer communities in Toronto contribute to the social economy and thereby counter the archive of queer history based largely on the perspectives of gay white men. Having an alternative space of making a living and building community continues to be important to queer and trans people living in Toronto and beyond. Indeed, in Canada and elsewhere, forms of identity exclusion explains why the social and solidarity economy sector (also known as the third sector) is a lifeline for so many.

There are times, however, when this same space in the social economy is troubling for Black women. Philosopher Olúfẹ́mi O. Táíwò (2020a) has made me rethink the role of identity in solidarity economies because emphasis on trauma can feed into a fetish for elites who, while willing to hear the issues, are not willing to change the system. In other words, elites will "listen" to stories about the Banker Ladies, but neither compensate nor validate these efforts, nor will they use their powers to make necessary changes. Performative acts of solidarity occur in the academy all the time, while nothing really changes for those being oppressed.

The Banker Ladies chose to challenge the system long before academics made the links to political economies and race. Seeing the Banker Ladies as actors in development finance signals a move away from racial capitalism. Cedric Robinson (1983) explains that racial capitalism is a phenomenon that allows powerful social forces (read: white) to dominate less privileged groups in the markets. It is positive that many scholars now recognize the colonial aspects of development finance (Alami and Guermond 2022; Tilley and Shilliam 2018). However, there remains a need to cite ROSCAs as an indigenous form of finance that pushes against exclusionary financial economies (see Baradaran 2015; Ardener and Burman 1996). Indeed, it is a form of finance which has been around for a very long time – in fact, long before microfinance and other such systems. The Banker Ladies who mobilize ROSCA funds deliberately interrupt the process in which raced financial exchanges take place. Through the very act of organizing their own monies collectively, they transcend their own trauma and make financial systems into something more.[2] The social and solidarity economy is both a place of refuge for Black people who experience pain and a space in which the Black/African diaspora builds new economies.

Women in the diaspora draw on mutual aid systems as a way of doing more for themselves, their families, and their communities. In *The Politics of Survival*, political scientist Gladys L. Mitchell-Walthour

---

2 Táíwò (2020b) made a point on an episode of the podcast, *The Dig*'s "Identity, Power, and Speech" that resonated with me – namely, these women are the ones making the difference and mobilizing the support needed to do something different; they are not waiting on anyone and never have. This podcast has helped me think through ideas that supported the writing of *The Banker Ladies*.

(2023) makes it clear that, in the United States and Brazil, what has helped women most are women's self-help groups and informal sharing of labour, rather than subsidies, which have been known to hurt them. As political economists, academics, and policymakers concerned about power, politics, and the allocation of social provisions, it is important for us to note the impact of racialized capital on the people we study, as well as how women of the Black diaspora use their own lived experience to build economic organization from within.

Canadian scholars Jack Quarter, Laurie Mook, and Ann Armstrong (2018) have a definition of the social economy which assumes that sectors can interact. It is one that makes perfect sense if governments and commercial businesses respected all citizens in the same way. The social economy in Canada and in a number of other places is defined as "a bridging concept for organizations that have social objectives central to their mission and their practice, and either have explicit economic objectives or generate some economic value through the services they provide and purchases they undertake" (Quarter, Mook, and Armstrong 2009, 4). This definition distinguishes the social economy from both the public sector (the government) and the private sector (corporations and for-profit businesses). This definition is unsettling for those of us who study intersectional bias and business exclusion. The authors' concept of "bridging" presupposes that the three sectors can "engage" and "interact" together. What happens when a segment of society is harmed, and so fears the state and corporations? That segment of the population will self-exclude rather than choose to engage with the formal sectors. This is what happening all over the world.

The meaning of "bridge" in the literature of the social economy is not sufficiently defined to consider those who are left out, or to recognize that racial capitalism is present, and that "overlapping" sector is not always possible for some organizations. As the Venn diagram shown in figure 2.2 demonstrates, the term "bridging" does not make room for groups who feel excluded. It seems to suggest that some actors of the social economy can negotiate with the dominant powers while others cannot, and so are left out. john a. powell (2021), an expert on civil rights and director of the Othering & Belonging Institute at UC Berkeley, suggests that in

Figure 2.2. Venn Diagram of an Interactive Social Economy
Source: Quarter, Mook, and Armstrong (2018).

order to "bridge," a system must take an extra step to identify and then stop the alienating politics, and to listen to and ensure that excluded groups and minorities belong.

Figure 2.2, "A Venn Diagram of an Interactive Social Economy," denotes overlapping across the three sectors. The diagram makes it clear that self-help groups, mutual aid, and ROSCAs would be in the shaded area of civil society – a segment which is not interacting. Although they are embedded in civil society, ROSCAs are purposefully detached, even thought much of the literature of the social economy assumes there is "co-operation," "partnership," and "interaction."

Being Intentional by Choosing the Term "Solidarity"

Many Black, Indigenous, and racialized people do not interact with the state, the private sector, or certain types of social economy organizations (e.g., NPOs) because of racial exclusion (Spade 2020b). Excluded people turn to localized co-operatives and informal collectives, such as mutual aid, self-help, and ROSCAs to meet their needs, and this choice does not require engagement with the other two sectors.

The term "social economy" is limited in what it means to people of the African diaspora, who have had to struggle and fight for survival, and who have had their rights compromised under racial capitalist environments. It is insufficient to define the actors in the social economy and then presume that all people can interact with the other two sectors. There are many actors in the social economy who resist, and remain detached from, the state and private sectors. Like so many feminist scholars, and especially those who belong to the DISE Collective, we advocate for the social economy sector in Canada to join the rest of the world by adopting the term "solidarity economy," which encompasses "conflict," "difference," "protest," and "struggle." Only then can we start to acknowledge the conflicts existing in the economy. The solidarity economy must go beyond "mapping" or "bridging" and is ready not to engage with elitist institutions in the formal sectors. When we apply an anti-racist feminist lens to mapping out the economy, we will soon learn that many forms of exclusion occur even inside of the social economy sector. Not all actors in the economy can engage or have partnerships with one another because allocations made are often based on identity politics and other forms of oppression. To assume an "interactive" social economy renders it complacent and somewhat complicit towards those people who experience harms.

The solidarity economy holds meaning for people in the Global South, for excluded minorities, and for the African diaspora because it makes room for militancy and disruption to serve as the means to transform exclusionary economic systems (Hossein and Pearson 2023; Loxley 2008; Thomas 1974). CERN member Ethan Miller (2010) points out that the *economía solidaria* reflects the people's movements in Peru, Chile, and Brazil, each of which is fighting to make major changes rather than to negotiate with, or accept, what already exists.

In my own teaching and writing, I now use "solidarity" or "co-operative economics" because these concepts speak to the idea of transformation. The Manitoba-based economist John Loxley (2008), who lived for some time in Tanzania, considered grassroots and community-driven alternatives such as co-operatives devised by Indigenous people to bring lasting transformation. The theory of convergence, where people come together, and was put forward by C.Y. Thomas (1974) and inspired Loxley, outwits the World Systems approach by focusing on local needs to make development options reach those who are excluded. Membership organizations focused on change seems key here for challenging economic inequalities (Banks, Hulme, and Edwards 2015). In adding the word "Black" to the social economy is my own way of ensuring that we remember the struggle, and the deliberate politicized action needed to fight for equity within the (social) economy for African-descended people.

The impact of solidarity economy is twofold: first, it provides a place for Black and racially excluded people to meet their economic livelihood needs; and, second, it enables the voices and contributions of people of the Black diaspora to be heard and seen. The African diaspora takes solidarity spaces seriously because they offer a concrete way to nurture each other, and to build up their communities. The dedicated role played in the solidarity economy by Black people and other racialized people, and in particular women, is absent from the discourse on voluntary and social services. Yes, Black people find themselves in the social and solidarity economy because of deep forms of racism and exclusion. However, this involvement also makes them architects in undoing the harms. Knowing who can give life lessons about pain offers an argument for Black theorizing that comes from within the community.

Black Women Knowing What They Do

Black women organizing in the solidarity economy is not new. Yet the academic literature, by and large, has failed to see the large numbers of excluded people who refuse to be organized through philanthropy or charity (Spade 2020a, 2020b), and instead they spend time ensuring the Black Social Economy reaches Black lives first (Hossein 2018b; Wright Austin 2023). More stories need to be shared so we can move away from one-dimensional understandings of Black people's role in the solidarity economy.

The persistent stereotype is that Black folks are always waiting for handouts. Progressive spaces let us know that Black people need help. The city of Toronto, where I live, has a population of 6.4 million, with 46.1 per cent indicating they are foreign-born (City of Toronto, n.d.). In Toronto, the absence of paid Black leaders in the non-profit sector is glaring. Many newcomers rely on solidarity and self-help groups organized by themselves to serve their own communities. The narrative of Black people's role in the economy is one-dimensional. They are seen as passive rather than active recipients of aid. The story of Black and racialized women leaders of co-operatives is untold. Even the literature about alternative forms of business does not draw on theorizing that reflects racialized peoples, and specifically Black women.

As Black and racialized groups meet their needs through the solidarity economy, they also become acutely aware of their exclusion in business and society. Even the progressive spaces where they find friends are often riddled with complexity and subtle harms. African American bell hooks ([1981] 2015) notes that progressive arenas can be sites of conflict for Black women because they are always being ignored. It is not enough to see Black women congregating in the solidarity economy as passive beneficiaries. They are the "doers." They make things happen, whether they are paid or not. For the allocation of monies to be fair, just, and focused on belonging, the resources in this sector must be determined by Black and racialized people.

Black women *politicize the solidarity economy* because of their lived experience (i.e., racial capitalism and structural violence). They have found a way to rally together and to make use of co-operativism to defeat commercialized markets. This is at the very heart of theory-making on the Black Social Economy. Existing work on the solidarity economy is not hearing Black voices. It does not invite Black women into the conversation about *how* capitalism can be transformed. The intent of the Black Social Economy is to bring the Black political economy into the conversation, and take note of the applied work being carried out by Black women in particular (e.g., through co-operatives) to stymie harmful commercial economies.

In *Canada's Economic Apartheid*, Canadian academic Grace-Edward Galabuzi (2006) holds that existing social justice institutions need to involve the very people who are oppressed, and asserts that this movement must be rooted in politicized action to effectively confront racial exclusion. For social justice to take root in the economy, Black and racialized people must serve as leaders within the solidarity sector, both in terms of designing programs (e.g., as managers and directors) and in funding the work (e.g., as donors). INCITE! (2017) stressed that racialized people, and especially women, need to be decision-makers in the fight for equity and social change, as well as the ones in charge of the disbursement of funds for solidarity groups. While Black and racialized people lead important work throughout the world, what they do continues to be ignored due to racism and sexism (Banks 2020; Davis 2017; Hossein 2016b, 2016c).

White Androcentric Views on the Social Economy

No mention of anti-Black or anti-Indigenous racism appears in what is being produced in mainstream economics. Nonetheless, the erasure of scholarship by Black people about solidarity economies is active. John McKnight and Peter Block (2012) remain vested in "community innovation," but they naively document white neighbourhoods bringing about change with or without capitalist agendas. They co-opt the term "cultural change" to refer to the ways in which white Americans can thwart business in order to be people-focused. Absent from their work is any critical analysis of the horrors of racial violence against African American and immigrant communities. This kind of storytelling of the "social economy" amplifies white privilege and erases Black people from being actors in innovation. Nowhere in their fixation on "cultural changes" do McKnight and Block consider cultures that are not white. These stories, and others that promote economic alternatives, cling to the notion that they are "shaking up" or "radicalizing social change" in the current capitalist system. But they are not. These scholarly contributions on economic alternatives and co-operating are a project of white supremacy.

Given the social and economic struggles of Black people, an understanding of the Black experience in business and (social) economics is long overdue (Mullings 2021; Kinyanjui 2019; Gordon Nembhard 2014a; Stewart 1984). As highlighted, the idea of "alternatives" fails to offer intersectional analysis. Androcentric white and mostly male experts (e.g., Michie, Blasi, and Borzaga 2017; Barton, Horvath, and Kipping 2016; Thériault 2012; McKnight and Block 2012; Hart, Laville, and Cattani 2010; Uttig 2010; McMurtry 2010; Bridge, Murtagh, and O'Neil 2009; Quarter, Mook, and Armstrong 2009) have dominated the discourse on the social economy and co-operatives.[3] These are the scholars who decide and define what the third sector is while seldom including non-white/racialized feminist scholars writing from lived experience.

The organizational activities of Black women have been shunted to the side, and I have been in rooms where Black women's political economy is described as "civil rights activities." This constant dismissal or (strategic) citation blindness of Black feminist political economy is not how we decolonize the library on the social economy. One would think these white scholars knew better about the immoral roots of the capitalist economy and racial capitalism; yet those writings about how to reform capitalism or rethink business using co-operativism have failed to think about epistemologies beyond the West. And they still draw on whiteness and privilege to study down certain communities. As early as the mid-twentieth century, Professor Oliver C. Cox (1948, 1959, 1964), who coined the concept of World Systems, notes: race, racism, and elitism are deeply embedded in global markets (Hunter 2000; Wallerstein 2000). Cox's World Systems theory holds that Europe, the metropole, stole and exploited the resources of the colonies in the Global

---

3 Note that Quarter, Mook, and Armstrong (2018) corrects this view, and the authors recognize a Black Social Economy.

South to build up their own riches (Rodney 1982). Aware of its deeply racist origins (Williams [1944] 2004), those in the solidarity economy had no interest in reforming the capitalist economy.

Groups working on the European binaries of Marxism versus commercial capitalism are so preoccupied by their own ideological battles that they do not see the racial exclusion of people (Escobar 2020; Willoughby Herard 2015; Robinson 1983). This is exactly the point of the writings of Marcus Garvey and how he felt that the Marxist left was blind to the racial politics (Lewis 1987; Martin 1983). Academic peer-reviewed books and journal articles continually overlook – or deliberately erase – the history of millions of Black co-operators is poor, and racist, scholarship. *Re-imagining Capitalism* (Barton, Horvath, and Kipping 2016), published by Oxford University Press, disseminates knowledge about "new ways" of doing business without even considering what Black people have to say, or accounting for their exclusions in the global economy. This book, authored by three privileged white men and published by a prestigious global press, is void of cultural diversity. A year later, *The Oxford Handbook of Mutual, Co-operative, and Co-owned Business* (Michie, Blasi, and Borzaga 2017) defined co-operatives over the course of 704 pages without considering any Black/African perspectives.

Scholars engaged in political and economic discourse need to correct how they use and cite literature on solidarity and social economies by historically excluded scholars in the Global South and North alike. During a plenary address given at the International Feminist Economics Association's annual meeting (Glasgow), Professor Nina Banks (2019) shared how Black feminist economic writing is obscured within economics, especially in heterodox and feminist economics. Black women writing on political economy routinely fail to be cited. Scholars genuinely committed to exploring liberation economics, co-operative studies, community-based alternatives, or solidarity economies must diversify the reading they do as part of their scholarship and cite a broader range of scholars in their own writing – with recognition that the lived experience of people has a role in economics and politics.

A Black Epistemology for the Solidarity Economy

Black and African descent people, one of the most disadvantaged groups in business and society, have turned to the solidarity economy for refuge. This sector has become a critical arena for this excluded group of people, allowing its members to engage in cultural, social, and economic activities. However, as noted above, the literature around the social and solidarity economy is silent when it comes to theorizing about, or documenting the practices of, members of the African diaspora. A Black epistemology in social economics requires a body of work theoretically underpinned by Black liberation and the lived experience of people of colour (Hossein 2016b, 2018b, 2019).

A Black epistemology rooted in the Black Radical Tradition is sorely lacking in terms of political economy, and especially Black feminist economics. The social economy is primarily analysed by white scholars, who focus on practitioners and donors (who again are mainly white) assisting a disproportionate number of people of colour. The Black Radical Tradition can contribute to the literature of the solidarity economy by including discussion and analysis about the Banker Ladies and their financial ingenuity in co-operativism. The Banker Ladies contribute to the Black Radical Tradition, not by theorizing or activism, but through their lived experiences and their capacity, against great odds, to maintain family, community, and social and economic solidarity.

The Banker Ladies show, through practice, how to live our lives sustainably and in peace with one another, even if the larger society is not ready for it. Through quiet, confident leadership, they demonstrate how we can take care of self, family, and community. The Banker Ladies transform things locally; they are not focused on growth and scaling up what they do. The imperative towards "growth" is an ideology, and not all people are convinced about living this way (Gibson-Graham and Dombroksi 2020; Escobar 2020; Federici 2019; Amin 2009; Gibson-Graham 1996). The overexertion of an anti-business stance can dovetail, in some ways, with corporate elite power lurking within the economy; the extremes of pro- and anti-market remedies do not often help those being excluded. Oftentimes elites on both sides underestimate the range of resources Black and racialized women organize on their own terms. For this reason, theory generated by scholars who reflect these communities' experience of exclusion brings inestimable value: it has potential to reveal the myriad ways in which people are proposing new kinds of economies.

Now is the time to draw on scholarship that engages in narratives that frame the discussion from different locations in terms of geography and class. Much of what we currently know about Black political economy resides in Africana studies and sociology. When former prime minister of Trinidad and Tobago Eric Williams ([1944] 2004) wrote *Capitalism and Slavery*, he set the record straight about the immoral and racist beginnings of capitalism. Capitalism is rooted in the trade of Black people whose forced labour made plantations profitable. This hostile and cruel system carried on because white men believed they were entitled to use Black people, who they viewed as inferior and less than human, as they saw fit. Today, the slave forts at Ouidah in Benin, at Elmina in Ghana, and on Goree Island in Senegal – all places I have visited – are reminders of the inhumane, torturous treatment of African people, and the deep-seated hatred directed towards them. Stuart Hall's (1992) "The West and the Rest" defined the colonial discourse that subjugated non-white people to an inferior position while elevating the culture and ideas of white people. Hall (1992) reminds readers to rethink the power dynamics that gave white colonizers the illusion that they were superior to others. Hall's point is echoed in the work of Oyěwùmí (1997, 122), who speaks to the phenomenon of "double colonialization" experienced by African women, who were separately inferiorized and exploited.

African Economies and the Persistence of Collectivity

An alternative reading of history makes it clear that white leaders robbed much of the Global South of its glorious wealth and resources. Guyanese historian Walter Rodney (1982), murdered by the state for exposing its social, economic, and political elitism, provides evidence of how white colonialists' grievous acts of thieving, extraction, and rape led to the underdevelopment of Southern countries. Rodney witnessed these behaviours firsthand in his own country of Guyana, where the Dutch, French, and English pillaged the country for gold and diamonds. He later encountered abuse in Jamaica and Tanzania, where powerful white leaders stole so many resources. Rodney's (1996, 1982) two books, *The Groundings with My Brothers* and *How Europe Underdeveloped Africa*, are seminal works that expose the class bias of elites who dominate Black and Brown people, and bluntly state that Europe and Europeans deliberately caused the underdevelopment of Africa and its diaspora to uphold a capitalist world economy.

The Master's plan of extracting wealth out of peripheral countries in the Global South, in order to develop the North, was a process that destabilized other economies. Europe was made possible because of the slave trade, and colonizers' extraction of goods, which effectively robbed the South of its own development. As if this theft was not sufficient, European colonizers ruled countries in the Global South according to their own agendas, destroying people's lands, cultures, and co-operative systems. The crisis of underdevelopment in the Global South is also tied to the experiences of Indigenous and racialized people in the Global North. White colonizers (or "explorers") terrorized and killed Indigenous Peoples in the Americas – to the extent that some First Nations communities and/or tribes no longer exist. Aboriginal people who survived were moved onto reserves, and their children were taken away to abusive residential schools in a ploy to make people assimilate and not resist when settlers usurped their lands. Settlers needed workers, and the idea of plantation economics was a way for white people to get rich fast.

For hundreds of years, white people used slaves for labour in the plantation fields across the Americas (including in Brazil, the Caribbean, Colombia, British North America [later Canada], and the United States) to generate profit and make themselves rich (Rodney 1982). In 1804, Haiti won its independence, having defeated the institution of slavery. In *Black Jacobins*, C.L.R. James

(1989) recounts how revolutionary leaders like Toussaint and Dessalines won the fight against slavery. Haitian American anthropologist Michel-Rolph Trouillot ([1995] 2015) suggests that Haitians did the unthinkable when they beat Europeans at warfare, freed themselves, and organized their own state. Payback for achieving independence from slavery in 1804 was a complete ostracization of the Haitian people for a hundred years, and a bill for billions of dollars issued by the French state.

Even after slavery was formally abolished, white supremacy remained. Colonial powers forced people to conform to their cultures and modern ways, dictating this approach as the way to "develop" and move forward (Brohman 1995; Hall 1992). While many countries eventually took the path of modernization, some African leaders – like Kwame Nkrumah, Julius Nyerere, Patrice Lumumba, and Jomo Kenyatta – emerged to experiment with African-based values and traditions, using them to counter the experience of colonization and the West's prescriptions for growth. An Israeli political scientist specializing in African politics and women's rights, Naomi Chazan (1994) documented how African people created their own communal and village associations when states failed to meet the needs of the people through modernizing.

African people have been long preoccupied with how to be self-sufficient. Even Tanzanian President Julius Nyerere (in power 1963–85) experimented with villagization, building on the philosophy of "Ujamaa" (Nyerere 1968). Ujamaa is a Swahili word meaning "economic co-operation" – the noble goal of pooling resources for the betterment of a people. Ujamaa is not self-interested, or focused on the profit motive; rather, it is about community well-being, and making space for others as fellow humans. Human rights activist Mahatma Gandhi spoke of "Gram Swaraj" (a Hindi term meaning self-sufficiency in the villages), and urged villagers to produce what they wanted and to be mindful of how they used resources.[4] India's Gandhi and Tanzania's Nyerere fought for their

---

4 Credit to Professor Christabell P.J. of the University of Kerala for reminding me of
   Gandhian economics of self-sufficiency.

country's liberation from a colonial power: England. Both imagined new worlds that could include *Ujamaa* and *Gram Swaraj* to develop their own countries. Neither of these men nor their people needed schooling on how to democratize, to organize collectively, or to "develop."

Africans who were enslaved and/or suffered through colonization have a shared history of a specific type of trauma. This trauma can bond people in profound ways, and encourage a strong sense of community. Every year, during Kwanzaa, many people of African descent throughout the Americas and Europe dedicate one day to Ujamaa. The racism embedded in plantation society and the capitalist business model was so profound that Black people revere co-operative economics, viewing it as something vital to their own survival. Diaspora leaders like Frederick Douglass, Sojourner Truth, Fannie Lou Hamer, Martin Luther King Jr., Elijah Muhammad, Malcolm X, and Marcus Garvey all carved out a space in America for the Black plight to be heard (Karenga 1993). Isabel Wilkerson's (2011) *Great Migration* is a story about African Americans who abandoned the racist South so they would not have to live in fear of violence. They moved to areas they believed to be safer, but plantation politics followed them everywhere.

Men and the Black Radical Tradition

This legacy of enslavement, colonization, and their after-effects on daily life stands at the core of writing in the Black Radical Tradition. Black male scholars produced work on political economy for a very long time; yet, their publications remain largely uncited and unknown (see Wallerstein 2000 for him correcting this issue with Oliver Cox). In writing *How Capitalism Underdeveloped Black America*, American scholar Manning Marable (1983 [2015]), influenced by Walter Rodney's (1982) work on white power, markets, and imperialism affirmed that capitalism, at its root, has always been fundamentally racist because it depended on the exploitation of Black labour. The idea that Black people could engage in business fairly was sabotaged because of the United States's racist context

(Marable [1983] 2015). In *Black Marxism*, political scientist Cedric Robinson (1983) set out a concept of racial capitalism that echoed these findings. Robinson argues that poor Black people will lose in the capitalist system because it continues the feudal system, which differentiated and tiered people using those of lower rank unjustly for profit and personal gain. These Black scholars challenged the myth of inclusion in the marketplace, showing that capitalist economies were not neutral, and that Black and other excluded groups would be dominated so long as a fundamentalist market economy fixated on commercial profits remained intact.

The American capitalist system was born out of bigotry. It was a system that upheld "race" and racial bias (Robinson 1983). For centuries, white people have used fear and violence to subjugate African people in order to develop their own wealth (Rodney 1982). Many rich white Americans benefitted from the slave trade and slave labour on the plantations, a story that is often left out by scholars when they re-imagine capitalism to talk about responsible business. Some of the forefathers of these scholars engaged in businesses that penalized and hurt people of colour. The perverse nature of capitalism has led to ghetto markets that have destroyed or co-opted Black families into a lifestyle of drug-trafficking, prostitution, and crime (Rodney 1982). Yet business professors Leon Prieto, Simone Phipps, Lilia Giugni, and Neil Stott (2021) are reviving the story of the Bluefield's experiment, in which people organized a co-operative store for students at the institution. Despite the exclusion African Americans have endured, they created a co-operative as an economic alternative.

Notwithstanding all this pain and suffering, Black people – those born and bred in the West – need a place to call home. Professor Maulana Karenga is the founder of Kwanzaa – the philosophy of "Kawaida" in which the idea of community outreach is embedded. It was created to ensure that the Black diaspora could own its legacy of being African and appreciate their own contributions to human civilization, as well as uplift themselves (Karenga 1997). The question is whether we can use the concept of Kawaida in business. Karenga's (1972, 1975, 1997) body of work dares to move Black people forward using their own frames of reference and by building up community-focused projects. At its heart, this work requires valuing one's own culture. Black people must reject control and domination, and instead embrace the philosophy of Kawaida as a form of liberation. This coming together as a people is a radical form of economics. Values of sharing and co-operation are at the foundation of Kawaida, and can be useful in thinking through what is meant by radical economics and the Black Social Economy. Karenga (1972, 1975) advocates for members of the African diaspora to share cultural treasures that describe Black people as thriving rather than preoccupied with their oppressors' ideas, or bound up in the politics of oppression that interrupts their humanity.

In *An Afrocentric Manifesto*, Temple University's Molefi Kete Asante (2007) lays out the thinking behind "Afrocentricity" and the need to study Black people from their own experience. Karenga aptly defines Afrocentricity as a "quality of thought and practice rooted in the cultural image and human interests of African people" (1988, 403). Asante's (1980) *Afrocentricity* is a body of work grounded in the social situation of Black people living under oppressive systems. These works should be configured in economics because the reasons Black people lose out in business are part of the experience of being Black. Afrocentricity must not be boxed in or limited by a set of prescriptions; rather, it is a standpoint theory, one which acknowledges that excluded people have a right to knowledge-making.

There exists a Black epistemology rooted in exposing the evils of capital, capitalism, and markets. Much of this work is published in the *Review of Black Political Economy* and the *National Political Science Review*. Through these venues, Black academics exiled from the mainstream disciplines of politics and economics have been sharing a sound body of knowledge that reflects the Black experience in economics and life. Cameroonian philosopher Achille Mbembe (2017) explains that the category of Blackness was conceived by white people to terrorize people of the Black diaspora. That these racist harms continue in today's world is the legacy of the transatlantic slave trade. This kind of knowledge-making disrupts the canons. The very people we study and who live in harm's way – that is, Black and racialized people – can benefit from theorizing that is situated in a political context and written with lived experiences in mind.

The fact that Black epistemology rooted in the Black radical tradition has not infiltrated the fields of social or political economics is not due to a lack of material. Nor has radical and heterodox economics literature been any more inclusive of Black scholarship, despite claiming to be spearheading critical economics. No, the field of radical and heterodox economics also remains a very white space. Incorporating thinking produced from the perspective of Black epistemology rooted in the Black Radical Tradition would disrupt what we think we know, and set a historical precedent in interpreting how people of colour engage with the social and solidarity economy. It would also serve to counteract the wickedness of racism and explain hardship through stories that come from within.

An excellent starting point in explaining how racialized people come together to do good is the Underground Railroad, which was an intricate system of informal ties and co-operation that helped enslaved Black people escape from the United States to Canada. This organization was essentially co-operative in nature, with people opposed to slavery working collectively to free fellow humans. The story of the Underground Railroad is essential to a full understanding of issues of co-operation and the social economy in North America. One of the most popular conductors was American slave Harriet Tubman (Davis 1983; Conrad 1943). At the Freedom Centre in Cincinnati, Ohio, the Underground Railroad is viewed as a third-sector organization – one that relied on its members in the United States and Canada to provide housing, money, transport, food, and support to people escaping lives of brutal violence. Despite the glaring evidence of this co-operative organization, neither the literature of radical economics nor that of the social and solidarity economy refers to the Underground Railroad's role in the beginnings of co-operativism.

Black scholars in the West with first-hand knowledge of slavery and human bondage have thought long and hard about how economic freedom might liberate Black people. As highlighted before, it was W.E.B. Du Bois who advanced the theory of "group eco-nomics" among African Americans, as a way to counteract white people's need for cheap labour and would exploit people individu-ally. This concept of "group economics" is a fundamental aspect of Black liberation theory in that it breaks away from individualism to co-operation, and a theory that can assist in the theoretical framing of the social and solidarity economy for those who have been his-torically excluded. Du Bois's (1903) powerful essay collection, *The Souls of Black Folk*, described collective forms of African business among the Bantu people of southern Africa, historical knowledge that is inspiring for Black people. Du Bois knew all too well how extreme market fundamentalism changed the nature of society, and documented how African people engaged in business none-theless (Haynes Jr. 2018). Pooled economic activities helped these people withstand oppressive white power, Du Bois maintained. "Group economics" would inspire African Americans to create co-operative businesses, and bond together in the face of a racist environment. Du Bois's work is vital for public and co-operative economics, and it is puzzling that social economists writing in Canada and the United States do not reference his highly relevant work.

Economics professor James Stewart (1984) wrote one of the first scholarly pieces to examine co-operatives within the Black community, pronouncing group business to be the way to help disenfranchised Black Americans. He recounted the story of the Opportunities Industrialization Centers (OIC) movement out of north Philadelphia. One of America's oldest self-help NPOs, the OIC was started by a charismatic Baptist preacher, the Reverend Leon H. Sullivan, who carried out work rooted in collective busi-ness and self-help (Stewart 1984).[5] The OIC had been launched in response to racism against African Americans in the business sec-tor (Sullivan 1969). Sullivan mobilized his congregation to support

---

5 From 2001–4, I worked at the international headquarters of OIC International in Germantown, Philadelphia. While there, I carried out extensive field trips to country offices in Nigeria, Ghana, Guinea, Niger, and Liberia.

the OIC, which opened its first office in Philadelphia to help Black youth acquire trade and business skills so they could be self-sufficient and avoid abuse (Sullivan 1969). Additional OIC offices were soon opened across the United States with further ones established in a dozen African countries (Stewart 1984).

Jamaican-born social entrepreneur Marcus Mosiah Garvey was a powerful Black liberation theorist. While living in Harlem, New York, in the 1920s, he introduced a philosophy of racial self-reliance in business to counter mainstream business practices (K'adamwe, Bernard, and Dixon 2011).[6] Garvey was a migrant worker, and an activist committed to social enterprises and co-operative businesses such as the Universal Negro Improvement Association (UNIA) and the African Communities League (ACL), which helped with the economic development of Black communities around the world (Marable [1983] 2015).

Garvey's message, which he brought to his conferences for the Black diaspora, remains relevant to the lives of Black people outside of Africa (Hossein 2016b, 2016c, 2016d; K'adamwe et al. 2011; Martin 1983). During Garvey's lifetime, the UNIA had a very active membership. The association is still active in Montreal's Little Burgundy (near Atwater Market), as well as in several American cities, including Atlanta, Detroit, New York, Philadelphia, and Washington, DC (Marano 2010). Garvey's own upbringing in colonial Jamaica combined with his lived experience as a migrant worker in Panama and Costa Rica no doubt made a mark on his ideas of how to make business work for the Black person (Hill and Bair 1987; Lewis 1987).

Black people around the world have been deeply influenced by Garvey's teaching on Black empowerment and the implementation of self-help to achieve advancement. (See figure 2.3, "Bust

---

6 I presented a paper on Garvey as a social entrepreneur at the Global Garveyism Symposium held in Richmond, Virginia, on 23 April 2016 (Hossein 2017b). Fellow panelists Ula Taylor of the University of California at Berkeley, Michael O. West of the University of Pennsylvania, and Keisha Blain of the University of Pittsburgh provided many comments, which I incorporated into this chapter.

Figure 2.3. Bust of Marcus Garvey, Front Yard at the Small Business
Association, Kingston, Jamaica
Source: Author's photo.

of Marcus Garvey," which stands in front of the Small Business
Association of Jamaica in Kingston, Jamaica, in recognition of his
efforts to push Black people to be self-reliant in business.) Many of
the Banker Ladies whom I interviewed felt inspired by the African
pride and business ethics of Marcus Garvey.

Black liberation theory's concepts of "self-help" and "co-opting
business" to support the community from within are useful in analysing the social and solidarity economy. In *Up from Slavery: An
Autobiography*, Booker T. Washington ([1901] 2013) gave meaning
to the ideas of Black self-help and business, outlining ways that
marginalized people in the Americas could be part of the economic
system. Washington's philosophy was that people should pursue
self-help and make use of business to carve out their own way in

Figure 2.4. Statue of Booker T. Washington in Liberia
Source: Author's photo.

life. Many Black people appreciated this analysis, making Washington one of the great leaders of the time. His ideas spread to the continent of Africa through a number of vocational and technical training schools (see figure 2.4).

Washington's belief that Black people should train and develop their industrial trade skills for the marketplace was controversial to some because it did not challenge how racially segregated the environment was (Meier 1975). The Black community was divided on whether to engage or disengage with the market economy in its existing state. Nevertheless, Washington established the National Negro Business League to support Black entrepreneurship, launching it at a time in US history when Black people were being lynched. He also funded anti-lynching groups. Working within the economy, and determining ways to counter exclusion, have been undercurrents of the Black Radical Tradition.

The Black Social Economy is rooted in race, business, activism, and lived experience. The challenge for the Black Radical Tradition has been to move from pure liberation theorizing to Black feminist praxis. This change is necessary so that critical political economy is informed by the lived experience of Black and African descent women and their role in economic co-operation. Learning from the Banker Ladies' lived experiences and practices of collective engagement will expand the body of work in the Black Radical Tradition.

Drawing on the Abundance of Africana Feminist Political Economy Theory

Liberation theories of the Black Diaspora react against the erasure of racialized people in the political economy who experience cultural domination by white/ened people. The voices of Black feminist economists are often missing: that is, their work is not cited in the literature of the political economy while publications critiquing racial bias in the social economy often do not name Black women scholars. On the rare occasions a publication does cite a Black woman scholar, discussion of the contribution often appears as a sidebar. In this section, I present Black feminist theory in political economy. This body of research, which takes a critical stand on markets and politics, forms the basis for understanding market politics from a Black feminist perspective.

Black feminist writing about politics and economics is hiding in plain sight. The research is simply not being treated as required reading in disciplines such as political science and economics despite the fact that these disciplines ought to occupy themselves with issues of power, provisioning, and justice. Black feminists like bell hooks and Patricia Hill Collins, who examine such erasure in the academy, speak about the importance of lived experience. In *Ain't I a Woman*, hooks ([1981] 2015) demands a rightful place for Black women, arguing that their life struggles are a form of theorizing. This makes sense when we consider Black Canadian women whose contributions to the economy and society have been effaced.

It is not surprising that Black people are ignored in the social and solidarity economy. Take the extensive field work in South Africa by American political scientist Tiffany Willoughby-Herard, who dares to push the field of political science to include Black feminist thought. In Willoughby-Herard's (2015) book *Waste of a White Skin*, she recounts how, as a lesbian of Haitian roots raised in Detroit, she sees the value of examining class and other interlocking oppressions in the study of poor white South Africans. Her daring work exposes the racism within global philanthropy and family foundations, which exist to maintain white power while outwardly portraying that they are "helping" marginalized Black people. What Willoughby-Herard (2015) argues is that philanthropy, especially that which is corporatized work pursued under the guise of doing good, counters the achievement of racial justice.

In *Demonic Grounds*, Katherine McKittrick (2006), a feminist geographer at Queen's University, makes it clear that women of the Black diaspora who have had to endure sexism and racism in society have not been passive beneficiaries of the system. Instead, these women are making social justice (economic forms of it) take hold, which is, at the end of the day, what helps people stay human. The struggle borne by Black women is not subsidized by charities. These women build their just economic systems through their own labour (Gordon Nembhard 2023; Banks 2020; Harrison 2008). Emory University's Dianne Stewart (2007) wrote one of the first articles to tie the ROSCA system to Black feminist theory. In Stewart's case, she explored ROSCAs carried out by Jamaican American women. These community-based "Pardna banks," as they were known, built commonalities between women, were practised across economic strata, and provided a coping mechanism while also offering an emancipatory potential for women to dream and thrive.

The Banker Ladies are very much part of the Black Radical Tradition, which is feminist and intentional about co-operative economics. African American businesswoman Madam C.J. Walker, who was dubbed America's first Black female millionaire, built a beauty empire around Black hair products. She dedicated her life to improving business norms that would put Black people's needs first. Despite many intentional acts to ensure her funds advanced Black issues, she was pushed aside by male activists – especially Black male leaders. Still, her modest origins as a washerwoman in St. Louis informed how she did business, and how she lived her life. She always remembered her early experience, and so she donated a portion of her profits to human rights for Black people (Bundles 2001). Madam Walker's business acumen is instructive for Black feminists because her motivation was not about "getting rich"; rather, it was about helping others and making a difference in the world. Madam Walker's life story, recently retold through the Netflix mini-series *Self-Made: Inspired by the Life of Madam C.J. Walker* (directed by Kasi Lemmons 2020), is a testament to her struggles, and the racism she encountered in the United States.

Long before America's Rosa Parks, there was Canada's Viola Desmond. An iconic figure who, like Madam Walker, was in the beauty business, Desmond showed Black women how business could be co-opted in a way to fund self-help groups from within, and assisted several in developing their own livelihoods in cosmetology so as to avoid exploitation in the marketplace. By the 1940s, Desmond was a successful businesswoman living in Halifax, Nova Scotia. She also made history for getting arrested for refusing to move from her paid, front row seat in a racially segregated cinema. Desmond's act of defiance challenged racist policy, but she was only given a "free pardon" years after she died (Reynolds 2016). In Canada, Desmond's life and actions are revered because she symbolized the financial freedom and the fight for human rights (in 2018, I visited the Canadian Museum for Human Rights in Winnipeg, Manitoba, to see this documentation on her life). She found the racist rules of the day morally repugnant, and recognized that she could resist because she was self-employed and revered in her own community (Reynolds 2016).

Black feminist political economy critiques commercialized capitalism and corporatized philanthropy. African American scholar Jessica Gordon Nembhard, who grew up in an intentional community and who spent time at the University of Saskatchewan expanding her knowledge in co-operativism, knows first-hand about the depth of co-operativism among Black people and Black women specifically. This circumstance is noted in Gordon Nemb-hard's (2014a) foundational work *Collective Courage* where she documents the role held by co-operatives in Black people's lives in the United States, clearly demonstrating a strong history of economic collectivity. Nembhard's work challenges the co-operative sector to see that African Americans created "intentional communities" to eke out a living in a racist society. Co-ops had to operate under the radar because of the traumas encountered by Black people in white-dominated society. The concept of intentional communities is very relevant to Black women co-operators who build co-ops in tandem with community members and with the intention of stymieing the impact of discrimination in their daily lives.

In her work *Outsider Within*, anthropologist Faye V. Harrison (2008) analyses the impact of the global structural financial systems imposed on countries in the Global South such as a Jamaica. She deepens her analysis using the life story of Mrs. Belulah Brown of Kingston, Jamaica. After losing her job, Mrs. Brown found ways to organize with community members for mutual aid. Harrison's (1988) early work recounted how Jamaican "higglers" (small business traders) drew on Partner banks to sustain their businesses and to bring goods to alienated people. Their work was daring because it was carried out during colonial days. Imagining business as a way to help each other, on everyone's own terms, underlines how women choose to do business collectively. This body of work is important to the Black Radical Tradition because these women, often economically marginalized, are contributing to economic development plans. They are never remunerated for these acts of giving and building up of civil society.

To grasp fundamentally how finance and business can be done differently, I recommend *Downtown Ladies* by Haitian American anthropologist and artist Gina Ulysse (2007). This book expands Black feminist political economy by examining the informal economy of Jamaican higglering. In *Downtown Ladies*, Ulysse captures the voices of the "Downtown Ladies," or the higglers, many of whom are also Banker Ladies. The "Downtown Ladies" live in, or emigrated from, the Caribbean region. They innovate within the realm of small business trading to counteract the economic unfreedoms that exclude the kind of business they do. They organize independently and collectively, and they do business differently and informally. They contribute goods to a group of women routinely ignored by formal commercial systems. Through claiming and co-opting economic resources, and by experimenting with how the market functions, Jamaica's Downtown Ladies disrupt "business as usual" and refuse exclusion from the business sector.

This determination to organize collectively while taking care of one's own family is equally evident in *Poto Mitan* (co-directed by Renée Bergan and Mark Schuller 2009), a film with which Ulysse was involved. The film documents the lives of three Haitian women, all of whom leave multinational corporations targeting poor women to do low-paying and hazardous work. These women turn to the Haitian ROSCA Sol, which supports their ambition to engage in self-employment and enables them to dedicate time to local issues of concern to women, such as domestic violence. By sharing the lived experience of three women who deliberately chose small-scale business over salaried factory work, the film offers an invaluable contribution to our understanding of how women of the African diaspora regard work and enterprise development.

A great deal of academic writing in economics and political science is detached from empirical research. Regression analyses seldom explore life stories or explain why people do what they do. Through their edited collection, *Theorizing Empowerment*, University of Toronto scholars Notisha Massaquoi and Njoki Nathani Wane (2007) show how African Canadian feminism is distinct from the US experience. The book reveals how much of this circumstance has to do with the diverse immigrant presence, ensuring that Black Canadian feminist theorizing can only be understood in the plural. The learning here is that the concept of lived experience for Black women is very much part of knowledge-making in the Black Canadian political economy. The varied experiences of the African, Caribbean, and Canadian-born Black feminist diaspora are different, but there is alignment in terms of activism and engagement in care work. Black diaspora feminists are contributing to the Black Radical Tradition by bringing the immigrant and the Global South experience to community and economic organizing.

Attention to Africana feminist political economy has been ignored or siloed by most disciplines. Black feminist economist

Nina Banks (2019, 2020) has pointed out that the community is an important site of activity for Black and Latina women. It is the place where they carry out non-market group activities to address the needs of those who are made vulnerable by society, and who are not being considered by the public and private sectors. It is Bank's (2020) work that has made me think about the compensation due to the Banker Ladies. Banks (2005, 2008, 2021) dedicated years of research to uncovering the life of Sadie Tanner Mossell Alexander, the first African American to earn a PhD in economics. Though not easy Nina Banks (2021) spent years combing through archives to put together the story of Sadie Alexander, a Black woman who was unable to secure an academic position as an economist because of her gender and race. Alexander could only find work in the industry as an actuary; eventually, she retrained in law. After editing her speeches and other writings (2021), Banks concluded that, as a social justice lawyer, Alexander was always concerned about economic issues related to African Americans. This story about Sadie Alexander, a Black woman economist denied the opportunity to work in her profession because of her race and gender, is precisely the kind of intersectional, feminist political economy discourse that can guide the Black Radical Tradition in new ways.

American political scientist Sharon D. Wright Austin (2007), the child of sharecroppers in the South, wrote *The Transformation of Plantation Politics*. For this volume, which explores plantation politics and economy in the Mississippi Delta, Wright Austin surveyed dozens of communities. She found that capitalist trickle-down economics that came with the onset of development and casinos failed to change the economic standing of Black people in the area. Research for Wright Austin's (2018) next book, *The Caribbeanization of Black Politics*, involved surveying 2,000 Black immigrants from Cape Verde, Haiti, and other Caribbean islands, who had taken up residence in Boston, Chicago, Miami, and New York City – all US cities that have major Black populations. Wright Austin's works make it clear that new models for economic co-operation are needed, and that when Black Americans see how mainstream systems exclude them, they may look to group economics as a viable way to change structural inequities – a practice aligned, too, with a political sense of group consciousness to some extent.

It is a deeply Black feminist imperative to share cases about how and why Black people, and especially Black women, engage in self-help and rely on each other to address economic and societal exclusions. Black feminists see ties between economic exclusion and the factors of race and (hetero)patriarchy, and so reframe questions on co-operativism considering the lived experience and multiple oppressions taking place. Africana feminist political economy takes note of co-op systems that Black women lead, mostly in hiding, and in the informal terrain because of the discrimination they encounter. Black scholars writing on the diaspora Katherine McKittrick (2006) in Canada and Jessica Gordon Nembhard (2014a) in the United States have been helpful in highlighting that the act of "hiding" only meant that these women were building humane and alternative systems to support livelihoods – and to live away from the harms they endure. The Black women scholars theorizing about Black women's economies that is present in this inventory of works – studies which rely on extensive empirical research – are very much a part of the Black Radical Tradition. This tradition of Black women's political economy is also absent from the canonical literature on social economics and co-operativism.

A Black Social Economy and its Africana feminist epistemology can equally contribute to the Black Radical Tradition, which has been largely masculinist. There is a need to expand and make room for Black Banker Ladies, women who show through lived experience that they take up politicized economic actions to address business and societal exclusion. These ideas, which emanate across the diaspora from a large body of Black political economy scholarship, are rooted in lived experience and Afrocentric conscientization. This work is needed for a sound understanding of solidarity economics. This theory making can only be useful if the stories of Black diaspora women are told in practice, as well as cited in analyses articulated by Black women scholars. It is unacceptable to draw on poor Black women's ROSCA systems and solidarity economies without recognizing the agency these systems provide, as Black feminist scholars have conceded. By tying Africana feminist political economy to the solidarity economy, this chapter addresses a chasm in the literature. Students and academics concerned about economic and political transformation should not only be accessing this body of literature but using it to decolonize and culturally diversify the inner workings of our world.

Opening up the way we tell stories means looking beneath the surface. In the hundreds of interviews in which I have engaged, I found that Black women view themselves as co-operators when they are involved in mutual aid groups that co-opt resources in a way that is grounded in group economics. This kind of co-operative economics is at the very core of Black political economy. As their personal stories make explicit, Black women who are excluded from business create their own co-operatives. The lived experience of Black women who engage in ROSCAs, self-help, and mutual aid has been shaped by the communities from which they come. Black and racialized people have a vast arena of theories, ideas, and concepts on which the field of economics can draw. They will aid our discussion about how the field can move towards building inclusive economics.

chapter three

ROSCAs: An Antidote to Business Exclusion

ROSCAs are a form of mutual aid and co-operativism practised around the globe. Russian theorist Peter Kropotkin ([1902] 1976), who wrote extensively on mutual aid, found that all species rely on one another for their survival and that humans are no different. Mutual aid, and coming together, also genuinely makes us happy. During the COVID-19 pandemic, strangers rallied to help those in need by buying groceries or running errands. These stories were some of the most important during the lockdown. Commoning and informal networks based on trust and reciprocity have been brought back into the modern world.

In 2020, Black protests in the United States, Canada, and Europe highlighted anti-Black racism as systemic for those who live in white-dominated societies. Exclusion of various kinds have driven women and especially those of the African diaspora to rely on each other; the women who organize ROSCAs hide what they do because of the dangers they perceive. The Banker Ladies in this book told me that they fear reprisals for organizing banking co-ops and they are scared that their activities will be seen as "illegal." A film called *The Banker Ladies* (Mondesir 2021) was produced to expose the anti-Black racism in business and society at large, as well as to illustrate the gendered aspects of why and how Black women engage in co-operativism.[1]

---

1 Canadian filmmaker Luke Willms will release a film, *Unbankable*, which looks at how African people worldwide, including the Banker Ladies, have had to discreetly engage in banking co-ops. See the trailer for the film online at Willms (2023).

For these women, ROSCAs are an invaluable antidote to the racial and gender oppression they experience. They are lifelines in the face of continual inequity.

Black women-led ROSCAs also teach us about business models that offer a sense of purpose and belonging. An expert on civil society, john a. powell (2021) makes it clear that belonging is about letting people be different: "Belonging is based on the recognition of our full humanity without having to become something different or pretend we're all the same," he explains. "We are always both the same (humanity) and different (human), and are also multiple and dynamic, constantly renegotiating who we are." In response to being excluded, the Banker Ladies make spaces to listen and to hear those left out for being different. They purposefully organize ROSCAs to serve as places of belonging and to figure out how to make these systems work internally, so that the group banking system meets the financial and social needs of their members.

Given their focus on local co-operation, it is highly unlikely that ROSCAs will become redundant since these intentional communities, with their emphasis on the collective, counter exclusionary politics in the markets. This chapter stands at the core of the book's main argument: that the African diaspora draws on ancestral knowledge to create ROSCAs that carry people forward. Black women who organize ROSCAs (regardless of what they are called locally) do so to contribute to solidarity economies. Susus in Ghana and Equub in Ethiopia are legacy systems that continue to guide diasporic peoples to resist harms and exclusions. In this chapter, I discuss the persistence of these systems, their mechanics and how they work, and why ROSCAs represent a quiet form of resistance.

ROSCAs as a Globalizing Force

ROSCAs are a worldwide phenomenon. No matter where you go, there are ROSCAs; they appear in countries of the Global North and the Global South (Hossein and Christabell 2022). In 2002, the International Labour Organization–Geneva commissioned *Informal Finance in the Informal Economy*, a report designed to capture how trust mechanisms among people run deep, and to explore how such financial systems endure the test of time, irrespective of modernity (Aliber 2002). *In Their Own Hands*, co-authored by development practitioners Jeffrey Ashe and Kyla Jagger Neilan (2014), documents the stories of women who use ROSCAs, and shows the powerful impact of group finance where external subsidies do not play a role.[2] For *Portfolios of the Poor*, Collins et al. (2009) surveyed hundreds of people's financial diaries in Bangladesh, India, Kenya, and South Africa. Their study revealed that ROSCAs represented the most trusted financial device among those surveyed.

In *The Poor and Their Money*, Stuart Rutherford (2000) reveals ROSCAs to be among the most reliable and trusted forms of financial co-operation. ROSCAs involve people coming together in a simple way to help one another access goods. They were practised centuries ago, long before formal banks existed. People still belong to ROSCAs because these groups are grounded in a spirit of helping one another. It should be noted that most people do not use the term ROSCA, which is a term academics adopted to understand this concept of group banking. People from around the world use the relevant local indigenous name when referring to this form of group financing.

In the Vernacular

In *Take Back the Economy*, Gibson-Graham, Cameron, and Healy (2013) make it clear that stating institutions in their local names is important. In Ethiopia, the world's most ancient civilization, people still use the terms Equub and Idir, as they have for thousands of years. I met dozens of women in Bahir Dar, an Amhara Region of Ethiopia, who use Equub as their primary way to save and lend money. Ethiopians now living in Toronto, Canada, have brought

---

2 See case studies from the book at the website, Ashe and Jagger Neilan (n.d.), dedicated to sharing through open access.

the Equub system with them. "The Role of Informal Organizations in Resettlement Adjustment Process," carried out by Getachew Mequanent (1996), was one of the first studies to examine ROSCAs in Toronto. This study, which showed how newcomers from Ethiopia drew on Equub to settle into their new city and country, was one of the reasons I wanted to carry out field work in Ethiopia. I wanted to explore Ethiopia as a source country because of the great extent to which the Ethiopian diaspora uses these systems.

While living in the Amhara Region, I noted there were many banks in Ethiopia. However, the main state bank – Commercial Bank of Ethiopia – proved difficult when it came to financial transactions. There was a rigidity. I soon learned that self-employed Ethiopians felt unwelcome in formal banks (focus groups, October 2018, Bahir Dar). The same had been true for women vendors I had met the previous year in Makola Market in Accra, Ghana. They complained that commercial banks, as well as alternative banks like microfinance banks, had become so complex that they preferred their own "natural" banking systems called Susu (focus group, 13 July 2017, Accra).

Local names for ROSCAs are wide-ranging: Susu in Ghana; Hagbad in Somalia; Janjui in Cameroon; San in the Dominican Republic; Esusu or Ajo in Nigeria; Itega or Chama in Kenya; and Gbeh or Eso Jojo, Monee, Moziki, or Asusu in francophone Africa (e.g., Benin, Congo, Togo). Cameroonian scholar Margaret Niger-Thomas (1996) writes about Janjui (a local ROSCA) in Cameroon, where the women use them to take control of their lives when men leave them or move away to be migrant workers. In Sudan, people call them Sandooq. Neighbouring Egypt refers to them as Gama'yia. Sri Lankans have Cheetu. Indians refer to ROSCAs as Chits or Kitties. Pakistanis call them Community. Iranians have Sanduuq, which refers to a box of funds. My time in Kolkata and Kerala confirmed Indian people's knowledge and affection for these banking co-ops (interviews and meetings, November 2018 to January 2019). India, like Ghana, has legislation recognizing the role of ROSCAs. In Southeast Asia, Vietnamese refer to them as Hui while Filipinos call them Paluwagain. For Indonesians, it is Arisans. For Japanese, it is Kou. For Koreans, it is Kye. For all the aforementioned countries, ROSCAs are very old practices that have endured despite modernity (Annisette 2006; Ardener and Burman 1996; Niger-Thomas 1996; Izumida 1992). In the Americas, local names for ROSCA also vary: Mexicans have Tanda or Ronda while Jamaicans have Partner/Pardna. For Peruvians, the name is Junta. Ecuadorians use Caja. For Bahamians, it is Asousou. Haitians use Sol. Trinidadians use Susu while Bajans have Meeting Turn. In the United States, Canada, Australia, France, and the United Kingdom, ROSCAs go by numerous names, a reflection of the many diaspora groups who live in these countries.

The Staying Power of ROSCAs

In the 1960s anthropologist Clifford Geertz (1962), who studied ROSCA systems in Indonesia, referred to them as "middle-rung institutions" that would become redundant as modernity reached remote areas of Java (Indonesia). Geertz (1962) argued that Arisans (Indonesian ROSCAs) would die out as modernity approached and when increased banking opportunities with commercial lenders emerged. Yet, Arisans did not fade away with the arrival of a far-reaching modern banking system, substantiating the contrasting position Shirley Ardener would take in 1964. Three decades later, Ardener and Burman (1996) remained confident ROSCAs would continue to grow for social reasons.

ROSCAs remain the mainstay financial system for most people in the Global South because they function efficiently, offer low defaults, involve very small transaction costs, and require little paperwork (Hossein 2016b, 2016c; Collins et al. 2009; Rutherford 2000). As unregulated financial groups, ROSCAs provide group support, quick access to savings, and credit among people who belong to the same socio-economic groups (Figart 2014; Hossein 2013; Ardener and Burman 1996; Geertz 1962). These banking groups also provide a sense of belonging, comfort, and camaraderie absent from mainstream financial systems, which often make people feel excluded. ROSCAs also place the power to decide how money gets used into the hands of ordinary people.

Mutual aid and community-focused groups have grown within countries and across developed countries because people want to experience inclusivity in society and business (Gibson-Graham and Dombroski 2020; Banks 2020; Hossein 2018c; Gibson-Graham, Cameron, and Healy 2013; Ardener and Burman 1996). In the Netflix series *Live to 100: Secrets of the Blue Zones* (directed by Clay Jeter 2023), the Moai system, a co-operative and sharing economy, was a key factor for the people in Okinawa, Japan, known for living very long lives. The act of being with others and not alone was also important.

Being in a group and doing things informally as ROSCAs do is what makes them distinctive. In Ghana, the academic couple, social worker professor Ellen Bortei-Doku Aryeetey and economist Ernest Aryeetey (1996) outlined the ways in which market women used their social networks, mostly informally, to tap into those people who could assist them meet their financial needs. The women never considered that they were "unbanked" because they had kinship and social networks that could help them, both socially and financially. Guyanese historian Maurice St. Pierre (1999) explains that money clubs – known as Boxhand – were in existence in Guyana since at least the 1600s, when African slaves rotated funds among each other. Faye V. Harrison (1988) considers the legacy of Jamaican higglers who chose to use Partner banks (discussed later) to meet their financial needs. These Partner banks were (and still are) quiet forms of protest against business exclusion.[3]

Black women step up to organize savings in the community so that they can do business (Hossein 2013, 2014a, 2014c). As highlighted in the previous chapter, the documentary *Poto Mitan* (Bergan and Schuller 2009) follows the lives of three women in Cité Soleil, one of the largest slums in the Americas. The women reject low-paid, risky factory work, and instead turn to Sol to help them develop their own businesses. They are *poto mitan* ("pillars of strength" in Haitian Kreyol), shouldering the needs of society through self-help. *Poto Mitan* reveals that business exclusion loses every time when women turn to Sol. However, we should

---

3 See also Katzin's (1959) work about higglers under colonization.

not reduce ROSCAs and the work of the Banker Ladies to coping mechanisms. ROSCAs are a gift that allow citizens to devise their own ways of sharing money to help others who are left out of business.

Over centuries, women have primarily been the ones perfecting ROSCAs. In doing so, they demonstrate the capacity marginalized people have to build mutual aid financing groups for their own survival and to live well with others. They do not sit idly by while others alienate them. This kind of collective economics flies in the face of commercialized business rooted in exclusionary practices. Karl Polanyi (1944) was the first to make this important point in *The Great Transformation*: if capitalism carries on its destructive path of alienation, people will rise up and carry out a "Double Movement" to show a different kind of economic system. Not all people feel there is only one way to do business. In fact, the norms valued by the Banker Ladies – who are self-sacrificing and care about making economics conscientious in orientation – are very different from those held by dominant financial markets concerned with profits over people. The Banker Ladies are a real-life Double Movement.

Doing mutual aid every day helps women manage exclusion. As mentioned earlier, one of the most impressive co-operative business movements on this planet is the work done in Hausa by the Nigerien *mata masu dubara* (meaning "women on the move"). Thousands of local women have created village banks (Grant and Allen 2002). Development expert Julia Smith-Omomo (2019) credits the ROSCA system of the Congolese – called Moziki and Osusu by Liberians – for helping in the post-conflict rebuilding of people's homes. The women using ROSCAs are locally situated. They are residents of the community where they live, and they are vested in bringing about social change. The Banker Ladies, no matter where they are located, are drawing on indigenous African systems they know and trust to build social cohesion in a society.

What ROSCAs Mean to Descendants of Slaves

In the edited collection, *Beyond Racial Capitalism*, Hossein, Wright Austin, and Edmonds (2023) show how Black/African-descended people – from the United States and Canada to the Caribbean, Brazil to Ireland – have created self-help groups in inhospitable environments for centuries. African people in the Caribbean, as well as in other parts of the world, have been deeply affected by enslavement and colonization (see Mintz 2010; James 1989). Academic studies by Gordon Nembhard (2014a), St. Pierre (1999), Mintz (1955), and Du Bois (1907) show that African-descended people in the Americas use business to uplift their racial group. In *Collective Courage*, Jessica Gordon Nembhard (2014a) posits that any form of organizing by African Americans was a life-or-death matter because co-operation in business among Black people was viewed as subversive to the individualism of American capitalism. Du Bois's (1907) work on group economics documents the ways in which groups in southern Africa at that time supported joint- and community-oriented businesses.

During critical moments in history, persons of African descent have rethought how to organize their social and business lives. In the United States, the "giving circles" movement have taken hold (Eikenberry 2009). The movement involves groups of people coming together to pool resources out of mutual interest and to fund causes in which they believe. These giving circles, usually white in membership, have the goal of organizing grassroots fundraising for charities. American scholar Angela M. Eikenberry (2009) refers to giving circles as a "new" form of philanthropy or grassroot philanthropy. Yet, there is not much "new" about giving circles because Black people and immigrants, particularly women of colour, have a rich history of contributing and sharing goods with others especially through ROSCA systems (Hossein, Wright Austin, and Edmonds 2023; Barclay, Fullwood, and Webb 2019; Banks 2020; Ardener and Burman 1996; Light 1984; Vélez-Ibáñez 1983).

Giving groups by grassroot women is not new. ROSCAs have been embedded in community for generations, particularly in the US context, with women investing in local projects. US-based scholars have documented the ROSCA systems: Carlos Vélez-Ibáñez (1983) with the Mexican Tandas and Diane Stewart (2007) with Jamaican Americans and the Partner banks in times of business exclusion. Ivan Light's well known work on ethnic entrepreneurship revealed the use of Kye and Hua among Koreans and Chinese in Los Angeles and more recently Patricia Campos Medina et al. (2023) show how Tandas are used as a lifeline for Indigenous and undocumented workers in the states of New Jersey and New York.

As in the United States, Indigenous Peoples in Canada have had co-operative type systems such as the potlatch. In *For All the People*, John Curl (2012) documented the Navaho traditions of potlaches and the history of pooling goods. Leanne Betasamosake Simpson (2020) locates the sharing economy that took place prior to colonialism and continued during the colonial period, often under the radar. Canada's immigrant communities – particularly those who have had to endure anti-Black racism – continue to turn to ROSCAs as a way to meet livelihood needs. As highlighted before, Mequanent (1996) was one of the first scholars writing about the use of Equub among Ethiopian newcomers to Toronto.

ROSCAs in the Black Americas

Some of the early forms of collective systems come out of Haiti. In my earlier work, I note that Haiti, the first Black Republic to free itself from captivity in 1804, did so through a co-operative system. They then had to deal with a string of despotic personalities and remained isolated for a hundred years; its hard-fought freedom would have undermined the slave trade (Heinel and Heinel 2005; James 1989). Haitians responded to this isolation by internally developing a robust system of konbit, gwoupmans, and various local co-operative systems (Hossein 2014c).

In the Americas, the centuries-old work of Black Banker Ladies started under conditions of enslavement and the struggle for freedom, the effects of which continue into the present day. There is no sign of the Banker Ladies letting up on this work, even as modernizing development projects abound. More than three decades after Clifford Geertz (1962) predicted ROSCA systems becoming redundant in Indonesia as modernity took hold, feminists Shirley Ardener and Sandra Burman (1996) countered his idea, having found that ROSCAs were spreading to Western countries as an integral aspect of migration. Early on Hossein (2013) also found that across the Americas that the Banker Ladies, who belong to the same socio-economic class, demonstrate that there is a need for the kind of community development work they do.

ROSCAs remove the politicized aspect of aid that exists when poorer women depend on elites. The Banker Ladies reach excluded people, providing them with ways of joining together to co-opt goods and realize their dreams. History shows that Africans and people of the African diaspora have had to rely on these collective systems to survive. The ROSCA system of mobilizing social capital from within is still relevant in most societies.

ROSCAs as a Quiet Resistance

Doing business in and for marginalized groups takes significant courage since this work can be seen as a form of resistance against the negative impacts of capitalism. Recall Gordon Nembhard's (2014a) argument in *Collective Courage* that economic sabotage, lynching, and murder were very real risks faced by Black folks as they tried to create co-operative economies for themselves. The Underground Railroad, which "smuggled" thousands of people out of slavery through informal collectives, was also life-threatening work (Du Bois 1907). Whether under slavery, during the Jim Crow era, or in modern times, the lives of Black people have been vulnerable. Remaking economies has been the one sane way to keep living.

Black people do not do business in the same way. That is a given. However, many of the troubles they endure as a group have made Black people conscious about the need to co-opt business precisely so it works for the group (Davis 2017). In a sense, the concern is to grab hold of the concept of business as a people's concept, and then find a way for business to liberate or free people from their difficult positions in life. ROSCAs, and the women behind these institutions, have been quietly advocating for this very idea: there is a humane way to do business in society.

For my book, *The Banker Ladies*, I studied 443 Black women in the Caribbean and Canada who choose to organize or participate in ROSCAs. However, their involvement in ROSCAs does not mean that they do not also use mainstream banks. Some certainly do. However, those who use both systems are making a point: individualized banking does not meet their needs completely. The Banker Ladies are quietly saying no to the prevalent commercial banking model, and they are proposing their own co-op banks as an alternative. Formal banks in the Caribbean and Canada may make noise and advertise about a commitment to "equity," "diversity," and "downscaling" (to reach low-income customers), but these gestures are often hollow. Subsidized development finance often replicates the same, or similar, exclusions as formal banks (Hossein 2016c).

The Banker Ladies stand by ROSCAs as a form of banking for those who are under-banked, have limited access to trustworthy finance, and/or who feel excluded in business. During the course of eight years, I asked hundreds of Black women in six countries: "Do you find that by organizing ROSCAs you are resisting mainstream lenders?" Eighty-three per cent ($N = 368$) of the women I interviewed responded: "Yes." For them, having their own co-operative banks constituted an act of resistance (see figure 3.1). The women explained to me that ROSCAs are where they "pool," "come together," "bind," and "share" monies. This act of coming together is a form of resistance. I must also note: 9 per cent of the women preferred not to say anything ("Don't know") because they found the question to be political in nature, and there is a fear of answering some questions.

The decision of the Banker Ladies to bring solidarity into the banking world defies outright the logic of commercial banking, which perceives banking as an individualized rather than joint activity. The Banker Ladies choose co-operative banking, the precise opposite of how conventional formal banks operate. In *Governing the Commons*, political scientist Elinor Ostrom (2009) found that people co-operating and sharing goods is perfectly logical since many people are not motivated by self-interest but rather by community well-being. Ostrom's research on the commons recalls that people organize collectively, along a set of principles.

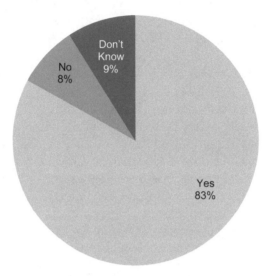

Figure 3.1. ROSCAs as an Act of Resistance in Canada and the Caribbean
(*N* = 443)

In conjuction with her colleagues, in 2009 Ostrom received a Nobel
Prize in economics. It recognized her for investigative travels
that countered mainstream understanding of how people engage
in localized development. Ostrom's work also suggests that
people of the Global South, or from other non-Western cultures,
are experts in co-operation because they already do this work.
ROSCAs are born out of crisis, with ordinary people making conscious decisions to bring these institutions into being. The Banker
Ladies, often already stretched for time, nonetheless make the
effort to create banks on their own terms.

Many scholars have documented that ROSCAs are about coping, meeting basic needs, and socializing. However, ROSCAs
mean more than that to Black people. Elites vested in the conventional commercialized system worry when Black women organize
money co-operatively and come together to discuss politics. When
Black women form a ROSCA, they take on risks by doing business using a collective model. The women I interviewed said that

forming a ROSCA helps them to "push against" formal banking systems, and stops them from feeling "left out." The women told me something is "wrong with the existing banks" and that their informal banking co-ops "reach people who have nowhere else to go." Those running these co-op banks see their implementation of ROSCAs as conscious equity work. In other words, ROSCAs represent taking a political stand against inequality. The Banker Ladies stand up to exclusion.

In a political stand against biased finance and the commercial banking model that dominates their society, the Banker Ladies propose an alternative form, one rooted in the collective and rooted in the communal life. Pre-capitalist communal and co-operative systems have a place in the economy, and the Banker Ladies demonstrate that truth. Akin to Kropotkin's ([1902] 1976) work at the turn of the twentieth century, Karl Polanyi (1944) acknowledged in *The Great Transformation* that the economy is embedded in social relationships, and that not all people would agree to industry disrupting their social life. As stated before, the Banker Ladies take care of their social lives. They are the real-life "Double Movement" to which Polanyi referred, proving the point that finance and social identity cannot be insulated from each other.

The Business of Exclusion

Social exclusion refers both to the process of inequality among groups in society and structural access to resources. For example, in Canada, social exclusion constitutes the inability of certain groups or individuals, such as Black Canadians, to participate fully in Canadian life due to structural inequalities in access to social, economic, political, and cultural resources (Galabuzi 2006). Across the Western world, Black people have been uprising under the banner of Black Lives Matter, opposing sanctioned killings of innocent people and systemic exclusion of basic opportunities and rights (Táíwò and Mbembe 2021). Black women – the mothers, wives, and sisters – have paid a dear price for this violence.

The work of the Banker Ladies responds to a deep-seated bias and racial violence in society.

Even in Canada, where the federal government espouses a policy of gender equality, plenty of evidence shows Black and racialized women struggling in the Canadian economy and society. Canadian political scientist Miriam Smith (2005), who has studied social movements, maintains that the right to organize collectively is a vital human right residing at the core of democratic countries. Yet the ability to organize collectively is being increasingly threatened and co-opted by a market-driven society. In *Depoliticizing Development*, John Harriss (2002) argues that the concept of social capital has become a tool used by modernizing forces – for example, the World Bank's use of it to undermine those fighting for equity and justice.

In *Hard Choices*, economist Jerry Buckland (2012) examines the financial exclusion of Canadians in major cities, such as Toronto's neighbourhood of Parkdale, which has a large immigrant population. Solutions for dealing with banking exclusions and bias are often alternative financial institutions (AFIs) that are deeply invested in grants and subsidies. These programs do not address the structural issues associated with formal banks; they are simply side projects to reach those who cannot access formal finance. Negative forms of AFIs, such as private financial companies like Money Mart, dominate the sector. It is microfinance institutions (known as MFIs) that constitute the helpful kind of AFI. For the past four decades, the development sector has been fixated on professionalized microfinance, which mainly involves (white) foreigners going to Global South locales to help Black and Brown women have "access to finance." These MFIs, among them Grameen Bank, BRAC, and FINCA, address exclusion by appearing to make access to finance possible (Roy 2010).

Work on AFIs largely ignores the role of ROSCAs as a form of co-operative banking (Hossein 2016c), although some critics have pointed out the limits to neo-liberal, commercialized MFIs (Bateman 2011; Baruah 2010; Rankin 2001). Westerners still travel to foreign lands to critique imposed micro-banking systems – but do not recognize the diverse, already existing financial economies of ROSCAs in which Black and racialized women take part all over the world. The West prides itself on spending money to help foreign women economically, yet remains blind to the business exclusion occurring in its own backyard. Stories and images of how professionalized microfinance banks help African women dominate the discussion; however, the ways women of the Black diaspora (those born, bred, and living outside of Africa) organize mutual aid receives little to no attention.

The ROSCA as a form of AFI is not even a unit of analysis. Yet, these entities are the go-to banks for racialized minorities and excluded people throughout the world (Collins et al. 2009; Rutherford 2000). When I started this research in 2010, I experienced keen interest from others when I discussed ROSCAs in the Caribbean context but received much less support when I said I wanted to examine use of ROSCAs by women of the Black diaspora in Canada. Co-operative experts with whom I worked with quite simply did not believe that these informal co-operatives mattered much in the context of a developed country because they had "never heard of them." By contrast, I saw ROSCAs everywhere because I was rooted in Black diaspora communities. I learned that, while Caribbean women in the region could flaunt the ROSCAs they made, this was simply not possible for Black Canadian women.

Progressives interested in "alternatives" were not ready to see that Black and racialized women living in a developed country would choose to make their own co-operative institutions because of deep forms of exclusions endemic to mainstream banks and co-operatives, including credit unions. To understand the business of exclusion, we must recognize that there are many people vested in keeping certain groups from telling their stories. After working for more than a decade in international development, I know that Canada is vested in development finance and in teaching other countries about access to finance. Yet, right in Canada, there are many Black Canadians enduring bias and discrimination from the Big Six banks. In Canada, ROSCAs are therefore essential to meeting the needs of thousands of people.

How Do ROSCAs Work?

ROSCAs have many modes of operation, depending on the group and where they are located. The structure, rules, and policies they follow vary according to the preferences of the group. Usually, members come together to pool and share monies. Most groups are led by women who are pragmatic because life has made them this way. In Ghana, focus groups (2017) composed of women from Makola Market explained to me that they did Susu to meet their financial and social needs; for them, issues of "race" and racism were not relevant motivations. As Susu members, they felt no danger in being part of their groups. Nor did the women consider Susu to be an inferior or underdeveloped form of co-operative.

Ethiopian women with whom I met in Bahir Dar (2018) organized Equub groups for practical reasons: formal banks were not nearby or required too much formality. During this trip, I also met a group of young male Bajaj drivers (drivers of small taxis) who pooled money on a weekly basis (focus group, 27 October 2018, Bahir Dar). One driver, Addisu, joined an Equub group not only for consumption, but also to invest in things that would improve his life. Bajaj drivers face social stigma because of the work they do, so this Equub was an important financial mechanism for its membership. According to Addisu,

> (Laughing) You know Equub! Yes, Equub is the most important thing in this country. Everyone uses Equub because it saves us. Every week I make 1,000 birr [US$37] payment to my group of 66 members. We meet every Sunday mornings in Kebele 14 to decide how to share the money. I am able to do many things with this money for my work. (Addisu, 27-year-old male Bajaj driver, 22 October 2018, Bahir Dar)

ROSCAs may be informal and not legally registered, but they are structured. An elected executive (e.g., president, vice president, treasurer, secretary) makes the decisions for the larger membership. If there are any controversial matters, the executive brings the issues to the full membership for a vote. Before a ROSCA is launched, the following elements are hammered out: the length of the term; rules for sharing monies; and how to deal with any form of delinquency. In a focus group with Somali women (2017), participants revealed that informality creates anxiety about theft of funds since these systems are not recognized. For this reason, the group decides, as a whole and in advance, the mechanics of managing risk that are most beneficial to the membership.

Each member of a ROSCA generally makes a fixed contribution to a collective fund for a specific period of time (e.g., on a 6- or 10-month cycle). The amount of money contributed and the duration of the fund varies, depending on each group's needs. This fund is usually allocated to members in turn, depending on the rules for allocation on which members agreed. For example, in a group of 10 women, each member might make a contribution of $250 per week (or $1,000 monthly). At the end of the month, a pool of $10,000 would be available to share at the monthly meeting. The executive and the members determine the needs of individual members, and then distribute the "hand" to members accordingly. One member of the group may receive the full $10,000 (called a "pot" or "hand").

ROSCAs are not profit-oriented. Many ROSCAs do not take any fees from members or charge them interest, although some do – again, these determinations are up to the specific group. Meetings are often held in someone's home, and members may bring food to share. Sometimes larger ROSCAs organize a meeting at a community recreation centre, with the group bearing the cost. In such a case, a small service fee might be exacted. One thing quite apparent in these groups is how much members value self-regulation. They take the time to make sure rules are clear to everyone who joins, and people who join a group undergo a careful vetting process.

ROSCAs Are about Politicized Social Solidarities

The Banker Ladies are leveraging their cultural know-how in financing to politicize social capital. Political scientist Marion Orr (1999) demonstrated in relation to the Baltimore school system, Black social capital may create solidarity in the face of systemic racism, but it is too far removed to convince those with political power to bring about the necessary reforms to improve education for African American children. The Black community did not trust white leaders, while Black social capital did not work across racial divides. In the end, corporations came in to manage education. Political scientist Sharon D. Wright Austin (2007) later drew on Orr's (1999) concept of Black social capital to expose the elitism of the plantation economy in the Delta region of the southern United States. Wright Austin (2007) contends that people need their own economic base in order to transform politics.

Being denied access to opportunities in finance, business, and society pushes Black people to organize to promote community development. Political scientist Danielle Pilar Clealand (2017) shows how Afro-Cubans draw on Black consciousness as a political tool to fight for racial equality. In *Race and the Politics of Solidarity*, political theorist Juliet Hooker (2009) was the first to point out that racialized minorities, when alienated by a system, will group together because of various intersecting and overlapping identities. Being Black is one of the identities that matter. Hooker's (2009) insights into political solidarity helped sharpen my own economic focus because she clarified people are constituted of many overlapping solidarities. As cited earlier, *The Politics of Survival* by Gladys L. Mitchell-Walthour (2023), helped me to understand that welfare payments alone do not advance the social positioning of their recipients. In her empirical work in the United States and Brazil, Mitchell-Walthour (2023) found that caring, mutual aid, and helping is what made a difference in Black women's lives – this is the Banker Ladies, and this why they are the vanguards of solidarity economics.

African-descended Banker Ladies in the Caribbean and Canada are building solidarities that take on the work of redoing business on a co-operative model. They are also organizing co-ops along multiple trajectories of identity: being women, being Black, being marginalized, and, for some, being Muslim or francophone. The Banker Ladies do not represent "social capital" projects engineered by political elites. These women, who remain outside of formal solidarities, can only build co-ops through racialized (and ethnic) solidarity. Through their activities, they make their own kind of social capital. In *Active Social Capital*, Anirudh Krishna (2002) troubles conventional thinking about social capital. In this work, he demonstrates how, when young people from lower castes are educated, they activate a new form of social capital that challenges the antiquated norms of village life – to the horror of their parents. The Banker Ladies also remake their own forms of social capital – in a way that defies academic definitions of what the concept means because ROSCAs take root in places that are marginalized and excluded. While I was doing my research in the Caribbean, particularly in Jamaica, I heard that crime and violence limited social capital. I could not accept such assertions as truth because I was highly aware that Caribbean women were organizing Susu, Partner, and similar systems to bring together their own social capital.

The sample I met with is not small for an in-depth qualitative study that took years to do. The 443 ROSCA users whom I interviewed are Chief Banker Ladies, and these women represent thousands of women who make known the meaning of collective action whenever they go underground to do business. Business is rooted in trust, reciprocity, and mutual aid. ROSCAs organized by these women stand in opposition to, and express criticism about, ordinary markets and government elites. In light of the hostility they endure and the risks to which they are exposed, the Banker Ladies own their groups and are not swayed by "outdoor people" or elite capture. Their clear understanding that they are doing what they want, while using an informal mechanism to achieve their intentions, is what makes their communal systems threatening. Through the countermeasure of ROSCAs, the Banker Ladies reveal that the neo-liberal business system, with its trickle-down effect, does not work (Birch et al. 2017; Austin 2007; Harvey 2007; Escobar [1995] 2012). The Banker Ladies refuse to be complicit with state leaders who only seem vested in minor reforms rather than in changing the economic system. It is not always clear how ROSCAs bring about change, but as a political scientist, it is very clear to me that the women who organize ROSCAs and other shared money systems do so to contest elite-run formal banks.

Collectivity to Combat Exclusion

While many Black people participate in capitalist economies as low-wage earners, the Banker Ladies show they can also be fund managers, producers, and entrepreneurs. Much of what Black people of the diaspora do remains in the informal economy. They use informal spaces out of necessity. For many people, the informal is a way of keeping safe and away from hostile work environments. Birch et al. (2017) in *Business and Society: A Critical Introduction* push us to rethink the view that it is only possible for business to behave in one way. Exploring the ways that Black women do business reveals these alternatives.

In *World on Fire*, Amy Chua's (2003) concept of market-dominant minorities is useful since it explains how a highly classed and racialized private sector developed in many countries around the world, and how racially distinct economic elites have exploited the labour of other racialized people. By the time the Banker Ladies move and settle in places like Canada, the United States, or Europe, where white dominance matters, to survive and thrive, these women co-operators start building mutual aid financial groups. They are able to do this because they are drawing on their previous experience in communal forms of business rooted in self-help and mutual aid. Again, the work of Kropotkin ([1902] 1976) is important here because it demonstrates how minoritized groups have had to rely on mutual aid to preserve themselves and evolve.

For the Banker Ladies, who carve out their own rules and remake notions of business, their work can be liberating. Capitalist markets do not recognize the alternative forms and systems of commerce Black people use to build self-reliance because these systems are not invested in the interests of the elite (Haynes Jr. 2018; Gordon Nembhard 2014a). The work of the Banker Ladies puzzles most people who analyse business and social exclusion. That puzzlement arises because these women show that social capital is alive and well in low-income communities with high levels of violence, and, moreover, that co-operative economics is thriving in commercialized societies. The diamante poem below helps to visualize, through words, who the Banker Ladies are.

Who Are the Banker Ladies?

Activists

Proud   Daring

Revive   Build   Sustain

Co-operatives   ROSCAs   Solidarity Economics   Self-help groups

Resist   Renew   Change

Brave   Conscious

Women

Combating Business Exclusion

Coming together to help one another during rough times is a sure sign of Black people's commitment to reacting against business exclusion in society (Hossein 2018a). In *Take Back the Economy*, Gibson-Graham, Cameron, and Healy (2013) show that diverse economies are grounded in community. People – particularly those who cannot fit into mainstream business – have turned to home-grown community economies (Gibson-Graham 2006). Many people, who simply want to be involved in the economy, turn to collective, member-owned models – both formal and informal – that determine the sharing of dividends. To ignore the impact of mutual aid groups and the conscious decisions that women of colour do business differently is to undermine this quiet form of resistance in an era of corporate greed.

Many of the Black people with whom I spoke know they are left out of the economic and political system. Black studies professors Rinaldo Walcott and Idil Abdillahi (2019) coined the concept of BlackLife because of the pain that Black people must carry in white society, a reality which leaves them constantly rehashing their trauma. The Banker Ladies understand the pain associated with BlackLife and refuse to wait around for aid; instead, they make their own financial co-op systems. As I said before and underline here, it is the work of geographer Katherine McKittrick (2006) that has truly advanced an understanding of African descent women in various terrains who are often made absent even though they are very much present in society and business. In the past unacknowledged, erased, and harmed, these women are the ones now engaging in sites of political opposition. The Banker Ladies of the African diaspora encapsulate the whole of this phenomenon. These women co-operators are not waiting on philanthropy to rescue them; instead, they are building membership-focused economic systems that cannot be co-opted or commercialized.

chapter four

Acknowledging the Caribbean Banker Ladies as Co-operators

Caribbean women create ROSCAs to take care of the needs of their communities and to show that co-operatives have a place in society. These women also push against commercial banks that fail to engage in diversified lending and exclude certain groups – namely poor Black women. In the Caribbean case, women – often but not exclusively from low-income areas – create ROSCAs to mobilize local financial resources and help one another (Besson 1996; Levin 1975). The Banker Ladies dedicate plenty of their own time to developing these groups and mentoring members. They employ their talents to uplift their communities and address inequities. They are not remunerated for these economic development efforts. Nonetheless, the Banker Ladies continue to engage in this community work without expectation of payment from the state or society. Even when they do not participate in ROSCAs themselves, community members are very much aware of them.

It is no secret across the Caribbean that Susu, Partner, and Sol all represent a legacy in the Americas (Bergan and Schuller 2009; Annisette 2006; St. Pierre 1999; Harrison 1988). In the 1940s, anthropologists Melville J. Herskovits and Frances S. Herskovits

This chapter borrows sections from my earlier journal article Hossein (2016b) titled, "Money Pools in the Americas: The African Diaspora's Legacy in the Social Economy," which appeared in *The Forum for Social Economics* 45, no. 4 (October): 309–28, https://doi.org/10.1080/07360932.2015.1114005. Reprinted by permission by Taylor & Francis on behalf of the Association for Social Economics.

(1947) examined kinship among African descendants in a Toco village, where they documented the use of Susu – a system designed to include those who have been alienated from commercial foreign banks and/or formal commercial finance (John 2020; Hudson 2017; Hossein 2016a, 2016c, 2016d; Ryan and Barclay 1992). During colonization and the complex period of post-colonization, self-employed women, known as higglers or hucksters, carried out co-operative forms of business to support each other through complicated times (St. Pierre 1999; Katzin 1959).

This chapter examines five country-specific cases – in Jamaica, Trinidad and Tobago, Grenada, Guyana, and Haiti – to show how Black women co-operators revamp colonial financial systems through African ideas of Kombit (understood as collectivity in Kreyol). In these countries, elites who deny poor women access to finance are nonetheless the first ones to respect ROSCAs organized by the Banker Ladies, which include Susus, Partners, and Sols. It may be that some of these elites – though not all – had mothers who relied on ROSCAs to pay for their schooling and family expenses. Some members of the elite even join ROSCAs because these systems are so culturally ingrained into the social life of the Caribbean. In fact, Susu, Partner, Sol, and Boxhand are co-op systems being copied by commercial banks today. Commercial banks roll out products such as "Mama Sol" or "Partner Plan" to attract new borrowers. Bankers in the islands know full well the appeal these banking co-ops hold for Caribbean women.

Through focus group discussions and one-on-one interviews, I learned that Caribbean women ran co-op economies grounded in friendship. However, they also made sure to reach people who were excluded. This economic co-operation towards creating an open economy, work in which they engage ever so quietly, receives praise from local elites, who nevertheless remain distant from these very women.

Local Needs Come First

Everywhere one goes in the Caribbean, ROSCAs are seen as a vital part of life, especially among Black women. C.Y. Thomas's (1974) convergence theory boils down to making self-sufficiency the economic concept that matters most in terms of resisting exploitation by capitalist firms. The Banker Ladies converge on local needs and productivity to do what is needed for those who are denied opportunities. Together with my colleague, political scientist Kadasi Ceres, who is based in Guyana (Hossein and Ceres, 2022), we credit C.Y. Thomas's convergence theory for making it known that a focus on local production outwits extractive commercial forms of business, creating a space where people-focused development can take place.

The ways in which diasporic Black women outwardly show gratitude for ROSCAs depends on their context. None of the Caribbean women participating in a ROSCA that I met within the region feared reprisal. They were not concerned that their actions might be labelled "illegal" or likened to a "Ponzi scheme." In fact, the Susu and Pardna banking systems they use are sources of giving, support, and people are grateful for what these women do in society (Hossein 2021b). The work that comes naturally to them – such as caring for others, self-help, co-operating and community business – may be influencing hardcore commercial bankers to think about the financial product lines that they offer.

It is not a stretch to imagine the impact ROSCAs have had in the world of banking. Kenya's Njeri Kinyanjui (2019) has shown that Chama systems are most relevant for market women conducting business in Nairobi, and their attitude towards business is actually about sharing and kindness and not about caring only about oneself. In Ghana and India, people, and especially women, have engaged in their ROSCA system so much that their governments have integrated aspects of the ROSCA system into their formal economy because the people demanded that they do this (Agarwal 2020; Christabell 2009; Bhatt 2005; Bortei-Doku Aryeetey and Aryeetey 1996). Where there is a level of trust for the state, citizens demand that the state actively involve informal collectives.

People around the world are insisting (or have already done so) that their local co-operatives are part of the financial ecosystem because it is one that values human provisioning. In India, for example, there are millions of people who belong to self-help group systems (Bhatt 2005; Devika and Thampi 2007). In *We Are Poor but So Many*, Ela Bhatt (2005, 46), the founder of Self-Employed Women's

Associations (SEWA), one of the world's largest self-help groups in the world, asks: "Why do we not revitalize traditional Indian economic structures instead of neglecting them?" This question gives voice to the need to recognize indigenous knowledge embedded in money systems with which marginalized women are already quite familiar. The ROSCA system, locally called Chits or Kitties, led to the development of Chit laws because of the demand for such institutions (Hossein and Christabell 2022; Sethi 1996). In the Kudumbashree case in Kerala, India, the state formalized development and brought in Sanghas (informal women's groups) to assist in local development. This was only achievable because local people agreed to the process (Agarwal 2020; Devika 2016; Devika and Thampi 2007). Local women are being hired and trained to develop capacity and engagement at the village level. Yet, we do not see such compensation being paid to the Caribbean Banker Ladies.

No Remuneration

While other places will hire and pay for the community development expertise of local women, this has not been the case for the Banker Ladies. While highly regarded for their contributions across the region, the Banker Ladies are not compensated for their work. The same is true in the United States. Achille Mbembe's (2017) *Critique of Black Reason* explains that Black people in the Americas were ruled by Code Noir, which involved meting out harms to members of the African diaspora because they were viewed as lesser beings. This persistent coloniality and racism permeated institutions, especially financial ones (Friedline 2021; Tilley and Shilliam 2018; Baradaran 2015). Given this deeply embedded racism directed at the African diaspora, and especially its women, it is clear why co-operative contributions by Black women are valued. In today's world, the activism of African American women is being revered for how it has bridged the gap in terms of economic inequalities. Work by feminist economist Nina Banks (2020) has made all of us realize that care economics still largely focuses on household work, failing to count community work as economically valuable. It is this work that made it clear to me that the Banker Ladies were not being valued or paid for their time and labour that it takes to mobilize and help community members.

The ways that Caribbean women organize money collectively (something they have done for generations) is certainly respected. Recognition and gratitude are their compensation for challenging the belief that there is only one way to conduct business in society. Still, their work is not incorporated into formal development plans. Nor are the Banker Ladies in the Caribbean remunerated for their labour, which contributes substantially to peace-building and stability in their communities, as well as providing financially just systems.

Inventory of ROSCAs in the Caribbean

The Caribbean's indigenous banks derive from long-standing, ancient traditions, which, in the past and the present, have taken a bold stand against unfair financial systems. The ancestors of the Caribbean people (like my own) are African or Indian. They came from countries that practised economic co-operation, and these systems travelled with them. ROSCAs may have been active in the Americas as early as the 1500s, putting down roots first in Brazil and Haiti. The experiences of enslavement and colonization cultivated practices of mutual aid and working collectively across the African diaspora. Black people were nourished by their own cultural systems and identities, alongside a conviction that an economic system that did not own humans was possible.

Enslaved West Africans drew on Susu, Esusu, and Asousou. After slavery was abolished, Indians who arrived in the Caribbean as indentured servants to live in the same logies (former slave lodgings) as the African people, went mostly to Guyana, Trinidad, and Jamaica (Reddock 1985). Their descendants held on to creolized versions of ROSCA systems known by the same names. The Caribbean people, whether of African, Indian, or Dougla (mixed African and Indian) descent, participate in co-operative

Table 4.1. Inventory of the Names of the Caribbean ROSCAs

Local Name	Country
Asousou or Esusu	Bahamas
Lodge	St. Lucia
Boxhand or Box	Guyana
Meeting Turn	Barbados
Partner/Pardna	Jamaica
Sol, *caisses informelles*	Haiti
Susu	Trinidad and Tobago, Grenada, St.Vincent

economics because it is part of their cultural heritage and set of traditions. Table 4.1 lists the names of ROSCAs in the Caribbean.

ROSCAs are comfortably familiar to the Caribbean people because they were raised by loved ones who were ROSCA members. Many children ran around making money deliveries to members. In the Caribbean, the work of running ROSCAs is, for the most part, carried out by low-income women who depend on them for economic support. While other segments of the Caribbean society do use ROSCAs, this study is focused on women who depend on ROSCAs for meeting livelihood needs. Office assistants and salaried workers organize Susus for special events, or to assist them with capital inflow when they operate a business on the side to help increase the family income. The Caribbean people, primarily Caribbean women, know about and join ROSCAs as an integral part of their way of life.

Methods and Data Collection in Five Countries with Hundreds of ROSCA Experts

This study of the Caribbean Banker Ladies adopted multiple methods to research the attitudes and motivations of lenders and borrowers in 14 low-income communities across five countries. Between June 2007 and December 2015, I held focus groups and interviews with 298 women who identified themselves as ROSCA leaders in Jamaica, Guyana, Trinidad and Tobago, Haiti, and

Table 4.2. Interviews with the Caribbean Banker Ladies in Five Countries (2007–15)

Method	Jamaica	Guyana	Grenada	Haiti	Trinidad	Total
Focus group sessions with ROSCA members (average 2–3 hours)	57	5	0	74	0	136
Individual interviews (average 1 hour)	89	14	17	19	23	162
Total	146	19	17	93	23	298

Note: These interviews represent close to 6,000 members.

Grenada (see table 4.2).[1] Being active users themselves, the women in charge represented the voices of approximately 6,000 people.

A ROSCA group in the Caribbean can vary in size, but the average is about 25–30 people. Haiti was an exception to this norm, with some of the largest groups, each with hundreds of members. The research conducted in Kingston, Jamaica, occurred in 2009 and 2010. Jamaica is the country that forms the main Caribbean case. Interviews were held mostly in the southwest part of Kingston, called downtown, south of Cross Roads. This area includes the neighbourhoods of Trench Town, Bennett's Land, Whitfield Town, Rosetown, Frog City, and the former prime minister's constituency of Denham Town and Tivoli Gardens.

In Haiti, I interviewed those living in the bidonvilles (low-income urban areas), first in 2008, then in 2010, 2011, 2013, and late 2015. These sites included Cité Soleil, Carrefour, Martissant, and La Saline, as well as Bel Air in Centre-Ville and Jalousie and Flipo in the hills of the chic suburb of Pétion-Ville. The focus groups were held in Bon Repos, a suburb of Port-au-Prince and Cap-Haïtien. In 2008 and 2010, a small set of interviews was carried out in Albouystown in Georgetown, Guyana, which is ethnically diverse.

1 On 12 January 2010, Haiti experienced a 7.0 magnitude earthquake that left 300,000 people dead and 1.5 million people displaced and living in tent cities. This situation affected data collection in the latter part of 2010 and 2011.

My work focused on the Afro-Guyanese and Dougla (mixed African and Indian) populations. In 2013, I interviewed 17 women in the Grand Anse valley, the bus terminal, and the central market in St. George, Grenada; and, to add diversity to the sample size, 23 Susu leaders in Trinidad Laventille, Beetham Gardens, and Sea Lots in east Port-of-Spain.

The research intention was to design interview tools so that people could tell a story and, at times, engage in dialogue. Some of the questions asked of business people engaged in money pools included: (1) What kind of financial provider meets the needs of persons in low-income (poor) communities? (2) With many banking options close by, why are ROSCAs prevalent among so many people here? And (3) Why do persons organize and join ROSCAs? Interview tools were standardized as much as possible to enable comparison across the cases. However, tools were adapted to fit local, contextual realities, such as in Haiti, where it was necessary to accommodate post-earthquake priorities. Two-hour focus group meetings of 6 to 20 people were held at neutral locations, such as community centres, schools, parks, street corners, outside storefronts, markets, or bars, depending on the area.

ROSCAs as Equitable Economies

In Jamaica, Haiti, Trinidad, Grenada, and Guyana, enslaved people have had to hide ROSCAs and pool goods to help one another, and to rebel against the inhumanity they encountered. This historical legacy of ROSCAs is something people still carry around with them – most knowingly. Enslaved people carried out market days and engaged in Buying Clubs because they imagined what freedom would look like (N'Zengou-Tayo 1998; St. Pierre 1999; Wong 1996; Witter 1989; Harrison 1988; Katzin 1959; Herskovits and Herskovits 1947). Today, the Banker Ladies are rejecting financial models that are alienating and minimize their contributions to business. The point of this book is to show that when Black women choose to organize financial systems based on a group method and focused on reciprocal relations, they are conscientiously taking on an activist co-operative role.

My Grenadian-born great-grandmother, Maude Gittens, migrated to Sangre Grande, Trinidad, where she would take on a decisive role in leading Susu banks for decades. She was a caterer and, undoubtedly, a well-respected leader in her community, but her pride was being a Susu lady. Her main role was to collect weekly deposits from members, women she had known her whole life. At some later point, she would give a lump sum of cash to each member turn. Members inspect the work being done, to ensure that distribution among members is equitable.

The structure of Susu varies from community to community. The rules are determined by members who discuss the fixed deposit to contribute every week. The Banker Lady usually has a business out of her home that allows members to drop off their deposits easily. The group decides how long they will engage in these weekly deposits, but a period of 10 to 12 months is common. Once all members agree on the rules and structure of the Susu, the Banker Lady launches the bank with the first intake of deposits. The Banker Ladies claim they lend out the deposits to members from the first day of intake to avoid having a large sum of cash on their person/premises. The system of rotation can take several forms, with variance based on group dynamics. Money can be allocated on a first-come, first-served basis, based on need, or by lottery (e.g., drawing names). Given that ROSCAs are a form of co-operative, the women who lead them are pioneers of collective forms of economic development. These women are quietly questioning the individualized business model.

Women who are precariously employed work in the informal markets, with many of them open air, selling and trading goods to get on with daily living. In that space, they continually talk across various cultural and class lines. In *The Point Is to Change the World*, Professor Alissa D. Trotz shares Andaiye's (2020) essay "Lessons for Organizing with Grassroots Guyanese Women." The essay explores how feminists in every aisle have largely ignored the role of housewives, when it is precisely in this space – the home and the markets – where women engaged about changes they want to see (see Antrobus 2004; Luxton 1980). Women informally sharing money in groups through a Susu, Boxhand, or Partner, are banking systems well known throughout the Caribbean.

In *Decolonial Perspectives on Entangled Inequalities*, Rhoda Reddock (2021) argues that in spite of the glitz of television shows and tourism depicting the Caribbean as a paradise, Reddock pushes back and argues that there is violence and gendered exclusions taking place that deeply affect women in the islands. So much so that the Caribbean women turn to economic alternatives, such as the sex trade, to make ends meet and to survive. The other kind of economic alternative women have always done in the Caribbean as a way to cope and meet their goals has been to co-operate with each other.

ROSCAs have played a vital role in the economic lives of the Caribbean women, especially those who work in the informal sector. ROSCAs have a place in feminist political economy – and in economics because millions of people are using these devices when formal financial systems are exclusionary. To open up economic possibilities, we must recognize Black women's use of ROSCAs in the region as vital to learning about gender and finance. The Susu, Partner, and Boxhand systems are a part of the region's history, but discussion about them is often missing from academic literature.

African people have held on to the arts, dance, and foodways – all social aspects important to a historical understanding of how enslaved people survived years of brutality. Another form of resistance has resided in African money systems rooted in collectivity. These systems have been kept alive for generations by the diaspora to help its members save money. Historian Maurice St. Pierre (1999) reminds us that pooling funds and having market days were always a part of the process for Black/African people working towards their freedom. Pooling earnings made from Sunday market day, then gathering together to share money in clubs without the masters' permission, were acts of defiance. Money pooling has a militant and activist aspect.

The Banker Ladies in Trinidad and Tobago and Guyana: Leading the Way

African people held on to the money pooling system because they knew it could help them be free one day (St. Pierre 1999). Indentured servants who came to be known as East Indian also held on to the ROSCA systems they brought with them. Both groups, colonized and treated without regard in the Caribbean, had brought with them important knowledge of co-op banking systems, which they then transplanted into their new environment. They did so because their long-term vision did not include living in domination, and they had ambitions towards owning their own lands.

Class-based racism and partisan politics in Trinidad and Guyana have interfered with people's access to finance (Hossein 2014a, 2015). Access to financial services has been complicated for people of African and Dougla descent in Guyana. In Trinidad and Tobago, commercial banks generally exclude the poor, and this is especially the case for people of African heritage – the reason being that commercial credit has been largely dominated by Indo-Caribbeans (2016). Formal bankers are culturally distinct from their borrowers in these countries because they differ from them in terms of class, culture, and sometimes gender (Hossein 2014c, 2016c). These bankers use politics in a way that deforms and limits micro-banking, and they do so out of personal prejudice rooted in racism and class bias.

A pervasive cultural narrative disparages the business acumen of people of African descent. The commercial bankers, usually educated men of East Indian descent, are hesitant to make loans to poor Black people (Hossein 2014b, 2014c, 2016c). Even within professionalized finance programs, the "norms" in commercial banks have influenced economic development programs to discriminate against people of African heritage. Nee, a 28-year-old Guyanese hair and nail salon owner based in Albouystown (a low-income area in the capital city), advised that money pools are a cherished tradition:

> Box help me start my own business. Yuh get all di money from people who believe in me. This here Box is a norm passed down from generation to generation, grandmother's time and it helps me. (Interview, Georgetown, Guyana, 11 May 2010)

At least 65 per cent of the entrepreneurs interviewed in Albouystown, Georgetown, said that they borrowed money from Boxhand because they could not access loans from a commercial bank or microfinance institution. In Trinidad, the largest microfinance bank is the state-run National Entrepreneurship Development Corporation (NEDCO), which has a history of partisan politics–influenced lending, with the result that 75 per cent of its loan portfolio was in arrears by July 2013 (field work 2013).

The fact that women are systemically excluded from formal finance provides the logic for aid agencies to make a major production out of development finance to "help" Black women. These "experts" fail to consider how the pre-existing system of ROSCAs, vested in mutual aid, is meeting the economic needs of these women. Even more disconcerting is that many of these experts belong to the Global North where their own banking systems are racist and exclusionary by design.

The Banker Ladies in Trinidad and Guyana who feel alienated by conventional business systems know they have ROSCAs at their disposal. The Susu and Boxhand banks are prevalent throughout these two countries since commercial banks are too limited to meet demand. The Banker Ladies fill this gap. While they do their business in a modest way, it is common knowledge that ROSCAs help all citizens. Even the elite bankers who turn the the women away recognize that these same women, the Banker Ladies, provide financial access – as well as caring support – to people typically left out of the economy.

Jamaican Partner Cultivates a Sense of Community

Over the years, I have learned that the Jamaican Partner is used by people from all socio-economic backgrounds. It is particularly a lifeline for those who have no other choice – like the women with whom I met in downtown Kingston. Politics in Kingston's main urban centre is marred at election time by violence, with local political elites making promises of handouts such as money, lodgings, and jobs for the very poor residing in the downtown core (Sives 2010). If they fail to deliver the vote for their candidate, they lose the handouts. So many academics in the region, namely political scientists Carl Stone (1980, 1986) have written extensively on "garrison politics," which is an entrenched process of political elites using residents in the downtown slums to carry out heinous crimes to assure votes and political victory in exchange for housing or other financial benefits (Sives 2010; Tafari-Ama 2006; Rapley 2006). Years of politicians and gangsters using poor residents to carry out their dirty work has led people to distrust political and business elites (Hossein 2016c; Gray 2004; Keith and Keith 1992).

The Banker Ladies with whom I spoke let me know that people living in so-called garrisons (housing developments set up to support a particular party or politician, often involved in political or drug turf wars) do not want to be controlled by elites or gangsters. Partner banks run by women untrained in formal banking, but with many years of expertise as co-operators, are aware of the local politics that can interfere in business. The Banker Ladies do not allow politicking inside their Partners.

After surveying 1,000 Jamaicans in Kingston, Handa, and Kirton (1999), economists based at the University of the West Indies at Mona found that 75 per cent of the Banker Ladies were women aged 26 to 35, who had organized Partners for an average of nine years. The women I interviewed lived in downtown tenements with corrugated metal tin roofs. Many of the unemployed women I interviewed did not have a formal bank account. Not having a bank account made no difference to them since they felt that they had a valid banking history with a Partner. One businesswoman, who requested anonymity, argued:

> Pardna is fi wi, and bank is fi di big man uptown [that is, the partner bank is for the poor (us) and formal banks are for the rich]. Yuh don't have to be rich or educated to throw Pardna. (Interview, 15 July 2009, Kingston, Jamaica)

Partner is by far the leading choice for how to bank. The women interviewed said it is the element of trust they value most. Unlike commercial banks, Partner is accessible because the women who run them are from the same socio-cultural communities as the members who use them. Members have come to know and trust them. Rickie, a 29-year-old bar owner, clarified the purpose of Partner and why people are loyal to these informal banks:

> Pardna. Live for dat ting. Most people here [in his low-income community] don't have go to banks. Dem [the bankers] don't know what's going on here and wi na know what's going on in their banks. Downtown know Pardna … it is the one ting here for wi. (Interview, 9 July 2009, Kingston, Jamaica)

Jamaican women running Partner banks for their communities exemplify the need to co-operate within the same socio-economic class group to fulfil people's needs, ensuring they are not waiting on handouts. The idea that Black and African descent women who have no training in finance can figure out how to make banking equitable is telling. The notion that they do not need prescriptions for how to "develop" from the (read, white) experts is radical economics. In my interview with a 52-year-old woman from Denham Town in Kingston, Jamaica, "Janet" reasoned that her Partner bank is culturally driven and respectful while commercial banks miss this basic understanding:

> Partna (ROSCA) is yuh heritage and yuh gro' wid it. I always inna Partna, it is life! My Partner pay school fees and … wid no roadblocks like the [formal] bank because Partner don't judge you and yuh get di money. [Translation: Partner banks are a part of one's heritage and you learn about it from growing up. I am always in a Partner because it is life! I use my Partner to pay for school fees and people do not judge you and you get the money.] (Interview, 22 July 2009, Kingston, Jamaica)

Partner banks are a type of ROSCA in which members know and trust each other. The women in this Partner refuse to listen to how they are to develop and "grow" because they do not agree with those ideas. Instead, they follow their own plans, support each other through self-help, embrace cultural traditions, and, on purpose, keep what they do small.

Partner banks offer people a place to save their money and from which to borrow money. Women said they preferred the Partner banks because there was "no rigmarole" (paperwork). The members consider the women who run Partner to be trustworthy. They like that there are few fees and that access to the funds is made easy. Millicent, a 66-year-old clothes vendor who had worked in Woolmers Arcade for 20 years, explained:

> Doin' business and sellin' is rough in the city, but as a small business person you have to learn to take it. Partner softens it … Partner is discipline because we can trow money every week. Faster and it's easy. A draw can help you in your business to thrive and to do X, Y, Z when nobody is there. (Interview, 30 March 2009, Kingston, Jamaica)

The Jamaican Banker Ladies are feminist economists of sorts because they are always thinking about exclusion and disparities, even though many of them dropped out of school early to find a job. The women I interviewed claimed that repayment rates are high (usually 100 per cent) because members trust these systems. Partner banks are deeply rooted in social relationships: they are there when nobody else is, and they help people and their communities develop self-confidence. Everywhere else in society, these women are not viewed as "experts." But when these women run Partner, they are. As a collective, they are the bosses. They decide, through group consensus, who gets access to the lump sum of money first; they assess the person's risks for defaulting, just as a trained loans officer would. The sustainability of these systems shows that they are viable.

Partner banks are made up of a group of people who know each other (sometimes they are related). Several variants of the Partner bank exist; and, although all are savings plans, many are also lending associations (Handa and Claremont 1999; Klak and Hey 1992). Each person's contribution to the Partner is called a "hand" and it is "thrown" (deposited) for a designated period; the pooled money is called a "draw." In some Partner banks, people draw lots to determine the order for obtaining a loan (interviews, March to July 2009, Kingston, Jamaica). "Charmaine" was very proud of her work as a Banker Lady because it increased her profile in the community. Like many others, she said that their membership extends beyond their community. Some women who move to the United States or Canada remain in Partner, making it transnational. It is thus not uncommon to hear that the whole membership is depositing to the same account.

The Jamaican Partner works effectively because peer dynamics ensure members comply with payment rules. The Chief Banker Ladies call for social sanctions when members disrespect the rules. During focus groups and interviews, many of the Banker Ladies told me that they do not put up with slackers, and that members who do not follow the rules are banished from banking. As noted in chapter 3, AFIs try to connect with ordinary people because they see a lucrative business opportunity. By contrast, these women co-operators understand the fundamentals of group banking. JN Bank has a product line called the Partner Plan. While people often joke that it is not the same Partner they know, lenders recognize the value of mimicking an African system of mutual aid to resonate with the masses.

A Vibrant Susu Culture in Grenada

The formal co-operative experience of Grenada developed under British colonization, which ended in 1974. In the 1930s, nutmeg and cocoa were important cash crops, and the colonial state created boards to manage these exports. In 1947, the Grenada Co-operative Nutmeg Association was formed to assist farmers in increasing their incomes by allowing them to bypass the middle-man. In 1951, the Colonial Welfare and Development Fund provided the financing to organize the quality of production (Steele 2003). In 1954, the Banana Co-operative Society was set up to assist trade with the Canadian Banana Company (Steele 2003, 338). Eric Gairy, Grenada's first head of state (two terms: 1967–74, 1974–9), was also the first political figure to come from a modest rural background (Sandford and Vigilante 1984). In the early years, Gairy was an anti-imperialist, committed to increasing the incomes of rural farmers through co-operatives. However, Gairy's mounting anti-local, colonial/elite rhetoric was met with poor governance.

By the mid-1970s, opposition grew against Gairy's undemocratic control and the violence of his secret police, the Mongoose Gang (Steele 2003).

Influenced by the US Black Power Movement and the Cold War, young, educated Grenadians from middle-class backgrounds rallied dissenters against the Gairy regime. The 1979 bloodless *coup d'état* by the New Jewel Movement (NJM) installed the left-wing state, the People's Revolutionary Government (Gentle 1989; Meeks 2001; Sandford and Vigilante 1984). Its leader, Maurice Bishop of the NJM, was impressed by Tanzania's Ujamaa (the Swahili word for unity, collectivity, or oneness). Put forward by Tanzanian president Julius Nyerere (term: 1964–85), Ujamaa advocated for moving villagers into farm collectives and was adopted into the NJM manifesto. Following an internal power struggle, and the assassination of Maurice Bishop and members of the New Jewel Movement, the United States invaded Grenada in October 1983 (Meeks 2001). The US invasion and occupation made local life difficult. Left to cope on their own, Grenadians turned to localized co-operatives such as credit unions and Susu. People were in distress and informal collectives offered one way for people to cope during crises. It is no accident that the country's largest co-operative bank, Grenville Credit Union, was created during this period of turmoil. US leaders were concerned about collective enterprises and viewed group organizing by colonized people as subversive, Communist, and anti-American. Grenadian people nonetheless persevered in their use of co-operatives, and they have a strong co-operative culture today – one in part attributable to the historical development of Susus on the island.

One cannot speak about co-operatives in Grenada without mentioning the impact of Susus on people's lives. People often participate in Susus informally, and in co-operatives or credit unions more formally. The Grenada Co-operative League (GCL) is the formal co-op network. It has 10 credit unions and a membership of 42,000, or 40 per cent of the population (General Manager, interview, 4 June 2013, St. George, Grenada). According to Devon Charles, the general manager of Grenville Credit Union, "community banks are not concerned about blowing their trumpets, but they are there to help people and co-operatives are not going away" (interview, 11 June 2013, St. George, Grenada). Ordinary Grenadians trust credit unions for their banking because of their roots in the community. Susu is also the most valued financial system that people use, whether they belong to a credit union or not. "Jingle," the owner of a food shop at the bus terminal in town, was sceptical that commercial banks could help small vendors. "Jingle" preferred a co-operative bank:

> Government and dem [commercial banks] say dey would 'elp business in market and [bus] terminal. But they only talk, talk and give no help to us. They fear we can't pay. So I don't worry with [their] empty promises and I go to my Communal [refers to Communal Credit Union]. (Interview, 16 June 2013, St. George, Grenada)

Susus in Grenada, like those found in Trinidad and Tobago, are based on a rotating system. To be clear, the Susu system and other informal collectives were always around in Grenada and the other islands. In times of crisis, reliance on these communal and self-help groups of various kinds became even stronger. In Grenada, Susus (money polling) and the Maroon system (labour-sharing projects) continued during the authoritarian regimes of Gairy (1967–74, 1974–9), the New Jewel Movement takeover (1979–83), and the US invasion in 1983 (Sandford and Vigilante 1984, 32) because people were under stress. The point is that these solidarity economy practices have existed for a long time in the region and became critical during economic and political crises.[2]

The Susu systems are based on daily or weekly plans, with each cycle spanning from 6 to 12 weeks. The Banker Lady manages the money collected from participants and usually charges a small flat fee (Besson 1996). People trust the Susu bankers. As "Mummy," an energetic elderly woman who has owned a mango

---

2 Susus predated the colonization experience and various political regimes and I credit Professor Eudine Barriteau at the University of the West Indies at Cave Hill for helping me highlight this point clearly.

and spice stall in the central market in St. George for more than 30 years, explains:

> Susu is di ting! [Susu is a good thing to have] You [can] get your money when you want it and nobody give you problem [referring to Susu banker]. You can say to the [Susu] banker, give me a hand [lump sum of cash] and she will because she know you and what you will do [with the money]. We bind (we come together) … no one can change this way. (Interview, 13 June 2013, Grenada)

Susu helps ordinary, self-employed people access large lump sums of cash from peers who know them. This kind of access would never be possible at a commercial bank, especially for poor persons of African heritage. "Mummy" tried several times to get a loan from the commercialized microfinance bank called Microfin (now defunct), but it involved a long, drawn-out process that was hard to follow. Members of the ROSCA were open about their difficulties in getting loans from banks, and in citing these difficulties as the reason Susu banks became so important (Hossein 2014a, 2014c).

Haiti's Sol: A Pioneer in Solidarity Economics

ROSCAs in Haiti are the very core of what co-operative development means to the Caribbean region. Haiti was one of the first slave colonies. The collective money systems used by Haitians, known as Gbeh (or Eso Jojo), originated in the Kingdom of the Dahomey (now Benin). French-speaking Benin and Togo, West African countries that Haitians claim as their ancestral lands, have always had strong traditions of informal banking co-operatives. Haitian Sols were born out of these enduring African co-operative systems – co-operatives were never new to the Haitian people, nor a project "introduced" to them by local or foreign political elites. While some colonizers interfered and introduced top-down control in their brand of co-operatives, an intervention which resulted in limited development (Develtere 1993), it was not the primary form of co-operative in these countries. Many Haitian people have vibrant co-operative economies today which they have been incubating for generations.

While Haiti has a large, formalized co-operative sector, ROSCAs far outnumber formal co-operatives. African ideas of Kombit (Kreyol for collectivity) come from Beninese ancestors who brought banking concepts to the Americas as far back as the 1500s, when slavery began. Oppressive country politics under leaders like Dessalines (1804–6) adhered to *politique du ventre* (politics of the belly) dictatorships, leaving the masses in a state of total suffering (Fatton 2007, 2002). Sols have assisted at least 80 per cent of Haitians in meeting their everyday financial needs. This collective approach to business is so well-known that political elites have enshrined Haiti's (1987) status as a co-operatist state into the preamble of the Haitian Constitution, meaning that co-ops are part and parcel of what it means to be Haitian. Political elites recognize the vital role self-help banking groups have played in the country's development, culture, and history.

The first Haitian co-operative was formalized in 1937 in Port-à-Piment du Nord, near Gonaïves, at about the same time that Haiti was occupied by the United States (Montasse 1983). More *caisses populaires* (credit unions) were formalized in La Vallée (Jacmel) in 1946, and in Cavaillon (South) and Sainte Anne in Port-au-Prince in 1951 (Colloque sur la Microfinance 2010). The growth of co-operative banks took place in the 1940s, which was a period of repressive politics. However, these formal co-ops owe their development to Sol, the "predecessor" that continues to endure. Despite being banned from organizing Gwoupmans (Kreyol for association) and co-operatives under the brutal reign of the Duvalier dictatorships from 1957 to 1986 (N'Zengou-Tayo 1998), Haitians continued to participate in Sols to meet their needs (Maguire 1997). Haitian co-operative scholar Emmanuel Montasse (1983) discovered growth in credit unions between 1951 to 1983, years Haitians were deprived of basic services.

In Haiti, ROSCAs – known as Sol or Soldes – are mobilized by grassroots people, especially those who are ignored. In times of extreme distress and the current political crisis, there is no doubt that people are relying on Sol to get by. Those who call themselves the "*moun adeyo*" told me that they see Sol as a way to feel a part of their community (focus group, 9 October 2010, Port-au-Prince). Most Haitians, whom I have interviewed over the years (2008, 2011, and 2012), had a sentimental view of Sol and were proud

Figure 4.1. Haitian Woman and Her Coffee Co-op Business, Cap-Haïtien
Source: Author's photo.

of its African traditions. Haitian women have used Sol to grow their businesses. In December 2012, I met with numerous Haitian women who own coffee co-operatives in the north of the country, near Cap-Haïtien. Sol has been an important financing device for assisting them in growing their businesses (see figure 4.1).

Local traditions of Kombit, Gwoupmans, and Sols have been invaluable for reaching economically excluded Haitians and are a testimony to the democratic spirit of the masses (Fatton 2007; Montasse, 1983). A mainstream banker whom I interviewed attested to the importance of Sols in Haitian society:

> … *caisses* belong to the Haiti people. The *caisses* are accessible, grassroots, and embedded into people's hearts because they focus on people's community, collectivity, and helping each other out, which are very important traits for us [Haitians], especially those of us who are poor. (Interview with local businessman, 2 October 2010, Port-au-Prince, Haiti)

Sols are created by people in the community. Members contribute a fixed amount, such as 100 gourdes (about US$2.50), every week or month for a cycle of 6 to 10 months, depending on the number of members. Members agree to contribute a regular, fixed sum during a stated cycle. Each group has a firm end date. Members can use the money for a specified period as indicated by the Chief Banker Lady, the "Mama Sol." Sols are organized by members who decide the fee structure. Some sols are completely free with no fees. Others apply a small flat fee for administration (focus groups, 9 October 2010, Bon Repos). Sols are trusted by their users because of their collective nature. Poor families have used these socially embedded banking systems for generations.

Unsurprisingly, Sol has had a profound impact on the Haitian people. Commercial bank Sogebank launched its "Mama Sol" product line in hopes of diversifying its clientele and, more imperatively, making ordinary Haitians want to bank there. As conventional bankers look for ways to expand their customer base, Sol is a name they hope will attract and convince clients (such as Madam Saras [women traders] and *ti machanns* [market sellers]) to bank with them. The very bankers who made it nearly impossible for some of these women to borrow money from formal financial institutions are now looking for ways to attract women running informal businesses; these women represent the vast majority of people doing business.

Sharing Known Traditions

ROSCAs are a well-respected business tradition throughout the Caribbean; the Banker Ladies have status – they are revered. When I first told people about this project, they were generally pleased and excited to talk to me about ROSCAs. (Interestingly, I had the opposite experience when I earlier worked on a formal microfinance project.) The Caribbean populations see ROSCAs as their own invention, but one for which they credit their African roots. The collective sensibility of women who bond together to engage in self-help is admirable and agential; they act with agency to show the world that business can be done humanely. It is their approach to co-operative business, and belief in the power of co-ops to open up economies that makes what they do original and important. While the Banker Ladies are free to share what they do, they remain independent and without any formal support for the work they are doing for society.

The Banker Ladies speak with pride and authority about ROSCAs. They are free to discuss what they do in ROSCAs and do so without shame or fear. They know people admire them for their contributions to co-operative building. All of the Caribbean women whom I interviewed told me that they use ROSCAs alongside conventional banking, but that their ROSCA matters most to them. Partner or Susu are the preferred banking systems in the region. Commercial bankers know this. For this reason, elite bankers are bringing the ROSCA system into their formal banks. As a result, the Banker Ladies are inadvertently influencing the formal banking sector to humanize finance.

Most of the Caribbean people know about ROSCAs. At some point in their lives, most of them have belonged to one or at the very least known someone who has. The Susu comes up often in conversation, theatre, and song. ROSCAs do not necessarily change people's social standing or make anyone rich, but that is not the point. ROSCAs assist excluded people to meet their social, financial, and political needs on their own terms. Unlike external funding, there are no strings attached or controls imposed on how members live their lives. Caribbean people are protective of these systems for this reason: it is development from the ground up, and it is reciprocal work that they know and value.

No matter where one goes in the Caribbean, women speak affectionately about ROSCAs. They point to things they were able to fund, including their children's education because of pooling money with other women. An article by Cheryl Harewood (2023) in *Nation News*, a national paper in Barbados, documented the adaptation of Meeting Turn by Angela Alleyne; as food prices skyrocketed during the COVID-19 pandemic, members pooled food items to help one another.[3] Whether the Caribbean women realize it or not, their work has made major contributions to the solidarity and co-operative economy. In writing this book, I came to appreciate the debt owed

---

3 Senator Crystal Drakes of Barbados sent me this story via WhatsApp (March 2023).

to the Caribbean people, who bring these systems with them as they migrate. ROSCA systems of sharing funds have helped the Caribbean people, as well as many other women. In a piece I published in *Stabroek News*, a Guyanese newspaper, I acknowledged that we should show gratitude to the Caribbean women for making Susu, Sol, Partner, and Boxhand known to the world; these co-operative banks were able to reach those left behind (Hossein 2021b).[4]

The Banker Ladies take care of people. The work they do is instinctive and cultural, and they use money to achieve this. The Banker Ladies are respected, loved, and valued for tackling inequities in business. In Jamaica, Guyana, Haiti, and Trinidad and Tobago, ROSCAs provide a way for women to bank when they are routinely denied access to formal finance. They offer members a sense of agency, validate local know-how and enrich the larger community. The Banker Ladies' form of development work prioritizes membership, and in doing this work, they draw on the love they have for self and community. Political theorist Myisha Cherry (2021) refers to this constructive use of rage to build up society as "Lordean rage." It is the type of rage that enables people who have been ignored and vilified to work through their pain by coming together and building. Yet, this work is not validated everywhere in the same concrete way.

The Banker Ladies do not receive the investments and support that they need to support the growth of the ROSCA system. What I know is that these so-called experts who come into their communities to study these mutual aid financial groups become the ones to access donor funds. They then create "social finance" or "group-based microfinance" projects, and they are the ones accessing subsidies to do this work and then engage these same women. The Banker Ladies and women in charge of these ROSCAs are never credited for this financial innovation. But the outsiders who come to the Banker Ladies study what they know and then "design" successful projects back to these women. This is precisely why social finance works so well – because they are using the very same ideas that these women have always known.

The intertwining of capital and slavery haunts Black people throughout the Caribbean. Moreover, this relationship between

---

4 The column "In the Diaspora" is edited by Dr. Alissa D. Trotz. It is a way of connecting Guyana and the Caribbean to many of us residing outside of the region.

Figure 4.2. Photo of the Bank of England's Exhibit, *Slavery & the Bank*
Source: Author's photo, 6 November 2023.

money and human enslavement is the origin of commercial banks in the region (Hudson 2017). As seen in figure 4.2, the Bank of England's *Slavery & the Bank* exhibit apologized for its governors and directors owning 599 slaves (Jolly 2022). These structural inequalities in world finance resulted in the plantation economy that tiered society along lines of class, race, and gender (Thomas 1988). These histories, which the Banker Ladies know well, have solidified a place for ROSCAs in the Caribbean solidarity economy.

No European invented Partner or Sol or Susu: the Caribbean people did, and they were innovations necessitated by the fact that they were a people living under circumstances of duress. Acknowledging the indigenous claims of ROSCAs, a heritage held on to for centuries by African-descended people in the region, disrupts the narrative that co-operative development is a colonial project. The Caribbean Banker Ladies are vested in what they do. The ethical business model on which they operate ROSCAs is committed to well-being, to values trust, and strengthens human connections in the world.

chapter five

Canada's Hidden Co-operatives: The Legacy of the Banker Ladies in Toronto and Montreal

Black women contribute in important ways to Canada's legacy of co-operativism, mutual aid, and building up of civil society. After 10 years of doing this research in Canada, the ROSCA is a global phenomenon that is surprisingly unknown to most Canadians. They may wrongly assume it is only located in the Global South. Even if people have heard of ROSCA systems, they assume they only have value in the Global South and do not see their relevance here. The number of ROSCAs users in the Global North is likely to be in the millions. According to Jeffrey Ashe (2023) of Grassroots Finance Action, he estimates that 83 million people in the developed world participate in ROSCAs. Yet in many parts of the Global North, these ROSCA systems, which are known to be active, are either ignored or stigmatized as illegal – which they are not. This stigmatization may explain why they are overlooked as a vital part of Canada's social economy (and why its users hide them).

For Canada's social economy to reflect its society, it must recognize the various informal co-operative forms that make up the third sector, and be driven by research and theory that is culturally diverse. The Banker Ladies "Blackify" economics by showing how co-operativism is a part of who they are. These women choose to form groups with other Black women, an action which shields them from feeling like outsiders in the country they call home.[1] It

---

[1] This use of Barrett's (2015) term "blackening" is broadened to include business economics for the Black/African diaspora in Canada.

is equally important to document that Black women are not only recipients of aid. They initiate self-help solutions on their own terms. This chapter engages with the role of ROSCAs for Black Canadian women and reasons why these systems remain so hidden. ROSCAs largely operate under the radar in the United States and in Europe for similar reasons (Hossein, Wright Austin, and Edmonds 2023). Michael Emru Tadesse and Esra Erdem (2023) document how Ethiopian immigrants to Berlin, Germany, used Equub to manage the financial exclusion they encountered.

My parents are Caribbean migrants. They moved to New York City (United States) in the mid-1960s during the race riots, then back to Guyana for a short visit before relocating to Toronto, Canada, in 1971 for employment opportunities and to avoid conflicts with their interracial marriage. Part of their adjustment process required tapping into informal networks. Many newly arrived Black immigrants draw on ROSCAs as they settle and integrate into Canadian life because it is usually the only form of financial access they have to a lump sum of money. They too use these funds in hiding because of the fear that what they do may be misunderstood. In an interview, a Banker Lady "Susan," a Black Canadian with African American roots and a mother of five children, explained to me that ROSCAs are a way for women who are left out of economic systems to group together to assert that they matter, and to do things for themselves:

> It is important for our people to build something for [our]selves. Not controlled by government. And create our own rules and circle of power. This is resistance. Susu helps us thrive as a people who have a business and social commitment to each other. What do you see? I see: Resistance. It's not about you or the men in our lives. It's about the group of us as women. It is joy. We need to see that for our own survival in this place we call home. (Interview, 18 June 2018, Little Burgundy, Montreal)

I grew up knowing about ROSCA systems because the Caribbean grown-ups around me talked about "Box" or "Susu." I knew them as a part of diaspora life. Later, working in development finance in parts of Africa, and then studying ROSCAs in Canada and across the Caribbean, I could see that African-descended people considered these ROSCA systems to be co-operative institutions. When I first started examining ROSCAs in Canada, it was an activity usually carried out by ethnic, kinship, or cultural groups. However, this circumstance has changed since I started doing this work more than a decade ago. In Canada, ROSCAs are also based on social class and, more and more, on affinities: with workplaces, schools, neighbourhoods, or common interests. I remember meeting a group of hospital orderlies in Little Burgundy. The orderlies explained to me that their Susu was made up of Caribbean people, as well as women from India, the Philippines, and white Canadians who found it a useful system.

Many Black immigrants from the Caribbean came to Canada during the 1960s and 1970s. They arrived from Jamaica, Guyana, Haiti, Barbados, and Trinidad. In later years, there followed an influx of Black immigrants from other countries, such as Somalia, Ghana, and Nigeria. Collectively they brought many skills to Canada (Mensah and Williams 2015; Mensah 2010; Galabuzi 2006; Tettey and Puplampu 2005; Winks 1997). Many new Canadians had a heritage of money pooling systems and brought these traditions with them to Canada. In this chapter about Canadian ROSCAs, I have also included what I learned from Canadian-born Black people. Some call themselves "Scotian" and have roots in Africville, Nova Scotia. Others trace their roots to the sleeping car porters and the Underground Railroad. Overall, the Toronto and Montreal focus groups were often very diverse: focus groups sometimes included people from the Middle East (Egypt) or South America (Guyana, Colombia, Peru). A disproportionate number of subjects in my study come from the Caribbean, Somalia, Ethiopia, and West Africa. I interviewed them in two very different contexts – Toronto, Ontario, and Montreal, Quebec.[2] People have been engaged in ROSCAs in Canada for more than a century.

---

2 In 2017, the *Canadian Journal of Nonprofit and Social Economy Research* (Hossein 2017c) published an earlier and more limited analysis of the content of my Toronto case study. Permission to use sections was granted by journal editor Jorge Sousa in October 2018.

The goal of this chapter is to raise awareness about the vibrancy of the ROSCA system in major cities. The Banker Ladies in Canada contribute to economic development in significant ways through mutual aid and co-operative building. In spite of social stigmas, the Canadian Banker Ladies are organizing against systemic exclusion. The Chief Banker Ladies in this study, with each of them responsible for at least a dozen women in the group, represent hundreds of perspectives. What these perspectives share is an awareness of being overlooked: the Canadian Banker Ladies are ignored in relation to their economic value to society, which is profound, given their goals of reaching excluded people. In fact, the Banker Ladies in Canada are stigmatized *because* of the informal collective organizing they do. These women are subjected to intense forms of anti-Black racism and misogyny. They are made to feel vulnerable when they should be recognized and compensated for the contributions they make to Canadian civic life. The harms they endure for being Black and as a woman is the reason many purposefully hide their ROSCAs. For as long as Black and racialized people have been in Canada, they have encountered racism in business and have retaliated by forming banking co-ops. It is time the Banker Ladies work receive recognition for their important work.

Racism in Canada's "Big Six" Banks

My family encountered systemic racism, the emotional trauma of which caused serious, lifelong consequences for all of us. It followed us as we moved around for several years; though my parents tried hard to hide their issues, they faced serious loss and precariousness when it came to finance. These experiences – of coping, of trying to survive – have stayed with me. It is no surprise, then, that my lifelong work has been to analyse financial access issues for racialized women; that my sister works in small business development for the state; and that my brother is self-employed. I chose my line of research enquiry because I saw financial exclusion at work in the business sector while I was growing up. My chosen line of enquiry into Black/African women and alternative financial systems in the informal sector has also created tensions for me within academe, particularly with white male faculty.[3]

Indignities experienced daily take a toll on people. For this reason, people choose to join ROSCA systems. In December 2014, Haitian-born Canadian Frantz St. Fleur was wrongfully arrested for allegedly depositing a fraudulent cheque of $9,000 into his account at a Toronto Scotiabank location, a branch where he had been a customer for 10 years (Alamenciak 2014). It turned out that his realtor had issued him a cheque. Scotiabank apologized profusely for this humiliating experience (Alamenciak 2014). St. Fleur brought a civil suit against the bank for the traumas he endured.

In January 2020, Maxwell Johnson, an Indigenous man, and his 12-year-old granddaughter were handcuffed by Vancouver police when the Bank of Montreal (BMO) suspected them of illicit behaviour (Sterritt 2020). There was no reason to question Johnson or his granddaughter's activities; Johnson had gone to the bank to open an account for his granddaughter. In February 2020, Egyptian Canadian Dana Ramadan went into a Royal Bank of Canada (RBC) in Toronto's west end. She says she was treated harshly by tellers, who accused her of illegal activities. The bank apologized and said its actions were intended to protect its client from potential fraud (Paradkar 2020). In April 2021, Kensha Spaulding was denied access to his own funds at a Toronto Dominion (TD) bank in Ottawa (The National 2021).

Such confrontations with banks are so commonplace that many Black, Indigenous, and racialized Canadians anticipate enduring such encounters when they go to a bank (Hossein 2017a). My Twitter message box often fills up with accounts from Canadians across the country about their experiences of racism in banks. These incidents of bias are examples of the many forms of economic discrimination faced by racialized Canadians, a phenomenon that has been heavily documented (Chin 2020; Gilmore 2015; James and Davis 2012; Das Gupta 2007; Galabuzi 2006). Given racist behaviour in

---

3 In 2020, I filed a human rights complaint with the Human Rights Tribunal of Ontario against York University due to systemic sex-based and race-based discrimination. The complaint is still pending at the HRTO as of February 2024 (no decision).

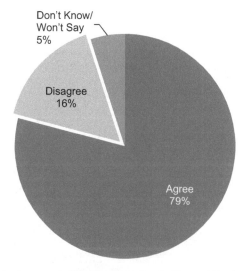

Figure 5.1. Exclusionary and Racist Attitudes in Formal Banks: "Do Black people from your community have a hard time getting access to their money or loans from formal banks?" (2015–17)

banking, it is understandable why racialized people choose to participate in alternative banking services; the racism exhibited towards racialized and low-income people makes it understandable why some minority Canadians do not trust mainstream business outlets. It is no surprise that money pooling systems have become one of the most important forms of banking for Canada's immigrant communities.

Dutch academics Julie-Marthe Lehmann and Peer Smets (2019) carried out numerous interviews with Ghanaians and Nigerians in Amsterdam who reported engagement with ROSCAs as a way of dealing with banking exclusion. The Canadian case is no exception in its bias against people who are Black/of African descent. For this project, I asked the Banker Ladies in Toronto and Montreal: "Do Black people from your community have a hard time getting access to their money or loans from formal banks?" In response, 79 per cent of the women said that banks were "racist" and "rude" to them (see figure 5.1). In further discussions, the women also stated:

"Black people and especially Black women have the hardest time getting access to loans." Some also mentioned that "deposited funds could also be an issue with withdrawing." These findings fit with my understanding of banking exclusion in Canada. It is a topic about which I have written in various opinion editorials.

ROSCAs Are Transnational

Most research on ROSCAs in the Global South tends to focus on its use as a coping device (Rutherford 2000; Bouman 1977; Geertz 1962). My own research on ROSCAs is an outgrowth of earlier Caribbean-based research I undertook, which examined professionalized microfinance institutions (Hossein 2013, 2014b, 2016c). Findings from this project revealed a back-and-forth with ROSCAs. Many of the Banker Ladies living in major North American cities, such as Miami, New York, Montreal, and Toronto, participated in ROSCAs in the Caribbean (Hossein 2016d). The Banker Lady "Shelagh," who I interviewed in Kingston, Jamaica's Coronation Market, told me several members lived in Toronto, and she could recount details about the city even though she had never travelled to Toronto. Similarly, there were Mama Sols in Port-au-Prince who had members living in New York City, Miami, or Montreal. Women I met in Toronto from Ghana, Sudan, and Sierra Leone confirmed that they belonged to ROSCAs in their home countries. The transnational aspect of ROSCAs challenges the presumption that solidarity economies are localized in one physical place. No matter where they reside, the Canadian Banker Ladies are clearly still connected to banking systems in their countries of origin (Hart, Laville, and Cattani 2010; Amin 2009; Blackman and Brooks 2002).

Methods

It is important to use methods that consider the lived experience of those who are oppressed. In the Canadian case, I took extra steps to ensure that people were anonymized because of the risks they felt for being in a ROSCA. The level of fear and worry were far more of an issue in Canada than in the Caribbean. The Banker Ladies in Toronto have every right to worry: the *Civil Remedies Act* (Ontario 2001) gave authorities the right to take away their money if at any point the police believed the funds to be unlawfully acquired. The women I met in Canada lived with a very real fear of police and government authorities with the power to trace and imprison them and/or the people they cared about and for. This is why I use aliases for my Banker Ladies in the Canadian case (as I do elsewhere) and provide fewer details about their location(s) overall.

Drawing on Black diasporic feminist theories has enabled me to go beneath the surface to unearth practices that were hidden. I do not allow theory to dictate the empirical work, but I use it as a way to guide and understand my findings. My interviews are driven by these overarching questions: "How do women of the same racial group organize ROSCAs in different political environments?" and "Are these women able to freely organize in public? And, if not, why?"

According to the 2021 census, 1.5 million people identity as Black in Canada or 4.3 per cent of the total population (Statistics Canada 2022a). I selected the city of Toronto, where I live, because it has the largest number of Black people (36.9 per cent); moreover, 52.4 per cent of Canada's Black population live in Ontario (Statistics Canada 2022a). Montreal has the second largest number of Black people in Canada at 6.8 per cent, including 179,000 Haitians (Statistics Canada 2022a). I used qualitative methods, individual interviews, and focus groups to gather data from direct users of ROSCAs in Toronto (102) and Montreal (43). As seen in table 5.1, in Toronto, two focus groups were held in each of the following neighbourhoods: 51 women in Warden Woods within southeast Scarborough (Toronto's east end), 21 in Rexdale, and 27 in Firgrove, the Jane/Finch community in Downsview (Toronto's west end).

It should be remembered that the women in the focus groups represent many other members of their ROSCAs, each of which has between 8 and 70 members. While the most common group size is about 30 members, the 145 women with whom I met represented about 4,300 women. I carried out a total of 208 interviews,

Table 5.1. Interviews with the Banker Ladies and Experts in Toronto and Montreal (*N* = 208)

Method	Toronto (*n* = 132)			Montreal (*n* = 76)			Total
	Scarborough	Jane and Finch	Rexdale	Little Burgundy	Montreal Nord/Jean-Talon	Côte-des-Neiges	
No. of Banker Ladies in the focus groups	51	20	21	5	0	7	104
Individual interviews with the Banker Ladies	3	7	0	9	17	5	41
Total interviews with the Banker Ladies	54	27	21	14	17	12	145
Toronto Banker Ladies				–			102
Montreal Banker Ladies				–			43
Individual interviews with business, government, and the community		30			33		63

Source: Author's data collection in Toronto and Montreal from 2015 to 2018 and again in 2022.

and 145 of these interviews were with the Chief Banker Ladies in the two cities (see table 5.1). I also carried out 63 interviews with leaders from co-operative, government, and community organizations, as well as the private sector. In July 2018, to get an alternative view, I hosted a follow-up session with members who were dissatisfied with ROSCAs; these women are not captured in this sample of current direct users. All direct users of ROSCAs whom I interviewed were Black women. The Chief Banker Ladies represent groups with memberships of between 8 and 70, which translates into thousands of Canadian women using ROSCAs. ROSCAs are far more widely used than people imagine.

During an eight-year period, I met with 102 Banker Ladies in Toronto, specifically in the Jane/Finch, Rexdale, and Warden Woods (Scarborough) areas. I chose these locations because of the high concentration of Black Canadians and presence of strong community organizations. These Toronto communities are dense inner suburbs; they are also low-income, with household incomes averaging less than $25,000 (Pagliaro 2014). The women interviewed had to self-identify as Black and be an active user of ROSCAs, and preferably be a leader of a ROSCA.

The Black community in Toronto is quite diverse, with Black women representing about a dozen countries. Mensah and Williams (2015) have detailed the heterogeneity of Black Canadians, and this sample is indicative of that research. Tettey and Puplampu (2005) share the experience of African-born Canadians, which they rightly note has not received as much attention as the Caribbean people. My study combines and speaks to the financial economies of the Caribbean and African-born Canadians (first and second generation). The following are the countries which the Banker Ladies came from: Antigua, Bahamas, Barbados, Benin, Burkina Faso, Burundi, Brazil, Cameroon, Colombia, Congo, Côte d'Ivoire, Egypt, Eritrea, Ethiopia, Ghana, Grenada, Guyana, Haiti, Jamaica, Kenya, Liberia, Martinique, Nigeria, Peru, Somalia, Senegal, Sierra Leone, St. Kitts and Nevis, St. Vincent, Sudan, Togo, and Trinidad.

The Montreal case is a small sample. It is worthwhile to consider the context of Quebec where Black people live alongside the grandiose reputation of the province's social economy (Bouchard, Cruz Filho, and Tassadit 2015). The Banker Ladies in Montreal are also quite diverse. Many of the anglophone Black women interviewed have Caribbean origins, namely from Jamaica, Barbados, Trinidad, Guyana, St. Vincent, and Grenada. They are called "Islanders" locally. There are also those with African American heritage, either through the history of sleeping car porters, or through families who moved to Quebec from Nova Scotia. People from the latter group are referred to as "Scotians."

Many anglophone Black people live, or have roots in, Little Burgundy and Notre-Dame-de-Grâce, in west Montreal. Côte-des-Neiges, Jean-Talon, Saint-Michel, and eastwards towards

Papineau, are where many francophone Black women live. They represent mostly Haiti and French West African countries, including Benin, Togo, Burundi, Cameroon, Congo, Côte d'Ivoire, Martinique, and Senegal. In Montreal, 43 Banker Ladies were interviewed over a two-year period. I first interviewed anglophone Black women, and then I expanded to Haitians and French-speaking Africans in the north and east ends of Montreal. In each of these cases, I also interviewed first- and second-generation Black Canadians with roots in one of the countries mentioned.

Some of the questions I asked the women in the focus groups included: "What financial services are available to women in your community to engage in business and meet other economic liveli-hood needs?" "How do you feel about ROSCAs?" More specific questions included: "Why have you joined a ROSCA?" and "How is your specific ROSCA organized?" Finally, "How do ROSCAs meet the needs of people as compared with commercial banks?" and "Given all the banking options in Montreal, why do persons join ROSCAs (e.g., Susu, Moziki, Partner, Ajo, Hagbad, and Equub)?"

The women debated the issues. At times, there were heated discussions among the participants on the ways they chose to organize their groups and why. For example, the Muslim Banker Ladies do not charge fees, feeling it immoral to do so, while the other Banker Ladies uphold small fees as a way to reduce the costs of running a ROSCA. The Somali Banker Ladies were particularly adamant about not charging fees. They also felt a separate focus group should discuss the subject of Islamophobia in business, and its impact on their lives, because of the particular stigma they endure as a group (see chapter 6). The anglophone Banker Ladies in Montreal also felt that language bias in the French-dominated province of Quebec was a form of exclusion. They wanted separate focus groups from the French-speaking Black women, whom they felt did not share their experiences. In addition to analysing data generated through interviews and focus groups, I conducted an analysis of the secondary literature to understand the politics of the English-speaking minority in Quebec. Black women interviewed felt strongly that the onset of Bill 101, which privileges French language and culture in business, education, and the workplace, created havoc in their lives

(McInnis 2016). Bill 101 was adopted on 26 August 1977, the result of the "Quiet Revolution" in Quebec. Through Bill 101, the Quebec separatist movement worked to take economic power from anglophones. For many Black anglophones in Quebec, this bill prompted an exodus to other parts of Canada, most notably to Toronto.[4]

During interviews in which they reflected on Bill 101 and their experiences of its impact, the women explained to me why ROSCAs have been so important to them. These mutual aid groups provided them with a way to cope, as a people, with both financial exclusion and social isolation. In response to being made to feel different, these women take it upon themselves to form ROSCAs. Indeed, ROSCAs have multidimensional appeal: they offer friendship and bonding between members, who share dividends. They are democratic systems; those who feel ignored or silenced come to ROSCAs and find they have a voice. Collectively organized groups, in business and society, are a quiet form of resistance.

Consider the work of African American scholar Patricia Hill Collins (2000a, 2000b). In *Black Feminist Thought*, Hill Collins (2002a) argues that Black women need theorizing to be conceptualized by people who have lived the experiences about which they speak (i.e., being poor, Black, female). Theoretical thinking produced by someone "who knows" resonates with marginalized, racialized people. The concept of lived experience is therefore crucial in analysing the impact of ROSCAs on Black women. Understanding what the social economy means for Black women therefore requires a dual approach: first, one must draw on lived experience; and, second, one must search out theoretical thinking that can speak directly to the systemic oppression experienced by racialized people. Black liberation theory makes it clear that ROSCAs can be a source of camaraderie and a way for excluded Black women to build strong economic lives. This study will shed light on the various ways in which Black Canadian women engage in finance and business in a developed country.

---

4 In any interview or focus group, time was devoted to unpacking the impact of Bill 101 on the lives of Black Quebeckers. Some people reflected on the stress they experienced over the dwindling numbers of their community brought about by the bias against them in favour of French speakers.

Findings: What the Banker Ladies in Toronto and Montreal Teach Us

This section merges the voices of the Banker Ladies in Toronto and Montreal to understand why Black Canadian women use ROSCAs – and why many hide the fact that they do. The women in this study come from many countries in Africa and the Caribbean. Many of the people whom I interviewed were also first- or second-generation Africans who were born in Canada. The countries represented include Jamaica, Trinidad and Tobago, Grenada, Barbados, Guyana, St. Kitts and Nevis, Antigua, Ethiopia, Ghana, Nigeria, Sierra Leone, Kenya, Tanzania, Somalia, Sudan, Egypt, and Liberia. The key findings include: the mechanics of how ROSCAs function in Canada; why women use ROSCAs even though they live in a financial centre; the stigmas that have made Black women hide their groups; and why the work they do counts as equitable finance.

Black Canadians make up one of Canada's largest non-European ethnic groupings. They represent the fastest growing racial group in the country, with a population of 1.5 million in 2021 or 4.3 per cent of total population (Statistics Canada 2022a). Toronto Metropolitan University's Grace-Edward Galabuzi (2006) found that African Canadians are twice as likely as those in the overall population to have low incomes, to be unemployed, and to encounter systemic bias that interferes with equal access to goods and services. Nearly all the women in this study have a household income of less than $40,000 per annum after tax, and they have always had to work supplemental jobs to make ends meet.

In the Statistics Canada article in *Juristat*, "Experiences of Discrimination among Black and Indigenous Populations," in 2019, 46 per cent of Black Canadians said that they feel discriminated against because of their skin colour and cultural identity (Cotter 2022). Media reports on gang violence and crimes also reinforce stereotypes that African Canadians do not contribute to society, and this view permeates the Canadian psyche (Austin 2013; James et al. 2010; Das Gupta 2007; Galabuzi 2006). In a focus group with young Somali women, the participants explained that when police raid the Dixon Apartments, they take away and confiscate their bags of money hidden in bedrooms; under the *Civil Remedies Act* (Ontario 2001) police are permitted to do this. These funds come from the Hagbad money collected and are not drug money (June 2018, Toronto). It is particularly difficult to be a minority within a minority, which is true of French-speaking Black people in an English-speaking society, or Muslim Somali women, or Black francophone women in Quebec (Madibbo 2012). Black women, whether they are francophones or anglophones, experience intense forms of business and social exclusion because of the colour of their skin (Austin 2013). Despite these challenges, in both Toronto and Montreal, Black Canadian women organize ROSCAs outside the purview of the state, using them to shield and protect themselves.

Why ROSCAS and Not Conventional Co-operative Systems

The Banker Ladies create community-driven financial systems in Toronto and Montreal, two of Canada's financial centres. ROSCAs cannot be viewed as a "foreign" activity. They have been practised for decades in Canada, moulded in ways that suit the Canadian diaspora. In the early 1800s, slaves who fled to Canada via the Underground Railroad organized "True Bands" to help people build their lives (AGO 2017; Bryan Prince, interview 2016). To supplement their incomes, Caribbean immigrants have participated in ROSCAs for 70 years. Indeed, this is probably a conservative estimate since Jamaican Maroons have been coming to Canada since 1796 (Walker 2012).

The Canadian story of creating alternative financial institutions (AFIs) is deeply grounded in the French Canadian experience of *l'économie sociale* (Fontan et al. 2009). In Quebec in the early 1900s, Alphonse Desjardins and his wife, Dorimene, first created the *caisses populaires* (credit unions) in North America to address financial exclusion of French-speaking and Catholic minorities (Mendell 2009; Shragge and Fontan 2000). As a student of the Canadian social economy, I wanted to include Montreal in this study so that

Figure 5.2. Desjardins Credit Union in Montreal (Beaubien)
Source: Author's photo, 2017.

the use of ROSCAs could be contrasted to the use of credit unions in a province that is revered for its commitment to co-operative and solidarity economics (see figure 5.2).

In the Toronto case, one issue that did not sit well with me was that Black women, well versed in co-operative banks, chose to bank with commercial lenders rather than with Meridian credit union because Meridian branches are not located within their communities. This was not the case in the Caribbean, where many women whom I interviewed belonged to a credit union because of similarities they saw between credit unions and their ROSCAs. I wanted to see if Black women in Montreal were more likely to bank with a credit union than their Toronto counterparts.

In Montreal, individual interviews were carried out with 16 French-speaking African and Caribbean women (interviews Montreal 2017). My research assistant, the child of Haitian parents but born and raised in Quebec, conducted the interviews. She found it nearly impossible to have the women meet in a focus group since they were worried about the authorities questioning their actions. A question that I asked French-speaking Montrealers was: "Do you bank with Desjardins? And why or why not?" Only one of the women interviewed said she was a client of Desjardins. The women in Montreal, French- or English-speaking, did not think Desjardins was concerned about them or their needs. I assumed initially that Black anglophone women could not bank at Desjardins because of the language issue. However, it soon became apparent that they snubbed Desjardins because of what they saw as its focus on "pure laine," meaning white French people.

Those interviewed did not like my question about why they did not choose a well-known, community-focused bank like Desjardins. When I raised the matter, Black women in Montreal who organized ROSCAs could see the inconsistency about choosing a commercial bank over a co-operative one. However, they did not agree that the Desjardins movement contested financial exclusion for all citizens. "Gisèle," a 50-year-old woman of Cameroonian descent who belonged to a Janjui, reasoned this way:

Je suis sortie de cet [Desjardins] établissement il y a longtemps et sans aucun regret. Ils n'embauchent pas beaucoup de communautés culturelles et on ne les voit à des postes décisionnels. [Translation: I left this bank (Desjardins) a long time ago and without any regrets. They (Desjardins) do not focus on or hire many of us from the community and we are not at the senior level decision-making positions]. (Interview, November 2017, Montreal)

In this study, Black women like Gisèle made it clear that a co-operative lender that is not diversified is not a place they trust or one in which they feel comfortable. Other Black women whom we interviewed, as well as community leaders, made this same point: even if they value the co-operative model, they are not joining a co-operative financial organization if it comes at the expense of being true to who they are as Black women.

Canada's Social Economy

The literature about Canada's social economy, as well as its practice, tends to focus on formal institutions, such as co-operatives and non-profits, with little or no attention paid to community-based organizations (senior manager, interview, August 2017, Chantier, Montreal; community banking executive, interview, May 2016; Quarter, Mook, and Armstrong 2009). Those who control the purse strings for the social economy at large tend to share a European cultural heritage, and they tend not to consider the ways in which racialized people are active participants in the social economy – even in the face of exclusion – and not simply its beneficiaries. In cosmopolitan cities like Toronto and Montreal, where a significant number of residents are foreign-born (Quarter, Ryan, and Chan 2015), it is most unfortunate that leadership in the non-profit and social economy sector remains extremely white (Hossein 2017a; McIsaac, Toupin, and Park 2013).

Canada's established history of the social economy recalls Quebec's Desjardins Movement (Shragge and Fontan 2000) and the Maritime Antigonish Movement (Alexander 1997). Notably missing from this historical narrative is the vibrant role played by the ROSCAs of racialized Canadians. Quebec's Chantier de l'économie sociale is a multi-million-dollar fund designed to assist in development of the social economy (Lévesque 2013). The Black women and community leaders whom I interviewed were unaware that resources are being considered for their neighbourhoods, and they were sceptical that anything would happen (interviews and focus groups, 2016, 2017, and 2018).

In Canada, the story of the solidarity economy should start by recognizing those writings on the Black political economy. The Underground Railroad was an economic act, as well as a political one. A co-operative network of people came together to help hundreds of enslaved African people escape from the United States into Canada; these individuals settled in places like Buxton and developed True Bands (a ROSCA) to set up house. Through personalized relationships, ROSCAs have helped people of the African diaspora build strong communities in their new lands (Hossein 2013; Ardener and Burman 1996; Herskovits and Herskovits 1947). ROSCAs are a form of liberation – a concept that resonates with the very people who engage in them because they see ROSCAs as an ethical business practice.

These banking co-ops have been helping people adjust to Canadian life for a very long time, but policymakers are not paying attention. In March 2021, I gave the Big Thinking Lecture, funded by the Social Sciences and Humanities Research Council of Canada (SSHRC), to policymakers and political elites (see Hossein 2021a). I argued that Black Canadian women are organizing self-managed co-operatives and have the expertise we need to grapple with anti-Black racism. The response to my talk from decision-makers has been flat. No one wants to acknowledge this body of work because it would mean changing elite-driven development models.

How Do ROSCA Systems Work in Canada?

The Banker Ladies determine how their banking co-ops will run. Generally, members organize a group with people they know and trust. Members "vouch" for any new person brought into the group, and they elect an executive with one person designated as the primary person in charge: The Banker Lady. The Banker Lady and the executive devise a set of rules which are then sanctioned by all members. Each ROSCA has a finite period. A ROSCA can range from a few months to several years, but a one-year time period is most common. Members make a fixed deposit every cycle (e.g., weekly, monthly) and the Banker Lady, in collaboration with the executive, creates a lottery system that determines the order in which each member can access a lump sum of money from the "pool."

ROSCA members decide how to allocate or distribute the "hand" (the sum of money to a particular member) based on need and by group consensus. There is no set rule. The members of the group are the ones who determine their own methods of collecting and disbursing money. Some organize social events (e.g., tea parties, dinners) while others are responsible for dropping off payments to the Banker Lady's house. During the COVID-19 lockdown while various stay-at-home orders were active, ROSCAs moved to online banking and e-transfer deposits. Some ROSCAs charge fees to administer the pool. Others do not. Several of the Jamaican

Table 5.2. List of Known Risks When Joining a ROSCA

Risks	Major concern (Yes/No/Mixed)
1. Bias and favouritism with regards to the ordering of the allocation of funds in turn	Yes
2. Size and delays in starting the pool	Yes
3. Mistakes, no paperwork	Yes
4. Default and late payments	No
5. Confiscation of funds by the police (Canadian case)	Yes
6. Theft and losses (internal or external)	Mixed, most are concerned about external theft. Some worry about when ROSCAs turn very large and internal losses can happen.
7. Lack of privacy, sharing personal details with a group	No
8. Negative perceptions and stigmas, such as being associated with drugs, gambling, money laundering, terrorists, pyramid schemes (Canadian case)	Yes

Canadian Banker Ladies require a fee of $20 to manage the Partner, especially if the group is large.

Know the Risks

The women who animate the thinking of the Black Social Economy demonstrate, through the organization and reciprocity of their inner circles, that it is possible to alleviate people's suffering and help them develop their own projects. However, doing this work involves some risk, something members understand. The flexibility of ROSCAs and their lack of paperwork can be helpful to the user, but this informality also means that there are risks associated with joining a ROSCA. It is by taking on these risks together, informally, that members' living conditions start to change – and usually for the better.

Most mainstream political economy theories do not acknowledge the risks assumed by people of colour when they decide to go against a commercial or corporate model. In the summer of 2017, I met with about 30 Banker Ladies, women who had experienced enough troubles with ROSCAs to know about the downsides (focus groups, July 2017, Warden Woods, Toronto). Even so, 24 of the 30 women said that they still participated in ROSCAs. Table 5.2 is a list of the main risks they identified. They appear in no specific order and two are specific to the Canadian case.

The risks are of concern to people who have never previously engaged with informal collective systems. The negative views are usually raised by people who do not know, or understand, the value of mutual aid. During interviews I have conducted over the past decade, I have found members to be aware of all these risks; they make sure to manage their exposure to losses. In the decade I have been researching these systems, potential risks associated with ROSCAs have seldom eventuated. In fact, members are more likely to repay a ROSCA group than a commercial bank because defaulting on people you know and trust (and live close to and see regularly) is unheard of.

During the interviews and focus groups, women seldom said anything negative to me about ROSCAs. I asked members why they are positive about ROSCAs. Their response: in the face of vehement forms of discrimination, economic co-operatives provide these women with the means for them to grow and prosper both individually and as a group. To my surprise, the matter of privacy was not an issue that troubled any of the Banker Ladies whom I met. I learned that ROSCA members would often meet in a large group to speak about each other's work and related issues. I now know that many of them knew and trusted each other long before they decided to form a ROSCA. They attend meetings with a commitment to uplift each other. Members said that they would often confide in each other about their plans for their funds when it was their turn. They seemed to consider sharing information as a form of supporting each other and not an invasion into their private affairs.

ROSCA members know about the risks, but they believe the benefits outweigh them. "Fardosa," a Somali-born Canadian woman and mother, explained:

> I am a Black woman. I am a Muslim woman. No one wants to look at me and I feel like a throw away. Hagbad [a Somali name for a ROSCA] is where we are special and we [are] making a bank. The risk for me is worth it for me. (Focus group, 26 March 2015, Scarborough)

The benefit of ROSCAs cited most frequently was that they involve little to no paperwork. However, lack of paperwork can also be a problem. A common stress factor identified by multiple users was that mental accounting can be faulty and mistakes are made when there are no notes. There is a risk that members can abscond with the group's funds since there is no legal recourse in Canada for retrieving these monies. While doing field work in Montreal, it was reported to me that, around 2012, a Montreal member caused a scandal by stealing thousands of dollars from her ROSCA. This woman has been on the run ever since. Even if found, there would be no way to take her to court as ROSCAs do not have a legal status. In Quebec, there is little to no public knowledge about this form of economic co-operation and mutual aid.

In my meetings with the Banker Ladies, I found that theft by a member happens rarely since the consequences are dire at the local level. Most groups apply a penalty, or a late fee, to address delays. Overall, the Banker Ladies did not find late payments and defaulting to be major concerns. It may be that the women who participate in ROSCAs have devised their own systems to make it unappealing to transgress the payment schedule on which the membership agreed. "Seynab" reported that her group has a system to penalize members who do not respect the will of the group:

> We keep her close. We watch her everyday. We visit her at her home and tell her to pay on time. If she is not doing this, we keep tabs on her. Then as soon as she pays everything, even if it is late, we ignore her after that point. She cannot learn about the next group and we will call people and let them know not to let her join. (Focus group, 20 March 2015, Firgrove)

The women who form a ROSCA have ways to monitor their members and their payments. Women who see ROSCAs as their only resort are more likely to pay on time. Members did have a major concern about the issue of unreliability of payments from other individuals within the group in case this misbehaviour affected them when it was their turn to receive the "hand" (or lump sum of funds). This concern related to timeliness. Delays in receiving the hand, or receiving a smaller hand than originally expected, threaten to interrupt the member's business (e.g., seasonal work, purchase of inventory). The late allocation of funds can undermine the achievement of a person's goals if the much-needed funds do not arrive at a time that aligns with a specific expense (e.g., school fees and supplies, weddings, burials, a seasonal harvest). Members also cited internal bias as a concern (i.e., the Banker Ladies favouring certain members over others, which can affect who gets the hand and when).

The actual default rate by members is low (Collins et al. 2009; Rutherford 2000). Women do not want to be boycotted from future groups, so they do everything they can to be timely with their payments (Somali focus group meetings, June 2018). The Banker Ladies told me they would rather default at a commercial bank because no one knows them there. A Caribbean woman in Toronto, who had been a member of a ROSCA for years, said: "I don't want to be blacklisted by the group, I need them" (interview, November 2017). There is shame associated with missing a payment because of the friendships they have within the group. Theft and losses sometimes happen for external reasons. For example, when someone from outside of the group steals money from a group member on their way to a meeting. House fires, or other natural hazards, can also cause losses. The women seemed less worried about these kinds of losses because there is not much they can do and members will cover for external losses. The women said that they would call a special meeting in front of everyone to explain why they have to make an extra payment and then they ask that each member do their part to share in the loss.

Canadian women identified stigmas associated with ROSCAs in Canada. These included ROSCAs being seen as systems that support terrorists, or which facilitate money laundering, drug trafficking, or other illegal activities. They worried about police raids of their homes. In the documentary *The Banker Ladies* (Mondesir 2021), "Ayesha," who lives in Toronto's west end, speaks about the vulnerabilities Black women feel when they join a ROSCA because the police can say that their activities are illegal and take their money at any point. Lack of public policy and education about these systems contributes to the suspicious and/or negative perception of them.

Most sceptics (who are uninformed) may be quick to describe ROSCAs as a pyramid scheme, which they are not. In South Africa, where the national Stokvel system has been misrepresented as an illegal pyramid scheme, the national network has had to educate the public on the difference. A 2021 Reuters article revealed formal commercial banks – afraid of losing customers to the Stokvel – as key players behind the fear mongering (Rumney 2021). To clarify, a ROSCA system does not operate on a profit-making model; any system that pays out dividends to a few members is not a ROSCA.

Over the course of hundreds of meetings, I learned about the risks faced by ROSCA members. When I ended the focus group about risk, I asked: "Who in this group uses a ROSCA?" Despite the risks the meeting participants had described, almost every hand in the room went up (and they were laughing). Indeed, the risks attendant on joining a ROSCA never dominated conversations I had with women who used ROSCAs. The women saw the risks as manageable in light of the larger financial and social rewards of mutual aid.

Economics as Community Well-Being

The Banker Ladies, whether in Toronto or Montreal, affirmed that the intent behind ROSCAs is twofold: they are implemented to meet the goals of members, but also allow those same members to "band together" as a community. Key components of economics are meeting people's needs and provisioning goods to help others. The Banker Ladies and the members of their ROSCAs show how money can be used to socialize and assist others so they will thrive in society. For "Natla," who is a 35-year-old married Sudanese Canadian, Sandooq (Arabic word for "boxes" [cash box], the local name for a ROSCA) gave her an opportunity to meet and talk to friends in her native tongue as she settled into her Scarborough (east Toronto) community:

> Who knows me here when I first come from Sudan [*pause*] … no one. I
> can't [could not] even speak English back then. I [was] feel[ing] alone. My
> children help[ed] me [to learn English]. My friends help me … Sandooq
> give me friends and Sandooq gave me a chance in life. I was able to do

much. I buy [bought] my airplane ticket back home and I bring my children there [for vacation]. Sandooq helped me so much when I first came to Canada; it was so cold. I swear to Allah (PBUH) for it. (Focus group, 26 March 2015, Toronto)

ROSCAs often provide a venue where women can meet and talk about their concerns. Many of the women with whom I met had similar views to "Natla." English is her second language, and it was hard for her to adjust to Toronto life. Thankfully, she was able to use her knowledge of ROSCAs to meet other Sudanese women. The diversity of Black culture is great, and the women with whom I met were divided along various identities, such as class, language, and religion (see chapter 6 for a specific analysis of Somali Canadian women).

Sometimes, the Banker Ladies would usurp my interviews or focus groups by engaging in debates with one another. This would result in me taking notes, but also moving my work to new levels of understanding in relation to the care and provisioning aspects of their activities. Many of the Banker Ladies in Canada, like those in the Caribbean, knew and respected the life of Marcus Garvey and his teachings on self-reliance and supporting the Black community. Black francophone women in Montreal revealed that pooling resources brought people together. In their meetings, the women revealed how they would help new immigrants settle down in Canada and adjust, and then help them to develop their own projects. "Noémi," a 28-year-old Congolese Canadian who uses Moziki or Restourne (a ROSCA in DR Congo), said:

Pour des gens de descendance Africaine comme moi, je vois dans le fait de faire des caisses [Moziki], l'opportunité de raviver une tradition communautaire ancestrale afin de s'entraider dans la société d'accueil et qui nous permet des fois d'accompagner ceux qui ont besoin d'argent. [Translation: For African people like me, I see Moziki as an opportunity to revive an ancestral tradition that we used in our communities and to help each other in our new homeland … And that (Restourne) sometimes allows us to accompany those who need money.] (Interview, 23 November 2017, Montreal)

"Virginie," a 40-year-old mother of Senegalese descent living in the area of Jean-Talon (Montreal), explained:

> Je suis d'origine Sénégalaise, où la tontine est très populaire, et j'ai poursuivi la tradition ici au Québec à mon arrivée. Pour moi, il s'agit d'une façon obligée d'économiser, de ne pas payer d'intérêt sur une dette ou des frais sur un compte bancaire quelconque. [Translation: I am of Senegalese origin, where *les caisses informelles* are well known and used, and since I arrived in Quebec, I continued the tradition. For me, it's an important way to save money and not to pay interest on a debt or fees on any bank account.] (Interview, 20 November 2017)

"Jean," a 50-year-old mother working various part-time jobs, who is an experienced and long-time resident, explained that joining a Susu is about the connection to others and making a commitment:

> I like to spend money bad bad [Translation: I like to spend a lot of money]. So if I put money inna bank, I will go and take it out because I always see something nice to buy. But with Partner I won't. Partner is a social aid. It's a commitment to a group. You must save money and help each other all the same. (Focus group, 18 June 2016, Little Burgundy, Montreal)

The Banker Ladies interviewed for this project attest that ROSCAs helped them when other financial organizations would not. "Mabinty," a 42-year-old married Sierra-Leone Canadian and a mother of five children, is involved in an Osusu so she can invest in real estate in her homeland, and she is doing this for her children's future. For her, Susu can help improve their standard of living.

> I make a house and I work hard all my life for my money. I am building [my] house for me and my kids. It's my foundation for my family when I am old. It is what I am doing here [in Canada]. Let's play this and win [referring to her Osusu] and to make it a different [lifestyle] standard for how we can come and help each other. (Focus group, 20 March 2015)

Why Do Canada's Banker Ladies Hide Their ROSCAs?

Black Canadian women hide their involvement in ROSCAs because they fear what might happen to them. Figure 5.3 shows that 145 Banker Ladies, based in both Toronto or Montreal, were asked directly if they hide their ROSCAs and, if so, why. More than 90 per cent of the women interviewed felt their involvement in ROSCAs to be perceived in a "negative" way by other Canadians (referred to as "outdoor people" [i.e., outsiders]). The Banker Ladies choose to hide what they do because they worry about reprisals, but they also hide to keep their ROSCA systems sacred and free from being co-opted by others. Black Canadian women with a legacy of colonialism and enslavement continue to fight for what they have (McKittrick 2006).

Hiding what they do is part of how they live. Secrecy is how they can thrive. I believe 90 per cent constitutes a conservative estimate of the number who feel stigmatized because they organize ROSCAs. Some women preferred not to answer the question, or said they "did not understand the question." After spending some time away from the data, and in the wake of getting to know the Banker Ladies better, I realized that avoiding this question made some of them feel safer because the trauma they had experienced as co-operators had been ongoing for many years.

The women with whom I met felt ignored and underappreciated for what they do. They recognize that keeping their ROSCA systems hidden is helpful, but agree that what they do is a service to society and not something to be obscured. Many women reported feeling "rejected" and "scrutinized" by regular banks; even a mundane task like making a deposit in a commercial bank can be a harrowing experience (Chin 2020). Still, those who critique formal banks never see ROSCAs as an option. Scholars Buckland, Robinson, and Spotton-Visano (2018) examine payday lending systems in Canada but do not mention ROSCAs as a way that women reduce dependency on such predatory lenders. Canadian economist Jerry Buckland (2012), who has done work in Toronto on fringe banking, does not consider the use of ROSCAs. Though these authors confirm elitism exists among bankers,

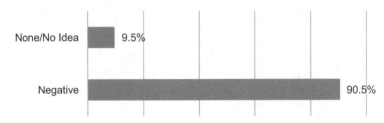

Figure 5.3. Stigma of ROSCAs among the Black Diaspora (*N* = 145)

something which makes low-income people and the women in my study feel unwelcome, they do not imagine that excluded people may be relying on their own community-based banks.

Women are creating their own banks in Canada. In my interviews, the poor treatment they received at banks was so bad and pervasive that it kept coming up as one of the main reasons for their participation in ROSCAs. As "Shondelle," who moved to Canada from Guyana as a child and now owns a small business, describes:

> I am very fired up about banks. I can't tell you how dem treat me. Bank man watch me nasty … when they [are] still in school. They minimize my credit card. It hurts. They think I am laundering for drugs when I am not. Who do these people [bankers] think they are? What dem don't know is that wi have Box [Boxhand is a ROSCA system]. (Focus group, 26 March 2015, Warden Woods, Toronto)

I know many of the communities well in the Greater Toronto Area where I conducted interviews because my family had either lived in those areas, had friends and family there, or my father had a business there. "Gloria," a 70-year-old Bajan Canadian former health care professional whom I met in Warden Woods, an east Toronto community, has lived in Canada for more than 40 years. She confided in me her experiences of working in Canada and her first-hand knowledge of bias in the formal banking system. For this reason, in her retirement she manages a large-scale Susu:

> You can't just go into a bank and say you want [your] money. These banks don't listen. But we know who will. We can … the Banker Ladies

can accommodate you. You can go to her and tell her what you need and she will listen to you. Tell me which bank man is doing this? (Focus group, 26 March 2015, Toronto)

Repeatedly, the Banker Ladies stated that formal banks are unwelcoming; bank staff are rude to them when they make deposits or withdraw money. Mistrust exists on both sides. Bankers, often university-educated and usually from middle-class backgrounds, are not sure how to interact with women from low-income communities (Buckland 2012). The Banker Ladies also notice the way tellers behave towards them, and so will often exclude themselves from mainstream business services. "Faye," a 40-year-old Guyanese Canadian and mother, explains that bank tellers are nervous and uneasy when people from certain communities want to bank at their branches, and all the women in the focus group agreed:

What can I say to you? The major reason most people I know felt that there is a stigma against Black people is when [we] live in certain communities here, such as Jane and Finch, Lawrence Heights, Weston, Rexdale. Dem [the tellers] does watch you so. The g'yal [in the bank] comes all jumpy and scared when I pass in there. I am there to bank, but I wonder what she thinking. I don't feel at ease when I go there. (Focus group, 20 March 2015, Jane and Finch, Toronto)

Most of the Banker Ladies identified race as the main reason they feel rejected by mainstream businesses, and they believe it is the cause behind why they are "watched" by tellers in a negative way when they go into a bank. They are surveilled and made to feel suspect. Even when cultural diversity among bank tellers is apparent, it does not make a difference in how the Banker Ladies are treated. They continue to feel excluded by these banks and those who run them.

Desjardins Co-operative Bank: Not an Option

I deliberately chose the province of Quebec as a place to pursue a case because of the rise of the *économie sociale* there in the 1990s.

I wanted to explore a case somewhere known for its strong commitment to co-operative economies, so I would have a robust comparison with Toronto, a city understood to have an individualized tendency towards the social economy. I hypothesized – quite incorrectly, it turned out – that Black people would be a focus in Quebec's social economy sector. Instead, I encountered a strikingly similar story of exclusion towards Black people, and especially Black women, during my Montreal case, despite Quebec being so revered for an *économie sociale*.

Through my interviews, I learned that Quebec's reputation for a social economy that "included the excluded" did not align with the experiences of Black/African descent people. The English versus French language divide consumes the lion's share of the discussion in solidarity economics. For example, in her edited collection *The Social Economy*, Canada Research Chair Marie Bouchard (2013) fails to consider the lived experience of Black and racialized people in Quebec. Contributors to her collection are primarily white scholars.

The Banker Ladies in Montreal interviewed during my project did not think that Quebec's social economy sector considered their economic or social needs. In fact, many of the Banker Ladies told me that they felt "penalized" for not being "white" and "French."

> A word on banks for you. [*pause, looking very stressed*] The big banks [referring to commercial banks] help us in Quebec ... and others that you mention like Desjardins do not care. Where are they? I will tell you where they are. They are there for the white French people. Their own. ("Leebert," 77-year-old Jamaican Canadian restaurant owner living in Notre-Dame-de-Grâce, Montreal's west end, focus group, 16 June 2016)

Montreal's Banker Ladies were more hesitant to criticize mainstream banks than those living in Toronto. It should be reiterated, however, that Toronto's Banker Ladies could rarely name a credit union because branches for them did not exist in their neighbourhoods. A study by Maiorano, Mook, and Quarter (2017) revealed that credit unions in the Greater Toronto Area were not to be found in lower-income communities; the few offices they did have were located in Toronto's more affluent parts. For example, Meridian Credit Union has offices at Yonge and Sheppard, the Danforth, and the Beaches. The same is true of Alterna Savings and Credit Union, with locations on the Danforth and downtown at Bay and College Streets, as well as City Hall.

Quebec's Banker Ladies reserved their harshest comments for Desjardins, a co-operative bank that they expected to do more for them, given its legacy. Participants like "Leebert" felt that credit unions, like Desjardins, have memberships of old, white, French-speaking people, whereas commercial banks like Toronto Dominion (TD) and Bank of Montreal (BMO) try to diversify their staff to attract non-white people and linguistic minorities. "Susan," a resident of Little Burgundy, is a Black Canadian whose ancestry hails from the African American railway porters. She stated emphatically: "To me those *caisse pos* [meaning Desjardins's *caisses populaires*] are there to help the Frenchman. I will not step into that bank" (interview, 18 June 2018). Several of the women I interviewed, including community leaders, were not surprised at the number of the Banker Ladies who refused to join Desjardins or other co-op banks. A woman of Haitian heritage who owns a small business stated unreservedly:

Desjardins is the worst (shaking her head). Always taking money from us but not caring about us. This is the caisses po or CP. They are a big fraud in my view. TD at least they have diversity and their employees are welcoming. Have you gone into a Desjardins guichet? It is white, white, white. Go and see ... Look, I am Haitian and I speak French fluently, and I am Quebecois. But I am never going to Desjardins. I want to see a bank that empowers me, not one that tries to assimilate me, and that is what Desjardins is trying to do. (Businesswoman, interview, 6 June 2018, Beaubien, Montreal)

Black women do not trust Desjardins. Both French- and English-speaking Black women have strong views about the exclusion they feel in Quebec's acclaimed *économie sociale*. The women reported that "alternative banks" (also known as AFIs) are there to help white French Canadian citizens, who are the majority in that province, and no other minority.

One community leader, "Ushana," took the time to explain the term "pure laine." It was a term that kept coming up during my interviews with Black women, including Haitian women. "Pure laine" (direct translation is "pure wool") refers to those of white French stock considered to be the "vrai" ("true") Quebecois. In interviews, Black women conveyed to me, over and over again, how they are made to feel like "new" immigrants even though their families have been in Quebec for generations. Immigrants and their descendants who don't have white skin have been made to feel like a threat to the French Canadian nation (Mills 2016). "Gemma," a 60-year-old Grenadian Canadian in a Susu, clarified the issue in this way:

> Black people do not know Desjardins at all, even the French Black ones because that bank is only concerned by white people. Commercial banks where I worked like BMO focuses on diversity issues whereas at Desjardins's tellers are all white, and they don't even speak English. [*Her face turns very serious.*] This Desjardins don't even know what we think, they have no clue how to relate to us as customers. They are so French and [they are] not willing to reach out and to touch the Black community. (Interview, 7 June 2016, in a Starbucks near Jean-Talon, Montreal)

This research finding was unexpected. I found that Black women in Montreal – both French and English – are alienated by Desjardins, one of the province's most prominent social economy actors. Black women were not alone in enduring this exclusion. Anglophone women whom I interviewed also explained they felt outside of the reach of the social economy because they did not speak English *or* French as a mother tongue. Though it could not be confirmed, many of the women interviewed disclosed Desjardins as sympathetic to the separatist movement. This perception of bias in the social economy is problematic for many Black people living in Quebec because of Bill 101. While this research was being undertaken, the president of the Chantier de l'économie sociale, Jean-Martin Aussant, was also affiliated with the Parti Québécois

(Radio-Canada 2016).[5] To the Black women and community leaders whom I interviewed, the involvement of the Chantier president in the Parti Québécois suggested that the Chantier assisted mainly white, French-speaking Quebecers. Since 2018, Beatrice Alain, a white woman of English and French heritage, has taken over as president. In my interviews with her, she confirmed she was aware of the racial bias of the Chantier. She recounted a troubling story of being called out for her white privilege at a conference in the United States, and noted that race/racism is "different" in Canada.

In a focus group in Montreal's west end, "Renée," a Banker Lady with roots in Guyana and a Montreal hospital worker, recalled ending her relationship with Desjardins after attempts to bank there:

> Let's just say [that] I went through lots of growing pains with Desjardins, so I left them. When I would go there [shakes her head] … all I remember is it was not nice and that the employees there had a very bad attitude towards minorities … They may be trying [to change] because they have to get us in their bank but they are not there yet. (Focus group, 18 June 2016)

In this small sample size of 43 Banker Ladies, 41 of the women did not have a positive experience with Desjardins. Nearly all the members, including outside community leaders, felt unclear about what the Chantier de l'économie sociale was doing for racialized minorities. Of the 43 Banker Ladies whom I interviewed in Montreal, only 10 (23 per cent) named Desjardins as their bank (8 of these women were francophones). This number is strikingly low given there is a *guichet* (branch) of Desjardins on every block. "Tina" explained: "I will go out my way to a commercial bank and pass by many Desjardins banks, but I prefer commercial bank [*sic*]." While "Tina," a 41-year-old Black Canadian from

---

5 More research is needed to understand the racial inequities occurring in the Chantier and to understand why Black Quebeckers feel excluded.

Little Burgundy, is in a Susu and values co-operative banks, she will not join a co-op that does "not respect" her:

> I do not dare go into Desjardins as no one speaks English. In RBC [Royal Bank of Canada] you can always get someone who speaks English with no hang ups. Desjardins does not worry about people like me. (Focus group, 18 June 2016, Montreal)

On my first trip to Montreal (2016), I anticipated that antipathy towards Desjardins would be felt mainly by English-speaking women. However, the francophone Banker Ladies with whom I conducted interviews also felt no affinity for Desjardins. I gained further insight into the distrust Black Montrealers feel towards Desjardins from "Kirlande," a Haitian Canadian activist:

> A commercial bank like TD celebrates 18 May as a Haitian Day with flags [showed me a picture on her phone of her local bank celebrating a Haitian holiday]. This makes us feel so welcomed. This staffing is mixed up with people from everywhere. At the caisse po, I was always feeling disturbed. They were not nice to me. I am a Black, French, and Canadian woman, and still I am nothing but a stranger in that bank. They do not want me there. (Interview, 9 June 2016, Montreal)

Given the historical relevance of credit unions, and Desjardins's original imperative to make banking inclusive for a linguistic minority, this study revealed that Black women do not feel a connection to (and in most cases, know the story of) the Desjardins movement. The women told me that they felt alienated by the movement; some believed members of Desjardins to be nationalists or separatists, and vested in white French pride (focus groups, Montreal 2016 and 2017).[6] These research experiences in Montreal are why I have coined the concept of the Black Social Economy. At the very core of the Black Social Economy are informal collectives,

---

6 Lévesque (2013, 30) held that the Parti Québécois has traditionally been in favour of co-ops.

such as ROSCAs, which provide refuges for people of the African diaspora to congregate and support one another.

Informality Reigns

For the Banker Ladies, informality does not imply a lack of processes, structure, or governance. In fact, the ROSCAs they operate are full of new forms of institutional remaking. In 2009, in Kingston, Jamaica, women debated whether or not the informal aspects of Partner banks were better. Jamaican women told me they "did not have any fear of reprisal" for joining a Partner, and they appreciated the flexibility of doing these systems informally. Most of the Caribbean-based women who use ROSCAs explained that people in their countries "appreciated" or "admired" the work done by them. Generally, the Caribbean Banker Ladies view formality as something they could pursue in the future. Many of the Canadian Banker Ladies were especially sceptical about formalizing ROSCAs. I asked them: "Do you want the legal formalization of ROSCAs?"

Figure 5.4 shows that the women consulted were divided on the issue. The reasons on both sides are compelling in terms of what more regulation would mean for women who feel marginalized in society. Thirty-seven per cent ($N = 54$) of the Banker Ladies were interested in online ROSCA systems. Demographically this group was composed of women who tended to be young and educated; many identified as Muslim from this group as well. In their opinion, legal regulation might better enable transactions without issues arising. Other Banker Ladies favoured legal formalities only if they worked to remove fearfulness about organizing their money groups. In a Banker Ladies Council meeting, women supported legal recognition, but not so much that it interfered with groups who wanted to remain informal (the Banker Ladies Council meeting, 22 April 2022, Toronto).

No consensus exists on whether to formalize ROSCAs. Of the women interviewed, 33 per cent ($N = 47$) had no opinion or seemed genuinely confused or ambivalent about what it would mean

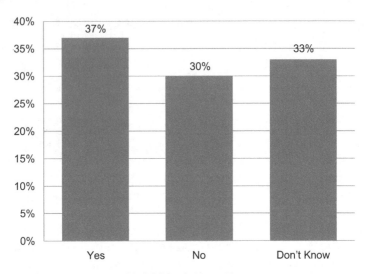

Figure 5.4. Formalization of ROSCAs (2015–22)

to legalize ROSCAs. Thirty per cent (N = 44) of the women with whom I met in Canada preferred being informal. They explained to me that to "grow too big" and formalize would mean losing track of their values and close connections. This group of women was very vocal on "being small" to avoid surveillance. Respondents let me know that informality was meaningful to them and that their ROSCAs would not be surveilled in the same way that formal institutions are.

These interviews prompt rethinking about how we understand the binary of formality/informality in banking. The Banker Ladies do not attach a negative connotation to informality the way the rest of society does. Some asked: "What is so special about being formal?" The women made valid points about why ROSCAs should remain hidden. Regardless of where the women stood on the informality debate, they agreed that the work of the Banker Ladies should be known. For this reason, they pushed me in 2018 to make a short film, *The Banker Ladies* (Mondesir 2021), to bring awareness and education to the public about what they do. The film's launch after the 2020 Black protests, and during the COVID-19 pandemic, helped people become more open to the reasons women of the Black diaspora engage in banking co-ops. The work of ROSCAs was no longer viewed with the same suspicion as informal networks and mutual aid became very important institutions in meeting people's needs during the lockdown.

When I began this project in 2007, studies about community building did not consider the role of women of the Black diaspora in economic development. In *Building Capital, Building Community*, Elson, Gouldsborough, and Jones (2009) overlook the role of ROSCAs. Their focus emphasizes cultural and linguistic differences between Ontario and Quebec, without consideration of the Black/African and racialized people who make up an important percentage of people reliant on the solidarity economy. As recently as 2015, former Ontario premier Kathleen Wynne's Social Enterprise Development Fund was valued at $1.4 million (Brennan 2015) and injected with a further $1.36 million in 2018; it did not have a single recipient organization led by a Muslim or Black Canadian. Similarly, during my analysis of Quebec's advanced social economy sector as it relates to the Chantier de l'économie sociale, I noted that its ecosystem also failed to address the local organizational activities of Black people or their contributions in co-operative development.[7]

The study of mutual aid, including institutions such as ROSCAs, has verified that people in the Global South have been organizing collectively for centuries. Even so, little is known in the West about ROSCAs formed by people of colour, even though people from the Global South move to Western countries in search of a better economic life. ROSCAs have become part of the financial landscape in major cities and towns which are home to large numbers of immigrants, and they are embedded in the financial and social lives of Black people (Hossein 2016d, 2018b; Handa and Claremont 1999). To manage their exclusion from business, the Banker Ladies – people who are often unbanked or underbanked themselves – turn to

---

7 See more about Quebec's trust fund for the social economy at the Chantier de l'économie sociale (n.d.).

ROSCAs. Although an alternative form of managing funds, ROSCAs are not seen by the mainstream financial community – or alternative finance providers – as a viable way to bank (Figart 2014).

When people move to Toronto and Montreal, they bring with them their foodways, their music and dance traditions, and their money systems. The names by which ROSCAs are known in a cosmopolitan city are many because of the various nationalities that live in a city. Some of those names include Osusu, Ajo, and Partner. All of these systems involve the pooling of resources. These long-standing traditions have helped immigrants historically as they settle down in Canada. As people migrate, they bring their culturally-specific versions of ROSCA with them, using them alongside other devices accessible to them (Smets 2000). ROSCAs have also become a common practice among second-generation Canadians who, like their elders, refer to themselves as the Banker Ladies, and manage and participate in these institutions (Blackman 2016; Blackman and Brooks 2002).

Hiding ROSCAs

The negative perception surrounding ROSCAs effectively stifles what the Bankers Ladies do, keeping knowledge of their work and contributions underground. ROSCAs in Canada are labelled illicit or illegal. The women whom I interviewed told me they are labelled as people engaged in "illegal" activities. They listed the following as crimes that had been ascribed to them by white Canadians: "gambling," "money laundering," "working as mules (drugs)," "terrorism," or "running pyramid schemes." When the Somali Canadian Banker Ladies participate in Hagbad, they are perceived to be sponsoring terrorist groups such as Al-Shabaab. The quote below from a senior expert on finance and debt in Canada highlights the ill-informed and dismissive attitude that prevails towards ROSCAs:

> As far as I know, these things (ROSCAs) are illegal. Aren't they?
> The underground economy is thriving. Such systems are part of the

underground economy and these people who use [ROSCA] systems are not legitimate. Why would people do this? Toronto has many legal banks and unless these people are into other things, then it makes no sense why they do this. Anyways, there is plain risk involved in these systems. (Interview, 15 February 2015, Toronto)

In the larger Caribbean and African societies, ROSCAs are regarded as time-honoured traditions. This is not the case in Canada. Though African Canadians respect and value ROSCAs because they have helped people adjust to Canadian life, they do not make this system of finance known to other people. This project took many years of research because it was imperative to build trust before ROSCA users felt comfortable speaking about their money clubs. My research assistant in Montreal found that women were afraid and would hang up the phone because they did not want to share details of their ROSCA activities with outsiders (RA notes, August 2016). The perceived threat of losing a system that is dear to them worried the women for many reasons. "Susan," a mother of five children and a Banker Lady from the Little Burgundy neighbourhood of Montreal, explained:

There is no legal framework in Montreal for this [Susu]. So we keep it discreet. Some of us worry and are scared ... Will the Taxman come? Is it illegal? Is it not? I also like to think about it this way. Think of corn rows we have in our heads. That Bo Derek [Hollywood movie star] stole that look from us. They always want what we have. To own what we do. Just to take it. We decided to keep Susu hush hush and it is our way of preserving it. Otherwise, there is no due respect from them for this sacred tradition we all value so much. (Focus group, 18 June 2016, Montreal)

As I moved around and talked to people, including elites and community stakeholders in the private and public sectors, I noted caution existed in relation to ROSCAs (figure 5.3 outlines the stigmas). The women were scared that the Canada Revenue Agency would confiscate their savings, fearing there were tax implications to using their money to assist each other. One woman, who insisted

I do not use her name or location, said: "We are supposed to be poor. Poor Black women are not able to save or to help anyone."

These women make self-sacrifices to save small amounts of money and use their pooled savings to help others. How could this be viewed as illegal? Nonetheless, they are made to feel unsafe. It saddens me as a researcher to know that in two major cities in Canada, Black women feel the need to hide their engagement in self-help groups. It was hard to listen to these women recount the many harms done to them.

A poignant question was asked by "Finella," a 51-year-old Banker Lady from Côte-des-Neiges, originally from Trinidad: "Why are we not more open? Why should we be? I know I keep my ting under the radar, so no government man cyant come and get it from me" (focus group, 16 June 2016, Montreal). Many of these women were told by (white) Canadian neighbours that ROSCAs are illegal. Like "Finella," Black Canadian women who belong to ROSCAs are made to feel that what they do goes against Canadian values. Tying ROSCAs to drugs and trafficking, or other illegal activities, is what makes the Banker Ladies turn inward, and move their groups away from the public domain.

ROSCAs are banking co-ops that use after-tax monies to "gift" other members of the group. There is no harm or illegality in doing this. I tried to reassure the women whom I interviewed that they could not be arrested for starting mutual aid financial groups that relied on funds saved from their after-tax incomes. The money pooled is their own savings – and they can use it as they want to, including to help others. Canada should be rewarding the Banker Ladies for the community development work they do, even honour them with development jobs. Instead, they have been made to feel like outlaws, leaving them (and their systems of aid) vulnerable to heinous forms of reprisal.

People who do not share a background with cultural groups that have a historical tradition of ROSCAs are less likely to grasp the savings aspect of this form of finance system or to understand how they help their members have access to a lump sum of pooled savings to do a project. While some stakeholders, usually white people (e.g,. bankers, finance experts, policymakers), admitted knowing very little about ROSCAs, others held on to the opinion that they were really a guise for illegal activity. Many experts saw the value of these systems in the "developing" world, but could not understand why these informal banking co-ops would be relevant in cities with many banking institutions. ROSCA users in Canada are discreet about their participation in these systems because they have experienced negative reactions when they share how ROSCAs have helped them.

A Montreal Banker Lady "Wilma," who came to Canada from Guyana four decades ago, explained to me: "Funny, back home everyone know I am in a Box. We don't have to sneak it. Den I get here to North America … We do Box and we are so quiet about it. In 'ere we live [meaning Montreal], we are secretive about our lives" ("Wilma," a 70-year-old grandmother in Côte-des-Neiges, focus group, 16 June 2016, Montreal). In Canada, nobody is taking note of the contributions of the Banker Ladies, or showing respect for the work they do; this is not the case with the Banker Ladies in their home countries. "Rachel," a 55-year-old Banker Lady also from Côte-des-Neiges, Montreal, runs three Susus with a total of 75 members. She is adamant that she is not doing anything wrong or illegal by having Susu groups, but reported that outsiders are quick to question or judge the Banker Ladies for what they do.

> People don't know a damn thing about it [ROSCAs]. They *imagine it is a bad ting* before they ask us what we do. As if we are hurting anyone … so they don't ask and we keep it as a secret. Anyways, my Susu is nobody's business and it is my only protection to help me when I need money. (Focus group, 16 June 2018, Montreal)

After I conducted my interviews about ROSCAs in Canada, it became clear to me that lenders (especially alternative ones), as well as the general public, do not know about these banking co-op systems – when they really should. I found the perspectives of bankers towards ROSCAs, as well as those of people working in alternative economies, largely negative. I would often prep the interviewee about racism in banking and why racism was a rationale for Black women to use ROSCAs, but it did not seem to matter. The only bankers who knew of ROSCAs had some sort of cultural affiliation. In general, the knee-jerk reaction of Canadian bankers was to criticize these systems, and they would become defensive about why Black and racialized people turn to these forms of banking rather than commercial banks.

The negative attitudes expressed by bankers and financial experts in Canada diverged distinctly from the discussions I had with the Caribbean banking experts. In the financial capitals of the Caribbean, such as Port-of-Spain and Kingston, bankers understand the affinity local people, especially low-income women, feel towards ROSCAs. There is no doubt in my mind that the COVID-19 pandemic made the Canadian public more aware of systemic racism. It is now public knowledge that mutual aid and informal institutions can help people, especially Black/African women, who are one of the most alienated groups in times of crisis. I sincerely hope the pandemic experience will help change the public's mind about ROSCAs in Canada.

Limits to Online Banking

Moving to a new place can be lonely and hard. Some people move from places where technology is not greatly valued or even necessary. However, in Canada, banks have made automated machines and internet banking the norm. In my interviews, I found that the older Banker Ladies, and especially those who are newcomers, prefer person-to-person contact and do not do online banking unless their children assist them (see figure 5.5).

Many women whom I interviewed said they have used ATMs to withdraw money. However, a significant number will not do large transactions at ATMs and 30 per cent of the women I interviewed do internet banking. The women who did do it complained that they relied on their Canadian-educated children to help them with their online banking if they used the online system. One woman said, "Who wants your child knowing about your money business?" "Monica," a 60-year-old businesswoman/cleaner from Warden Woods, states:

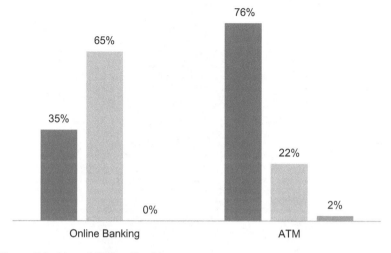

Figure 5.5. Use of Online Banking

Banks inna 'here [are] too much into technology and dem cyant see a person. Wit mi money, I want to see you. I want to see a man to gaff ... not a computer. Mi Susu is all about face-to-face [banking]. It's like old-time style. And mi a never give it up. [Translation: Banks in Canada are too much into technology and they cannot see a person. With my own money in the banks, I want to see person. I want to see someone to talk to and not a computer [too impersonal]. My Susu is all about face-to-face banking. It is familiar "old-time style" and I will not change this form of banking for anything.] (Focus group, 26 March 2015, Toronto)

ROSCAs: Seed Capital for Black Women to Run for Political Office

Lack of money is often the obstacle that prevents people of colour from standing up and running for political office. In Toronto, ROSCAs have been used by Black Canadian women to get a lump sum of money for their expenses needed to set up a campaign. The person who decides to run already has a group of voters who

Figure 5.6. Andria Barrett with an Election Sign Supported through a Partner
Bank
Source: Andria Barrett. Permission granted on 18 June 2021.

know about her intentions and can provide the needed community support.

Somali Canadian Munira Abukar used the ROSCA system to
fund her election campaign for a position on the City of Toronto
council. She believed that she could be a voice for Somali people
in her riding. Hagbad (the Somali name for a ROSCA) provided
her with access to the cash that allowed her to hold meetings and
organize her campaign. In 2021, Andria Barrett sent me an email

message that a Jamaican Partner (ROSCA) had provided the $3,300 she needed to make campaign signs for the next provincial election in her hometown of Brampton (see figure 5.6).

The ROSCA system may be a way to effect social change from the margins by making a lump sum of capital available to marginalized people seeking political leadership. This informal form of banking system is helping Black women gain both the capital and community support they require to formally run for political office. There is a lot of room for future research into how young, Black Canadian women are tapping into the informal collective financial systems they have known about since their childhood in order to engage in formal political systems.

Towards a New Public Policy on Canadian ROSCAs

My work as a political scientist is about inventorying: taking note of the various vernaculars of banking co-ops, which are formally called ROSCAs. What is important to note about ROSCAs is that they create a sense of belonging, help excluded people find a way to adjust, and contribute to building up civil society. The Banker Ladies organize ROSCAs as places of refuge. They set up ROSCAs to make places for excluded people to belong, to provide spaces where they can deliberate, and to offer a context where they can lift themselves up when they have been put down. The Banker Ladies in Canada are doing this work with absolutely no remuneration, and this situation endures because of an ongoing refusal to acknowledge ROSCAs as co-operatives.

Black and racialized women have been organizing informal banking co-ops in Canada for over a century, but we *choose not* to see them. We ask distracting and accusatory questions ("Where did they get the money?") when we should be praising this vital work that is built on a foundation of mutual aid. We should be seeing – and celebrating – the ability of ROSCA members to save small sums of money to generate a larger pool of funds, and their capacity to collaborate so that each member, in turn, can access a larger amount of money to realize personal goals. We choose not to see the effectiveness of ROSCAs for their users because to do so would mean creating a new way of engaging in community and co-operative development that involves the Banker Ladies (Black women) as the experts. The 145 Chief the Banker Ladies whom I interviewed in Toronto and Montreal, who represent thousands of members, have confirmed for me that ROSCAs are indeed part of Canada's solidarity economy. ROSCAs are reaching groups that have been ignored and traumatized by formal politics and economics. The Banker Ladies are experts in how to reach racialized and excluded people, and how to make their lives better – an important skill that is useful to all Canadians.

The Banker Ladies hide their banking co-op systems because of the anti-Black racism in Canadian society. They endure stigma, negative labels, and fear of reprisal. These women cannot express themselves freely about the self-managed mutual aid groups they organize. The use of the *Emergency Act* in February 2022 in response to fundraising by the Freedom Convoy truckers is worrisome for the future of informal finance (Canada 2022; Zimonjic 2022). Certain features of the act allow the state to clamp down on commercial banks, or restrict the use of non-bank platforms, such as crowd-funding and other social financial systems. While it remains unclear which of the laws on financial institutions will be retained, it is evident that surveillance of informal finance is now under state scrutiny.

Even though ROSCAs are the one sure way Black women counteract business exclusion, their potential for agency against oppressive social and financial systems can threaten political and banking elites. The Banker Ladies – regardless of birthplace, language spoken, or religious affiliation – experience intense forms of business exclusion. ROSCAs have been one sure way to reach and support Black women. ROSCAs are an effective antidote to racial capitalism. Rooted in mutual aid, ROSCAs are a pragmatic way for Black women to counter business exclusion and meet their needs.

Canada's Banker Ladies are not being remunerated for their contribution to community economic development. Of their own initiative, these women are building democratic institutions from the ground up. They are able to mobilize financial goods in communities where most people do not think there exists anything of value. They mobilize in the face of surveillance and mistrust in the idea of Black women having savings to give to each other. This body of work dispels the myth that marginalized women do not know how to save funds. The findings in this study show the ways in which ROSCAs are a new variant of co-operatives, but they are not being regarded as such. In my opinion, the fact that these banks are organized by Black women, and hidden from view, permits formal co-operators to deny these groups a rightful and acknowledged role in development.

Canada's Banker Ladies are bringing about change in quiet ways by holding on to honoured practices that migrated here as part of the cultural and financial traditions of the Caribbean or African immigrants. Experts of Quebec's social economy Marguerite Mendell and Beatrice Alain (2015) argue compellingly that the state is in a unique position to assist citizens in the co-construction of public policy in the solidarity economy – something previously done in the province of Quebec with the Chantier de l'économie sociale. There is a need for public policy to incorporate the work done by the Banker Ladies, and to remunerate them. Of course, the Banker Ladies are not waiting idly by for handouts; they are vanguards for what it means to do mutual aid, and how to build a meaningful, collectively owned economic system based on reciprocity and trust.

chapter six

Black Muslim Women Counter Business Exclusion

The violence against Muslims in Canada needs no footnotes or citations. These horrors are etched in minds around the world. In 2019, Quebec enacted Bill 21, which banned religious head coverings, including the hijab worn by Muslim women. In summer 2021, a Muslim family was run down by a white supremacist (male) in London, Ontario. In this context of Islamophobia, Muslim civil society in Canada has been enhanced by the work of Somali women creating banking co-ops. These co-ops are composed of individuals who come together to make regular contributions to a common fund that is then given to each member in turn. Somalis use a form of co-operative or group financing that goes by several local names. People from Mogadishu (the south) call it "Ayuuto"; those from Hargeisa (the north) use the term "Hagbad"; and for those from other northern regions, it is sometimes known as "Susu" or "Shalonga."[1]

In fact, Somalis are viewed as immigrants with business savvy. It is a characteristic in which they take pride. This chapter focuses on the use of Hagbad by the Somali community in Toronto's west-end communities of Downsview and Rexdale. This chapter illustrates a case of the stigma of being Black and Muslim in Canada and being

---

1 I use the terms Hagbad and Ayuuto interchangeably, but lean towards Hagbad. There is some speculation that Ayuuto comes from an Italian word, *aiuto*, means help and that the term arose during the Italian occupation of Somalia.

broken down as a result of Black Muslim women taking charge of their economic livelihoods.[2]

An experience of bias that leaves them being left out of society is not a new phenomenon for Somali people living in Canada. Migration from their homelands to Canada in search of a better way of life did not mean that things got easier for them. As Abdul Warsame, who lives in Rexdale and is a local leader among Somali Canadians, explains: "It's ironic; we fled Somalia to give a better, peaceful life to our children. And there's violence here, too" (Aulakh 2012). In other words, Somali people who immigrated to Canada fled war, warlords, and Al-Shabaab terrorists to escape death and suffering, only to see their Canadian-born children become victims of crime and murder (Bykova 2017; CBC News 2017; Ghebreslassie 2017).[3]

Women in Toronto's Somali community are joining together to make life better for their children, and they achieve this goal by using local systems they know and trust. In this chapter, I argue that the systems of Hagbad and Ayuuto stand at the core of what we mean by the solidarity economy. They offer an effective way of thwarting the impact of discrimination and Islamophobia by giving women the means to build their communities. Somali women, alienated for reasons of race, gender, and religion, are proud of the tradition of ROSCAs. In my original conceptualization of my project, I did not plan a separate focus group for Somali women. However, after numerous discussions, I decided it would be best to have one, as these women had certain unique and distinct issues from other Black Canadian women.

Mutual aid groups are not primitive or undeveloped co-operatives (Hossein 2018b; North 2016). They are designed by users who are thoughtful and pragmatic in their approach to banking. Somali women use peer-to-peer systems and, unlike other groups, have no alternatives for banking. As highlighted earlier, Canada is known for its tradition of economic co-operation. The

2 This case study draws in part on a recent publication about ROSCAs in the Greater Toronto Area (Hossein 2017c).
3 There has been an overrepresentation of Somali young men in Toronto's criminal justice system for some time.

concept of alternative financial services through member-owned institutions (i.e., as credit unions) is grounded in Quebec's history. Jean-Marc Fontan et al.'s (2009) edited collection explains how collectives became entrenched in Canada's *économie sociale* as a way to deal with corporate exclusion. In the early 1900s, Alphonse and Dorimene Desjardins created the *caisses populaires* in Levis, Quebec, to address the business exclusion of rural French and Catholic minorities (Shragge and Fontan 2000; Mendell 2009).

ROSCAs exist around the world – in Africa, Asia, Europe, and Australia (Roelvink, St. Martin, and Gibson-Graham 2015; Hossein 2018b; Gibson-Graham 2006; Ardener and Burman 1996). In Canada – specifically in Toronto, Ontario – Somali Canadians organize mutual aid groups with the goal of uplifting immigrant communities. The Somali women featured in this case emulate feminist leader Queen Araweelo, an ancient ruler who fought for the place of women in business and society (Mohamed 2014). The women whom I interviewed admired Queen Araweelo for carrying on the tradition of building solidarity economies in the midst of great difficulty. ROSCAs are a symbol of economic power for women.

Writing on the social and solidarity economy from the perspective of racialized women is one way to diversify knowledge sharing. My goal is to stimulate more diverse scholarship, particularly in social economic journals. The field lacks scholarly material focused on the experience of racialized Muslim women in the social economy. The goal for this chapter is to share the lived experiences of Somali women and to illustrate why Hagbad is the key to their self-help activities. Drawing on Hill Collins's (2000a) work, understanding the lived experience of Somali Canadian women is crucial to breaking down binaries and talking about finance from a Black, Muslim, and female perspective. It is important to move beyond looking at Black women's lived experience as a "case study," and instead consider how they live in business and society as a form of grounded theory.

This chapter is organized into five parts. First, I briefly discuss who the Somalis are in the context of Toronto, Canada. Next, I discuss my methods: that is, 71 interviews carried out in Toronto, Canada, home to the largest Somali population in the country. The third part of the chapter discusses findings in terms of the operations of Hagbad and shares insights provided by the 17 women, who represent hundreds of Muslim Somali women engaging in Hagbad and Ayuuto. The fourth part discusses the origins of the social and solidarity economy – specifically, how important the concept of lived experience within the Black feminist theory is to understanding the role of collectives in the lives of racialized Muslim people. That the situational experience of Black Muslim women can contribute to knowledge production is of a key importance. In the final part, I discuss the current experience of Somali people to provide some background on their migration and resettlement in Canada as Muslim people.

Knowing More about Somali Canadians

Within the Black community, Somalis hold a distinct identity – that is, their Islamic faith and Somali language. Somalis migrated to Canada because of war and the breakdown of a vibrant and free civil society (*Economist* 2016; Besteman 1999). Droughts and famine also played a role in dislocating people during the war. Somalis applied for refugee status and, with their families, started new lives in major Canadian cities like Toronto. All this moving dislocated them as a people. When they arrived in Canada, it was often with little money and limited education; this combination of circumstances made adjusting to Canadian life even more difficult (Ghebreslassie 2017; Nasser 2016; Mensah 2010).

Many Somalis who come to Canada (and the United States) are originally from Somalia, but others have arrived from refugee camps in Kenya, Sudan, Tanzania, Ethiopia, and Djibouti. This region of East Africa, also known as the Horn of Africa, was an important commercial centre in antiquity (3000–2000 BCE). The native homeland of the Somali people is one of the most ethnically homogenous societies, with much of the population having lineage or kin groups within a single ethnic group (Collier 2000; Lewis 2003). Regardless of complications associated with politics and the markets, the Somali people continue to conduct business by trading in gold, clothes, and foodstuffs with regional neighbours – a range of activity that has earned them an impressive reputation (Collet 2007).

Somali Canadians represent one of the largest ethnic groups and the fastest growing racial groups in the country (James et al. 2010; Berns-McGowan 1999; Kusow 1998, 2004), in part because of their complex political history. An estimated two million Somalis live outside of their homeland (Kleist and Abdi 2022). In Canada, most Somalis have settled in big cities, including Hamilton, Kitchener, London, Ottawa-Gatineau, Toronto, and Windsor, all communities in the province of Ontario (Mensah 2010). For a long time, Toronto and Ottawa have been the largest resettlement destinations of Somali immigrants and refugees in Canada (Collet 2007). According to the Somali Canadian Association, most Somalis live in the west end of Toronto, specifically in Rexdale and Etobicoke.[4] More recently, many Somalis reside in Calgary and Edmonton, Alberta. According to the 2021 census, there are 24,764 Somalis residing in the Greater Toronto Area and 32,500 Somalis across Canada (Statistics Canada 2022a; see also OCASI 2016).[5] While the annual flow of Somalis has been in the thousands since the late 1980s, Professor Joseph Mensah (2010) in his book *Black Canadians* has shown that immigration restrictions that came into effect in 1993 have made it difficult for Somalis to immigrate to Canada.

Somalis who come to Canada do not find resettlement easy. Galabuzi (2006) finds that Black Canadians are twice as likely as those in the overall population to have low incomes, to be unemployed, and to encounter systemic bias that interferes with equal access to goods and services. Statistics Canada data indicate that 50 per cent of racialized Canadians feel discriminated against or excluded from opportunities because of their cultural identity (Statistics Canada 2022b). Somali immigrants experience social exclusion from schools, work, and housing, and feel further

---

4 See more about the Somali Canadian Association (n.d.) online.
5 Canadian Somali community members say that these numbers are lower than the actual number because of their fear of government authorities and that the actual number may be higher.

stigmatized in Canadian society because of their dress and religion (Ghumman and Ryan 2013). They live on the margins, often in community housing, with many stressors experienced by the family.

Young Somali men, both immigrants and especially first generation (i.e., born and raised in Canada), have become negative targets in mass media, dogged by reports of gang violence. Somalis have been branded as non-contributors to society rather than assessed for why there is so much suffering and loss of young lives in their communities (Bykova 2017; James et al. 2010; Galabuzi 2006; Kusow 2004). Headlines such as "Black and 'Scared',""Somali-Canadian Shot Dead in Toronto Had Ties to Alberta Drug Trade," and "Why So Many Somali-Canadians Who Go West End Up Dead" are common (Nasser 2016; Appleby, Wingrove, and Mackrael 2012; Wingrove and Mackrael 2012). The news coverage deepens divisions and ostracizes Somali people. York University's Tokunbo Ojo (2006) has found that mainstream media distorts the image of Black Canadians while ethnic media outlets are unable to change these perceptions because they reach such small audiences.

Business exclusion and being shut out of mainstream social systems make young people vulnerable. Some Somali male youth may seek illegal work, such as selling drugs or weapons, to make a living (Berns-McGowan 1999; Hopkins 2006). Gun violence associated with young Black males in Toronto has been a subject of public concern for years and not only for Somalis (Global News 2017; CBC News 2017; Ghebreslassie 2017; Berns-McGowan 1999). Yet social funding steers away from this group, even though its members desperately need an injection of capital into their abandoned communities.

Somali immigrants thus confront a cultural context in Canada that has normalized the stigmatizing of Somali people (Global News 2017; Kusow 2004). The women interviewed unanimously report being denied opportunities because of their religion, language, and race. In 2014, Munira Abukar, a Somali Canadian woman, ran for city councillor in Toronto in the municipal election against the late Rob Ford (mayor of Toronto, 2010–14) in the Etobicoke Ward 2 riding. Abukar's election signs were defaced with racist messages (such as "Go back home") throughout her campaign (DeClerq 2014).

As noted in the previous chapter, Abukar's campaign funds came from Hagbad money groups (Munira Abukar, interview, 3 November 2017). What she received was more than funds to kickstart her campaign: the women who organized the ROSCA also provided her with the volunteer support she needed to keep her campaign going. The vandalism to which Munira's campaign signs were subject reflects larger society's hostile view of Somali people. Somalis are typically viewed as "welfare cases," draining the system with their claims of refugee status and made to feel that they are "less than others" or "foreign" (focus group, 2016; Carruthers 1995).

Somali Exclusion in Toronto

The intense and subtle forms of business exclusion experienced by immigrants in Canadian society – not all of it is overt – motivate Somali women to create banking co-operatives. Somali immigrants have particularly encountered a cultural clash between what it means to be Canadian and what it means to be Muslim. Somalis find that their religious values conflict with the "normal" financial practice of interest fees being applied when money is borrowed. Charging interest (known as *riba*) on loans is forbidden in Islam. Muslims therefore avoid loans that incur an interest charge.

While some Muslims engage in a workaround, many do not for sacred reasons. Mohammed Yunus, the founder of Grameen Bank, has referred to interest as "service fees" for observant Bengali Muslims. Similarly, when I managed a micro-credit project in Kano, Nigeria, in the early 2000s, the interest rate was called an "administrative cost." Somali women in this study made it clear that they are not interested in semantics. They simply will not engage with Canadian banks that do not consider how shariah – that is, Islamic religious law – must be applied to financing products. Financing products that recognize shariah do not involve interest. Those financial products that do exist, and are shariah-compliant, focus on mortgages.

Over the last four decades, Somalis have become a visible group in Toronto's demography, yet the banking sector remains ambivalent about meeting the need for halal business products. Establishing small businesses has been one way for Somalis to settle in Canada; however, challenges exist when it comes to supports for their businesses. Those challenges include restricted access to credit – made all the more difficult by a lack of alternative financial providers that take the prohibition around *riba* into account. If Somalis exclude themselves from banking, it is because systemic bias has excluded them.

Somali women who do business continue to face financial discrimination (focus group, 2016; Pagliaro 2014). They generally do not agree that, to build a life, they must develop a credit history that involves paying interest. Having little or no access to formal credit has in turn excluded Muslims from accessing business loans. Self-exclusion and business exclusion operate simultaneously, which has been a catalyst for the creation of self-help banking groups. Banking co-operatives like Hagbad have been an crucial tool for immigrants, specifically mothers. Hagbad has helped them meet their livelihood needs, including starting small businesses or paying for school fees (Hall 2011).

The traditional practice of Hagbad and Ayuuto is defined in the literature as a type of ROSCA or economic co-operative (Aredo 2004; Bouman 1995, 1977). While the roots of Hagbad are unclear, some Somali elders whom I interviewed were convinced this money system goes back many generations in several ancient civilizations in East Africa, such as Somalia, Ethiopia, and Kenya (Ardener and Burman 1996; Hall 2011). Women who moved to Toronto continue to draw on these ancient banking systems to secure a livelihood for themselves and their families. Hagbad has helped the Somali community in Rexdale for more than 40 years.

Research Methods

Data collection for this element of the project was difficult to achieve. It took months of planning to coax the women to come forward since they feared the research could further harm them. There is intense anti-Muslim rhetoric in Canada. After 9/11, it became particularly vociferous, evident even in statements issued at the highest levels of government, by the then-Conservative prime minister Stephen Harper's 2015 pledge to set up a hotline for barbaric practices to spy and report on Islamic people. This kind of overt social exclusion makes it hard for groups to confide in researchers. The fear of reprisal is real. It took months to build trust and to assure the women that this work would not make them vulnerable to the authorities, particularly with regard to taxes. The interview tools and form were reviewed by a human ethics committee and, as a result of this process, many of the names of the people interviewed were altered to protect their identities.

The research methods have a qualitative design. A total of 43 Somali women, all direct users of ROSCAs, were interviewed. In addition to the interviews with users (see table 6.1), empirical data was collected using semi-structured interview questionnaires with 28 individuals with knowledge of finance, particularly of alternative financial services and community development.

This case study on Somali women grew out of earlier interviews with more than 100 African Canadian women in Toronto and Montreal. These interviews are not included in table 6.1. In fact, tension surfaced in these early focus group meetings because Somali women refused to charge a fee to members for managing the ROSCA. Somali women felt they needed to have their own focus group sessions to address issues unique to them, issues that went beyond race and gender to questions of ethnicity, religion, and language. Somali women, many of them mothers, believed their experience as Black women to be distinct because of language (Somali, not English, is their first language) and religion (as Muslims). For this study on Somali women, I worked together with a research assistant, a Somali Canadian university student from the community. We carried out interviews in people's homes, or at schools, recreation centres, and workplaces – whichever venue the women participating thought was the safest and most convenient meeting place. Sometimes the work would be postponed because of a killing or harm experienced in the community. Although the work in this community took time, we built up a close rapport and the relationship blossomed.

Table 6.1. Interviews with Muslim Somali Canadian Women
on ROSCAs in Toronto (*N* = 43)

Methods	Interviews
Focus group discussion with women	17
Individual interviews with women	26

Source: Author's data collection in Toronto, Ontario, 2015–18.

Somali participants felt that the usual questions about ROSCAs did not sufficiently address issues of Islam and why they do business the way they do. To respect these concerns, I revised the overarching research question about faith to ensure inclusion: "Are Muslim women being excluded or self-excluding themselves in business and society?" and "How does Hagbad contribute to strengthening civil society?" Some sub-questions included: "What do women use Hagbad money for?," "How do you organize your specific Hagbad?," "Given all the banking options in Toronto, why do you use Hagbad?," "How do you feel about Hagbad?," "How does Hagbad meet the needs of people better than the commercial banks?" The participants discussed and debated these issues intensely with the facilitator, but also among themselves, speaking mainly in English but also in Somali (with English translation for participants who did not speak Somali and Somali translation for those with limited English skills). Almost all the Somali women in this study have a household income of less than $40,000 (gross) per annum and are either self-employed or working in low-paying and precarious jobs (e.g., office cleaners, bus drivers, grocery clerks, personal support workers [PSWs], school cafeteria cooks). Many of the women reside in low-income communities in Toronto's west end.

One of the early focus groups involved 17 Somali women. It was held in 2016 on a Saturday afternoon at a community centre in a social housing project. The participants were between the ages of 23 and 62. All worked full-time, often in childcare, or as school bus drivers, cleaners, security guards, or in school canteens. Just over half were mothers (47 per cent of whom were single mothers). Choosing a Saturday afternoon between mealtimes was the most convenient because it did not interfere with their workday, family schedule, or prayer time. Four women were first generation and Canadian born. The remaining 13 were born/raised in Somalia or neighbouring African countries, such as Kenya and Ethiopia. These 13 women came to Canada at various times over the course of a 40-year period. Since Hagbad groups can have memberships of 8 to 50 women, and sometimes more, every woman in the focus group represented many more women. Therefore, the focus group spoke for more than 200 women.

Findings: Camaraderie among Black Muslim Women

Many Somalis who migrated to Canada in the 1980s used Hagbad and Ayuuto to mitigate business exclusion. The women who were interviewed resided in the west end of Toronto, with easy access via public transit to all the major banks (Royal Bank of Canada, Toronto Dominion, CIBC, Bank of Montreal) with branches located within the community. Yet these women remain "underbanked" (and in some cases "unbanked"): they use commercial banks for salary deposits only. None of the women interviewed could name a single credit union because none had branches in their community – the closest one was located on the campus of a nearby university (focus group, 2017, Toronto). Having observed how community members struggled to access financing, these women took it upon themselves to innovate the banking services in their local areas.

While Hagbad, or Ayuuto, is not the only financial tool that Somali Canadians use, it is one of their most important forms of business finance. Hagbad groups require hard work and careful planning. Somali women who make a conscientious decision to form a group are invested in it, and work hard to ensure it helps all members. The women typically craft policy and organize members by group consensus. Members of an elected executive are tasked with collecting people's money, and then rotating it, in order to help one another achieve personal projects. Through this innovative financial self-help, which relies on a group dynamic of similar class origins and cultural backgrounds, Somali women have figured out how to make business inclusive, challenging Canadian banking norms that do not suit their cultural and social lifestyle in the process. As stated emphatically by "Munira," a 23-year-old Canadian of Somali heritage: "Ayuuto is a bank made of regular people. It is a bank that helps people *first* [my emphasis]. It is about reforming traditional banks to think about people. People don't trust these (commercial) banks anymore" (focus group, 2016, Toronto).

Discussions during the focus group helped to unpack what a ROSCA means for Somali Canadians, and showed how they are run and managed. The comments made by "Munira" reveal that Hagbad transforms how standard banks operate, remaking them with a focus on the collective. These innovative, self-selected groups come together with a common purpose; their creation spearheaded by women in the community who are in touch with one another and see the need for a ROSCA. During interviews, Somali women indicated they want to see their traditional banking system influence the Canadian financial sector so they can be a part of it. Studying informal, often hidden, co-operative banking groups validates the work of the women who participate in them. Recognizing the cultural aspect of the Ayuuto system, a form of mutual aid finance, is also a way to consider how Canadians can democratize financial services to include religious minorities.

How Does Hagbad Work?

Hagbads vary in structure since policies and rules are decided on collectively by the members of the group, which is usually run by women. Men also have Hagbad and Ayuuto groups, with many using them to buy used cars so they can operate taxis. Hagbad members epitomize the sharing economy because profit is not the imperative; rather, the intent is to pool and share resources. Members typically elect an executive, such as a president, vice president, and treasurer; members then vote on decisions, which are made binding for a specified period. Each member makes fixed contributions (a "hand") to a common revolving fund following a specific schedule (e.g., weekly or monthly). The money collected is added to a "pool," and then, over the duration of the Hagbad, funds are disbursed by the democratically elected executive to each member in turn (by a vote based on need). Here is a sample case involving a group of 10 women to illustrate how a Hagbad operates. Each member makes a monthly contribution of $1,000 for a 10-month cycle, which means, at the end of each month, a grand total of $10,000 goes into the group's fund. By the end of the 10-month cycle, each member will receive her contribution of $10,000. It must be emphasized: the Somali Banker Ladies do not take a service fee and the work they do is completely benevolent.

Hagbad is participatory. Members determine the needs of the individual members and distribute the "hand" to each member accordingly. There is no set rule for organizing money; instead, the membership of each group comes up with its own method of collecting and disbursing funds. The economic collective neither takes fees from its members nor charges them interest, making the system compliant with shariah. Pooling events – the occasions when members make their deposits – are usually held in someone's home, with the accompaniment of tea and fish sambusa (similar to Indian samosas). The fund is managed by the group's executive, and it relies on peer pressure to ensure members are timely with their deposits (focus group, 2016, Rexdale, Toronto). In cases of conflict, the group "manages" the person until the Hagbad reaches its end. However, the person will not receive invitations to join future groups.

Structural Exclusion in Finance

While the number of Canadians who do not use banks is low, it is unclear exactly how many people are underbanked (Buckland 2012). Many of those who avoid banks turn to fringe banking to cope – that is, they turn to money lenders, private finance firms (e.g., Money Mart), or alternative financial institutions like microfinance banks (Baradaran 2015; Buckland 2012).

Canadian Muslims, who make up about 4.9 per cent of the national population and 9.6 per cent of Toronto's population

(Statistics Canada 2022a), are excluded from banking. A quick internet search reveals that Canada lags behind many countries in terms of offering halal business products because there are few Islamic banks. Ansar Co-operative Housing Corporation and An-Nur Co-operative, which specialize in home mortgages, are the exceptions. Halal banking for small-business needs is missing. As a result, Muslims, like the Somali women in this study, cannot participate in commercial banks. Instead, they create Ayuuto to meet their needs.

Most of the women (82 per cent) interviewed during this study stated that, in general, the Somali community has a hard time accessing banking services to meet their livelihood needs. They felt their physical appearance as veiled women is a "triple whammy" behind why they are rejected: Black, Muslim, and female. All the women in the focus group were observant Muslims. Many of them viewed veiling as a marker of their difference, explaining that their veils made them feel "foreign" – even women born in Toronto felt this way. Some of them confessed that this difference in dress, combined with weak language skills in English, caused them to self-exclude from banks. Several women described negative and awkward experiences of trying to do business at banks. Somali women are conscious that, to some non-Muslims, wearing a hijab is viewed as an affront.

The women explained they use cash and cheques. They cannot use credit cards because they charge interest (*riba*), a practice which transgresses their faith. Their inability to use credit cards undermines their development of a credit history. Since establishing a credit history takes time, fringe banking options – including the use of Hagbad – are often the only way many newcomers can access money. Many women said they prefer using cash. They said that they would also use cheques if they have a bank. Even though a recent research by the Federal Reserve found that cheques are dead, they also found that African Americans are still using cash because of being unbanked (Van Dem 2023). Yet, the ROSCA groups the African diaspora relies on are never considered by policymakers as an important financial device. Black people will often turn to a ROSCA system as the preferred option to reduce their use of high-interest loans or other money-lending firms.

Asha, a mother of nine children, explained: "When we do not have a credit history, this denies us [Somali] people from getting money in banks. We Somalis don't follow the interest rule because it is *haram* [not allowed in Islam]" (focus group, 2016). In the same focus group, Faduma, a single mother and school bus driver, stated: "Ayuuto is for yourself. [It is] something for your life. It is about solving problems with people you like ... And you don't even [have to] worry about interest."

Canadian economist Jerry Buckland's (2012) *Hard Choices* proposes that banking exclusion in Toronto is complicated. Though dated, I did find that his idea that there is a deep-seated elitism among bankers making low-income people, especially women of colour, feel unwelcome in commercial banks still happening when I carried out my interviews. One woman in the focus group (who I cannot name), a mother of several children and who lives in the Dixon Towers (subsidized housing apartments) revealed to me that her very being and how she dressed (wearing a veil, speaking with a heavy accent) affected her access to business services: "When you are poor like me, this means [that] the banks don't give you a chance ... some of us look like this [imitates a banker looking at someone in a rude way] ... and we won't get any money" (focus group, 2016).

The 17 women who were interviewed unanimously reported that Hagbad or Ayuuto are viewed with suspicion by outsiders. "Ifrah" explained:

> Most people think Hagbad is wrong and they don't believe what we are doing in terms of helping ourselves. People think we are sending the money to Somalia, Al-Shabaab, money laundering. They think we mothers are terrorists but our home for a long time has been Toronto. We are not doing anything bad. (Focus group, 2016, Toronto)

Many of the women allege that money confiscated by police during drug raids was never illicit money at all but Hagbad funds. Self-help activities among Somali women are viewed as suspect. The women whom I interviewed were hurt profoundly by this perception. Of the dozens of women who were interviewed in

Montreal and Toronto, I found the suspicion of Islamic terrorism to be unique to Somalis. The women believe that Canadians do not consider what they do as an innovation, or a benefit, because they interpret Somali self-help initiatives as corrupt, with the funds associated with them collected to support terrorist groups. Even when Muslim women innovate in business, they are made to feel inadequate or are barred from accessing funds to help them grow, as reported in the *Globe and Mail* (Peesker 2018).

Muslim Somalis Contribute to Canada's Legacy of Self-Help

Self-help is a respected tradition in Canada. Canada's reputation as a world leader in collective institutions arose from its historical involvement in cases of social and solidarity economy, including: the Underground Railroad, the Desjardins Movement in Quebec, Aboriginal co-operatives like Arctic Co-operative Limited, the wheat pools and the Co-operators Group in the Prairies, and the Antigonish Movement among miners and fisher folk in the Maritimes. This tradition of self-help continues among immigrant women in the country's major cities, notably in Toronto where Somali Canadian women are pioneering ways for Black Muslim women to contribute to the social economy. Consider what "Zeinab" had to say about Somali women and their ingenious ways of creating a system that works:

> Banks and Canadians tear us down. They underestimate what we can do. We can do things for ourselves. I am doing great things for me and my family. And Ayuuto helps us to show what we can do. Ayuuto is original and I like it! No [copycat models are] needed. No thank you. (Focus group, 2016, Toronto)

Ayuuto and Hagbad fund many things in marginalized communities that otherwise would not find support – small-business ventures or side businesses, such as making handicrafts, selling snacks, and tailoring. Some certainly direct monies to help with consumption needs, but members of the group interviewed stated they used the money first and foremost for business purposes. Several women in the focus group shared that Hagbad has expanded beyond Somali women to include other racialized Canadians. "Lul," a 49-year-old Somali Canadian, told us:

> Hagbad is a kind of Islamic bank created by us [women]. If we had a Hagbad bank here that was formal and legalized we would not have to ever go to those banks and we just go to Hagbad. We don't have Hagbad bank as a Canadian bank to go to, so we do our own banking … this way and together. My friend is in Hagbad and she is not Somali … she is Vietnamese and other groups doing Hagbad because they find it useful to them. This is how we help Canada; we bring new things here. We need Hagbad [in Toronto] and that's what we going to do. (Focus group, 2016)

This kind of self-help by Somali Canadians reveals women taking charge of their finances to address their own needs and determine how monies will be spent. "Khadija," a first-generation Somali Canadian student, explains that while so many things in the lives of Somali women are dictated; in Ayuuto, women are the boss:

> For the older generation, Ayuuto is a connection to a lost homeland, and for the new generation, Ayuuto teaches independence and the ability to micromanage in ways we cannot do normally because we do not control how we live in this society. Ayuuto gives us the control we need to feel and be important. This is what this thing is all about. (Focus group, 2016, Toronto)

Hagbad as a localized form of self-help is missing from Canada's social economy. Indeed, banking co-operatives of racialized people receive little or no attention within the social and solidarity economy (Hossein 2017c). Despite this, Hagbad is transforming impersonal banking into a financial system that is indeed by and for the people. Amina, a 25-year-old ESL assistant, stated: "Hagbad is about helping each other. Banks can question me up and down [*she makes a face of not liking this and others laugh*] ... but Hagbad won't do that ... Hagbad is soooo sweet. We are Hagbad and no one is there to ask a lot of questions to make us guilty and feel bad ... and all that jazz" (focus group, 2016).

Hagbad systems are structured on lines of reciprocity and trust. When the women in the focus group were asked what Hagbad means to them, "Ifrah M.," a public school cook, explained: "Hagbad means that we are just here for each other. We know each other. Hagbad is about trust and it is the safest way to bank." In the focus group, "Zeinab," a 58-year-old widow and mother, stressed: "When a mother is sick or has a problem, we can organize according to her situation. Hagbad is about thinking about people."

At least 49 per cent of the women interviewed said they come together for Hagbad based on a referral system, while 41 per cent reported they knew other members of their group personally, either as close friends or family. In the case of default or late payments, the women rely on peer pressure to make members comply with the rules. Taking part in Hagbad means that people in the community get to know each other well. "Munira," a first-generation Canadian who lives in Scarlettwood Apartments (an affordable housing complex), stated, "Islamophobia and anti-Black racism is present and faced when we go see the bank tellers. Discrimination faced at banks is in there ... But with Hagbad, there is excellent customer service because you don't want to screw over your friends" (focus group, 2016, Toronto).

Hagbad's Contribution to Canadian Society

Hagbad is an important way for Somali women – and especially mothers – to help their families and communities through social and financial supports. The decision of Somali women to turn to Hagbad is pragmatic: by mitigating the impact of business exclusion, the system helps women to supplement family income with a side business. Through financial co-operation, they are able to support one another in their business endeavours. As a group, they come together to meet the financial and business needs of individual members – a process that formal banks fail to do. Through their collective organizing, these women build community, and they vitalize and innovate in the financial sector while contributing to Canada's civil society. These women teach their children the virtues of self-help, peace, and stability with the hope that they will become independent and caring citizens.

The Somalis interviewed were Black Muslim women from low-income socio-economic backgrounds who made a conscious decision to organize collective banks in Toronto's west end. In doing so, they took a stand against exclusionary forms of banking. Through their activities, they critique the Western form of individualized, commercialized banks and demonstrate the value of co-operative banks. A democratically elected executive of a Hagbad presents "new" forms of financial innovation. Somali women are clearly an integral part of economic co-operation and self-help in Canada. They also bring an intersectional perspective in terms of how we understand Canada's history in ROSCAs, mutual aid, and co-operatives.

Hagbad provides a powerful lesson in mutual aid. It also adds to Canada's history of self-help and disrupts thinking about Black people as a homogenous group. While race, gender, and class are markers for exclusion, so too are ethnicity, language, and religion. The Somali women interviewed speak Somali as their first language and wear a hijab as part of their religious duty. They reported they were "shaking up stigmas" and "liberating" themselves by creating democratic institutions that meet people's social and business needs. In interviews, the women told me and my Somali Canadian research assistant that counting Hagbad as part of the solidarity economy unravels the stereotypes of Somali people as "terrorists," "backwards," and "welfare recipients."

Hagbad purposely remains out of view – not because it is something of which these women are ashamed, but because of the ill-treatment they face in society. On top of being Black and female, Somali women confront the Islamophobia deeply embedded within Canadian society and deal with negative media attention: they are labelled as delinquents and viewed as people who operate against the "norms" (Munshani 2005). The women who use ROSCAs guard the Hagbad system closely because they know their activities are being scrutinized, even criminalized. Yet there is nothing illegal about forming a Hagbad, it is a mutual aid financial co-operative or ROSCA. In a quiet, pragmatic, and well-thought-out way, Somali women move around their neighborhoods organizing Hagbad to support and to help each other. The concepts of giving, reciprocity, and democracy are deeply embedded within the Somali Hagbad. These are the business ethics the Somali Banker Ladies perpetuate when they engage in Hagbad. The foundation of their social and financial innovation is steeped in a goodness that builds a strong civic culture.

chapter seven

The Future of Co-operation: Acknowledging the Black Feminist Economics in Public Policy

During a "Future of the Commons" lecture in 2012, the late Elinor Ostrom made it clear that when users of collective spaces, resources, and services choose to self-organize, they do so because they see what they have as valuable, and they do not want to be exploited. That is the future of co-operation – ordinary people making rules based on trust and reciprocity with one another and organizing life to protect the commons.

Joining a co-operative, ROSCA, or mutual aid group is about ensuring people have access to lump sums of money, so they can realize projects they see as important to their own lives. No matter the degree to which the Western world has pushed the economy towards individualized commercial businesses, community-rooted financial economies persist. In the face of global pandemics, the idea of people informally congregating to help one another will become even more essential and what truly matters. Indeed, this concept is gaining strength.

Nigerian feminist Oyèrónkẹ́ Oyěwùmí (1997) reminds us that Europeans inferiorized African people, especially African women. In doing so, they corrupted local African cultures by masculinizing religion, as well as their customs and norms. Colonizers were driven by their own commercial interests to interrupt and alienate certain groups of people (see Kinyanjui 2019; Stewart 1984; Marable [1983] 2015; Rodney 1982; Midgley 1981; Du Bois 1907). The response in international development circles has been to "fix" Black, Indigenous, and racialized people, and to "help" them "develop" in ways that are alien to their own cultural values, ethics, and practices (Betasamosake Simpson 2020; Escobar [1995] 2012).

We need to start considering, acknowledging, and writing about how people of African descent know what needs to be done. World-famous development scholar Arturo Escobar (2020) has taken his work beyond post-development: his preoccupation now is to document and look to people-driven activities. I am convinced that one of the main questions intellectuals and activists should be addressing today is the following: how do we imagine and create other economies, and modes of existing economically, that are different from the patriarchal racist capitalisms of the present day? This book demonstrates that the Banker Ladies have lessons to teach us about what it means to be an activist or a co-operator. They also offer valuable ideas on how to widen what we know as the Black Political Economy. The co-operative business model used by the Banker Ladies demonstrates their ingenuity in the face of denigration, and their ability to do a lot with seemingly little, all while enduring various forms of business and social exclusion.

The Caribbean Banker Ladies, although publicly recognized for their co-operative contributions, are not remunerated for the extra work they do. They are applauded for making do with what they have in the marginalized environments in which they live. By contrast, the Banker Ladies in Canada are ignored, and moreover, encounter extreme forms of anti-Black racism and sexism. They are taunted and vilified for the co-operative contributions they make.

As women of the African diaspora, the Banker Ladies carry their ancestral money systems with them, and they use them to build safe havens and places of refuge for those who suffer exclusion. The work done by the Banker Ladies is a part of the genealogy of finance – specifically collective finance – and it should be remembered and cited as scholars document "modern" financial economies, including the "fintech" sector. After many years following the Banker Ladies in a number of different countries, I have learned that these women find resources where it is believed there are none. They are leading the charge on social provisioning, using it to push back against racial capitalism. They accomplish this unremunerated work while being ignored, stigmatized, and vilified, and in the process, they expand the boundaries of what it means to be a co-operator.

Public Policy Ignores the ROSCA System as Co-Operatives

My study is unapologetically biased towards a group of Black women who have been overlooked for what they do. Over the years, I have met with a revolving door of feminist experts in government who keep telling me they "need to learn more about the Banker Ladies." For over a decade, I have been publishing about ROSCAs and Black people. My work is funded by research bodies, yet public policy on ROSCAs is still missing (Laforest 2009). I have participated in creating an open-access documentary film about ROSCAs, and authored many short opinion editorials which have circulated widely in Canada, the Caribbean, and beyond. Two major volumes have been published on ROSCAs in the Global South and among the African diaspora. In spite of this productivity, the political will to upset mainstream development and ensure ROSCAs become a part of social financial programs is still not there.

In my view, elitist experts vested in their understanding of economic development are not ready to incorporate the know-how of the Banker Ladies. The voices of hundreds of women of the African diaspora (multiply those by a factor of 22, and it becomes the voices of thousands), who oversee financial services for their communities, educate us about their contributions to politics and economics. They are the vanguards; the saviours of mutual aid and economic co-operation. Based on their own lived experience, they know what it means to engage in politicized action, with the intent of improving democracy from below and showing the world how to make commoning a part of our lives.

The Banker Ladies are not fighting for fame and attention. They do not compete for the spotlight. They are determinedly and successfully making finance equitable and inclusive. As illustrated by the cases featured in this book, the Banker Ladies quietly set out to do the financial group work that is needed for women in their

Figure 7.1. The *Partner Hand* Exhibit at the Bank of England, London (2023)
Source: Author's photo.

communities to thrive. They collect monies in their locales through camaraderie, friendship, and trust networks. These locales are often low-income communities – ones in which residents may endure violence. Outsiders to these communities find it difficult to imagine skilful organization and financial co-operation as possible within them.

The Bank of England has recognized the work of Jamaican and Caribbean immigrants, addressing financial exclusion through the use of the Partner banks. The Windrush generation in the United Kingdom countered business exclusion through various forms of economic co-operation known as Partner and Susu (see figure 7.1). Together with the bank's museum, Caribbean mother-daughter team Catherine Ross and Lynda-Louise Burrell of Museumand, the National Caribbean Heritage Museum, opened an exhibit on the Jamaican Partner banking system. It would do well for the Bank of Canada (and other central banks) to take note on how to make space for educating the public on ROSCA systems, as they have done in the United Kingdom.

The Banker Ladies are doing what they have seen done by the women who came before them. In turn, they share these lessons of financial abundance with the next generation. These co-operators create financial groups, which are vested in meeting livelihood needs, while also preserving ancestral systems of mutual aid, co-operation, and collectivity. A Black and feminist perspective on financial marginalization and informal co-operative economics is long overdue. The Banker Ladies enable us to gain insights into their lived experiences to see theory making that is inherently feminist in its design. Of vital importance is the fact that Black/African descent women in the Caribbean and Canada organize ROSCAs – a form of co-operative banking – to promote equity. Policymakers need to catch up on their knowledge and experience. The time for reading and homework has passed.

The formal world of co-operatives has ignored the contributions of Black minorities in the Americas. At the International Cooperative Alliance (ICA), no one is examining the co-operatives of the African diaspora. My colleague, who manages the Africa region at the ICA, has oversight for Black people worldwide; however, the unique cultural context for the African diaspora is not accounted for in the library of this global network. After decades of studying W.E.B. Du Bois, economist Curtis Haynes Jr. (2018) makes it clear that Black co-operativism occurs wherever persons of African descent take charge of their financial lives and recreate economies of care that are part of their heritage: an action that frees them from a heritage of being terrorized. This added layer of complexity is why co-operative networks should make room for the African diaspora.

It is no accident that a bias exists in economics that ignores the role of Black women in social provisioning, as well as the foundational ideas around the philosophy of Ubuntu ("I am because you are"). These contributions have been completely negated due to the white, Euro-Western pursuit of a commercial model. Capitalist business elites push, as the only way of making a living, a concoction of democracy tied to a trickle-down commercial business model. This model works to the detriment of many women of the African diaspora since it misuses and undervalues their labour. Nonetheless, Black women persevere. They organize, and stand firmly as vanguards of mutual aid groups, co-operatives, and solidarity. The Banker Ladies whose voices have been heard through this study reveal that they, too, are Black feminists who, through their own lived experience and innovative responses to challenging circumstances, are very much part of the Black Radical Tradition.

Crafting Policy on ROSCAs

The point of this book is not to provide a guide to creating a ROSCA system. Rather, my intent has been to raise awareness about the existence of ROSCAs, as well as to highlight the lack of recognition given to the women of the African diaspora who organize them, and who bring value to the economy and to society by doing so. The Banker Ladies organize co-operative economies while working full-time in the economy. They often do low-paying work that nobody else wants to do, but which we rely on as a society. They drive our buses, clean our houses, work in grocery stores and restaurants, and are our hospital orderlies and our personal support workers. During the COVID-19 pandemic, we deemed them essential workers; the rhetoric is that they are "heroes" and yet we still pay these women minimum wages. Even as they engage in waged work, these women are also managing banking co-ops with 50+ members. We do not hire the Banker Ladies to advise us on how to make business and banking "inclusive," but we should. Instead, we hire people lacking in lived experience and with limited expertise to theorize and waste our subsidies trying to "fix" issues of exclusion.

Hundreds of Black women engage in social and economic provisioning to enable those left out of formal systems. They make it very clear that these informal institutions, ROSCAs, are relevant in today's world. Governments and the policymakers who allocate budgets to human development now need to step up and listen to the women of the African diaspora, recognize the efficacy of their interventions, and incorporate their economic practices into those on offer for assisting in community development. Canadian scholars of the social economy Mendell and Alain (2015) refer to this kind of work by the government as one of co-construction with its citizens to deliver inclusive economic development. Our policymakers and those we elect should be leading the way to make budget lines to support the development of people-driven co-operative and mutual aid systems.

The pandemic has seen much discussion about the "re-birth" of mutual aid, co-operative groups, and ROSCA systems. So, our mission as a society should be to get people and their governments to understand the value of membership institutions, and going through a pandemic has been made this role of informal co-operative systems easier. People are now aware of banking co-ops as good and essential, and they have come to realize that more informality in our society would be beneficial. Below is a list of public policy suggestions that address global and country-specific needs for making ROSCAs an integral part of the economic ecosystem.

1. Credit the African Diaspora for Its Contribution to the Co-operative Sector

The Banker Ladies in Canada and the Caribbean – Black women who live in the Americas – do not abandon their commitment to making business inclusive, no matter the pressures with which they contend. Regardless of how many times they are pushed out of decent paying jobs or called horrific names, they continue to organize co-operatives for the betterment of society. The Banker Ladies take on commercialized banking systems by creating localized financial co-operative systems called ROSCAs. In so doing, they contribute to the varieties of co-operativism. Their endeavours broaden the concept of what it means to be a co-operator by encompassing informal types of co-operatives.

This book, *The Banker Ladies*, has policy implications because it shares information that can educate the public on the role of Black women in social provisioning and mutual aid. Feminist economist Marilyn Power (2004) argued that unpaid work, such as the act of caring for people, is very much a part of the sphere of economic activities that women do. The Banker Ladies who choose to do this financial and social provisioning work, often do the work in secret and without renumeration, are advancing the co-op business model to transform unequal financial systems. Through their emphasis on consensus and consultation, the Banker Ladies bring ethics into the banking system. In doing this work, they contribute to knowledge making from a Black feminist co-operator perspective.

A vital part of recognizing the contribution of Black people to development involves remembering that certain countries and people have a shared history of intentional underdevelopment (Mbembe 2017; Marable [1983] 2015; Rodney 1982). The brutality endured by Black people in the Americas and Europe is a story powerfully told by Colson Whitehead (2016) in *The Underground Railroad*. In this volume, Whitehead vividly describes the tragic life of fictional slaves Cora and Caesar. *Four Hundred Souls*, co-edited by Ibram X. Kendi and Keisha Blain (2021), depicts the struggles of Black American people through personal vignettes, demonstrating how the legacy of slavery haunts them to the present day. In these stories we are reminded about a racial solidarity that brings Black/African descent people together when they are harmed (Wright Austin 2007, 2023; Gordon Nembhard 2014a; Clealand 2017; Hooker 2009). When excluded people endure atrocities because of who they are, they bind together to resist that oppression and to make it less relevant to them.

People coming together to help one another under adversity is something Canadians know about too. In Canada, we can do our part about recognizing the business innovations of Black people. Our universities and public education system can be expanded to include co-operatives and member-owned businesses. When we teach young people about money, we can include modules on the ROSCA system. Currently, the focus on learning business is on the corporate version of the Monopoly game – how to be a sole entrepreneur. Recognizing other people and the ways they do business, building these systems into the current curricula will diversify the business models we use.

Recognizing that mutual aid is part of of the economic activities of humankind is important if we are to build effective policy in community development (Power 2004). When Russian theorist of mutual aid Peter Kropotkin ([1902] 1976) studied human and animal life, he argued that species by nature must come together and assist one another to ensure their own survival, especially in inhospitable environments. W.E.B. Du Bois (1907) promoted group economics because his research showed that African-descended people have a legacy of working communally, especially when they feel oppressed (Mullings 2021). In a rich discussion of state brutality against Black people, philosophers Táíwò and Mbembe (2021) remind us that trauma can bring people together – and this can lead to co-operative movements beneficial to all of humanity. The Banker Ladies combat wicked racism by building economic solidarity to take care of each other and to make the world a better place. Knowing this story is part of how we credit those who do this consciousness-raising work.

Knowing the history of the African diaspora is vital to acknowledging and valuing the contributions of Black people to co-operative development in the West and beyond. Jamaica's Marcus Garvey witnessed Black people working on the construction of the Panama Canal, on the banana plantations of Costa Rica, and on the docks in London, England (Blaisdell 2004; Lewis 1987; Martin 1983). Seeing Black people working in these jobs informed his thinking about self-reliance and supporting Black-led co-operative businesses. Black people around the world responded to Garvey's co-operative ideas, which inspired the founding of the Universal Negro Improvement Association (UNIA) – the largest and most influential anti-colonial organization in the world in the 1920s. The diaspora wanted co-op businesses that would address their needs in terms of health care, jobs, burials, and weddings. In *Collective Courage*, Jessica Gordon Nembhard (2014a) documents the history of co-operative businesses in which African Americans engaged and continue to engage to survive and to thrive. There is no shortage of theorizing about the Black political economy that helps us understand the informality of co-operatives among the African diaspora.

What we know is that adversity has served as a catalyst to create co-operatives in our world today. The Haitian people have enshrined co-operatives as a part of a core value in the republic's constitution because the country's informal traders, known as Madam Saras or *ti machans* (market women), use Sol and other *caisses informelles* to support one another, especially under brutal political regimes (Bergan and Schuller 2009; Fatton 2007). The Guyanese people are officially regarded as the co-operative republic because the Afro-Guyanese drew on Boxhand to buy farmland (St. Pierre 1999). Jamaican "higglers" (small business traders) have long used Partner banks to buy and sell, moving from the countryside to town (Harrison 1988). Trinis and Grenadians all have a rich legacy of Susu banking. The Caribbean people hold on to African traditions of ROSCAs as their preferred form of bank.

2. Recognize ROSCAs as an Invention of the Global South

It is time to give credit to the people of the Global South for expanding what we categorize as "co-operative systems." As mentioned earlier, the Bank of England and its museum collaborated with Museumand, the National Caribbean Heritage Museum, to make sure that Jamaica and the Caribbean people were credited with financial innovations. What I saw at this exhibit in November 2023 was that England's central bank, which once colonized many countries (remembering that its early board members owned slaves) in the Caribbean region, was recognizing the financial expertise of the Caribbean people when they emigrated to the United Kingdom. They then thought it important to educate the British public on the Partner banking system. Black, Indigenous, and racialized people all over the world rely on various forms of collectives and co-operatives to develop and enhance business in society (Betasamosake Simpson 2020; Begashaw 1978). Many ancient societies, such as the indigenous people of Ethiopia, Egypt, China, South Korea, Ghana, and India, have recognized the validity of informal co-operatives, and especially those known as ROSCAs or banking co-ops. There is much crediting and gratitude needed towards these countries when their citizens relocate to other lands and bring their financial technologies with them.

I learned a lot from other countries about the ROSCA system. During my sabbatical in 2018, I spent a few months in India. Since I wanted to understand the state of Kerala's legacy of solidarity economics, I visited there for an extended period to work with my close collaborator, professor of economics Christabell P.J. at the University of Kerala. Kerala has achieved phenomenal development in terms of literacy, gender equality, self-help groups, and co-operatives (see the works of Agarwal 2020; Devika 2016; Sandbrook et al. 2007 to learn more). Christabell and I are working on a series of projects about minorities who turn to various forms of co-operatives because formal corporate or state institutions fail them. Many of Kerala's achievements in development have been due to self-help groups, co-operatives, and the consciousness of its people, who continue to improve social well-being despite India's divisive, casteist, anti-Muslim fascist central government.

Amartya Sen (1999), the Nobel prize-winning economist from Kolkata, was deeply affected by the "economic unfreedoms" experienced by a Muslim poor labourer who was murdered by Hindu fascists when seeking work in a hostile anti-Muslim part of the city. Sen's life work was to think through human development whether in the Global North or the Global South. In a study comparing African American men to the people of Kerala in South India, he showed that, while African American men made more money in comparison, they were also more oppressed and had shorter life expectancies – largely due to the denial of opportunities. Keralites in general had better education, better jobs, less crime to worry about, longer life expectancies, and greater access to opportunities. Sen (1999) argues that African Americans lack freedom because of the structural inequalities blocking them from access to opportunities.

Indian women scholars have shown convincingly that self-help groups and mutual aid groups organized by women play a key role in equity and development (Agarwal 2020; Devika 2016; Christabell 2009). India has linked part of its Chit system to the country's formal banking system because citizens demanded this security and protection. A study by feminist economist Bina Agarwal (2020) shows the inner workings of class and caste bias in villages, and she reveals how Keralan women have sorted out these matters on their own terms. Mutual aid is prominent in their lives,

Figure 7.2. Ghana Cooperative Susu Collectors Association in Kaneshie, Accra

and has been for centuries. They are living proof that co-operative economics can exist side-by-side with individualized forms of capitalism. The state of Kerala has formalized Chit funds and tells the world that they are crucial forms of collective banking and should be regulated like any other financial institution.

In Ghana, Susu members also asked for a segment of their indigenous banks to receive some oversight and regulation by the Central Bank. In 2017, my colleague Samuel Kwaku Bonsu at the University of Ghana and I (2023) interviewed Susu members in several towns and markets in Accra, Tema, Kumasi, and Cape Coast. We learned that only a small fraction of the Susu system is regulated. The women whom we interviewed were pleased with this situation because it meant that the bulk of the Susu systems could remain informal, a status which was acceptable to the state. The Ghana Co-operative Susu Collectors Association is a national network that issues licences to individual Susu collectors (see figure 7.2). Offices are located around the country to facilitate the process for those seeking to formalize the Susu system.

In both India and Ghana, people have influenced public policy by asking that indigenous co-op systems become part of the modern economy. The Banker Ladies in the Americas are also trying to have ROSCAs recognized as a distinct form of co-operatives. This appeal is an important one to the formal co-operative system, which has generally ignored the ROSCA system. In 2022, the first-ever Banker Ladies Council was set up by a few women thinking through what it is they want. Often there is a tendency in society to tie the credibility of an institution to its possession of a formal status. However, ROSCAs are a distinct form of co-operativism that operate quite effectively in informal arenas because historically their users have been excluded from conventional systems. In the cases of India and Ghana, state officials have listened to the citizens of their countries, and so introduced pragmatic policies that recognize both formal and informal ROSCA systems as part of the financial ecosystem.

The ROSCA system, already acknowledged in other parts of the world, should similarly be considered part of the co-operative system in Canada, as well as other parts of the Global North. It is past time for South-North co-operation, with the Global South contributing its expertise in equitable co-operative banks. ROSCAs are co-op systems rooted in mutual aid. Conceived in the Global South, they have travelled as people travelled. These systems can help all people who feel excluded from formal systems – not just racially marginalized people.

3. Educate the Public on ROSCAs

The Banker Ladies do business from the ground up. Just because informal institutions do not stand out, it does not mean they are less relevant in the lives of minorities. Insights provided by *Take Back the Economy* (Gibson-Graham, Cameron, and Healy 2013) and exchanges on the Community Economies Research Network (CERN) listserv (which has hundreds of members globally) reveal that most of the world's transactions take place below the surface and are informal. Informal institutions are everywhere and deserve to be studied.

ROSCAs are tailored to the needs of those who participate in them. Scaling up activities, just for the sake of doing it, does not make sense. Schumacher's (1973) *Small Is Beautiful* exposed Western bias for growth. Schumacher (1973) gave a nod to theorizing from the Global South, examining Buddhist, Gandhian, and

Confucian economics, which emphasize the value of businesses that demonstrate caring and are considerate to living small. It is preposterous to think that for business to be meaningful, it must be large-scale. The Banker Ladies show that quite the reverse is true. So do Kerala self-help groups. Being big or small is not the relevant issue; rather, the focus should be on the work itself, and the needs of the people concerned (Christabell 2016; Gibson-Graham 1996; Thomas 1974). What matters is this: that people choose how to organize co-ops. The world-famous Mondragon Cooperative Corporation in the Basque region of Spain also demonstrates that going global can cause a co-operative to drift away from its mission of *putting people first*. ROSCAs are locally situated; the women who organize them are locally rooted.

The ROSCA system has become globalized with very little effort and without the goal of creating large conglomerates. Ordinary people move for new opportunities, and they bring these technologies with them as they settle. These groups are usually composed of people who know and trust each other. While some groups may have hundreds of members, it is typically established and long-standing members, people who already know and trust each other, who vouch for new members. ROSCAs are not perfect. They are not the magic bullet that will fix society's issues, but they do bring value to society by giving ordinary people a chance to organize financial goods in ways that makes them accessible to those who are marginalized (Annisette 2006; Rutherford 2000). The women who run ROSCAs need to be acknowledged as pioneers in co-operative finance.

Educating the public about the existence of ROSCAs is key to recognizing and promoting grassroots co-operative systems. The documentary *The Banker Ladies* (Mondesir 2021) was a first step in this direction. The intent is not to formalize these institutions but to recognize and see the value of what they bring. Authorities must be educated about the difference between illegal funds and those collected as a money pool by hard-working women whose only motivation is to help one another. ROSCAs are legitimate co-operative institutions, and harms meted against those who organize them – harms particularly felt by women operating them in the Canadian context – must stop. Hundreds of the Chief Banker Ladies, speaking on behalf of themselves and their thousands of members, state clearly and unequivocally that they are not terrorists, money launderers, or drug mules. Nor are ROSCAs pyramid schemes or gambling systems. More research funding must be directed at studying the financial exclusion of Black/African and racialized women – listening to what these women have to say and attending to how they develop alternatives to address business exclusion. With more knowledge about ROSCAs, Black women would not have to fear reprisals or arrest by police for being in a ROSCA.

4. Remunerate Black Women Co-operators

Both the critics and the cheerleaders of neo-liberal markets see the value of self-help. However, neither camp has recognized Black women to be co-operators. Black feminist political theory is missing from most economic and political science scholarship. In disciplines concerned about power, politics, and social provisioning, there is often no mention of Black feminist theory. Instead, European ideas are imposed on Black people's modes of economic solidarity and methods of organizing co-ops. The Banker Ladies pay no mind to the pressure to commercialize. They want to "just do co-operating" – their words, not mine – and do business with people they know and trust. However, their work takes a lot of effort and time, and these women are not paid for their vital contributions to community development.

The intent in this work is not to formalize these institutions, but to recognize and see the value of what they bring and to remunerate women co-operators for the work they do. Raising public awareness about ROSCAs will decrease fear of arrest and reprisal, and it will reduce the stigma currently endured by women co-operators. Public policymaking (not surveillance) can assist these women, so they do not feel the pressure to hide the needed contributions they do for society. At present, the Banker Ladies are not credited for the work they do, nor are they paid for their labour and time spent in building up civic engagement and making economic systems inclusive. Silencing and not citing the work they do for society and economy building is egregious and shameful.

We should be compensating the Banker Ladies for their efforts to address underdevelopment. These women are social entrepreneurs who care about community development.

Local elites in the Caribbean recognize the powerful impact ROSCAs have on the population – so much so that they have developed financial products that mimic these institutions. For example, Sogebank in Haiti has a "Mama Sol" product, while the Jamaican National Bank has piloted a Partner Plan to appeal to, and widen, their customer base. Local people know the difference, but they appreciate the fact that what they have been doing for centuries has penetrated conventional banking arenas. Why has this happened? As children, present-day bankers witnessed their own mothers doing Susus or Partner banks. In Haiti, many of the bankers whom I interviewed had mamas who used Sol to build a business or to send them to school. There is no shame in self-help through mutual aid groups. Mutual aid puts practical decision-making in the hands of regular people, so they can help one another on their own terms. Though certainly appreciated and valued, the Caribbean Banker Ladies are not remunerated for the social work they are doing.

The work of American historian Joshua Clarke Davis shows that, in the 1960s and 1970s, African American businesses were worker co-operatives focused on democratizing racial bias in the market. To describe them, he coins the term "activist entrepreneurs" (see also Wicks 2015). This concept of "activist entrepreneur" debunks the myth that only big firms like the Body Shop, Urban Outfitters, and Ben & Jerry's can bring business ethics into the marketplace. Small businesses run by African Americans did this work every day with a lot of risk. Dutch scholars Timo Korstenbroek and Peer Smets (2019), who have been writing about ROSCAs for years, recognize that it is "antagonistic organizers" like the Banker Ladies who push for social transformation.

The Banker Ladies work quietly without remuneration and are usually given no formal recognition for what they do. The Banker Ladies, who do not settle for second-class treatment, reorganize banking locally, relying on votes and consensus. The Banker Ladies are activist co-operators who regroup excluded people. They should be remunerated for this work, which brings such incredible value to society (Banks 2020). The Banker Ladies are carrying out a profound social good, addressing inequities in financial systems because governments, agencies receiving state subsidies, and private firms are racially biased against Black citizens and especially Black women.

In Canada and the Caribbean – both regions in which I have worked – programming around economic development is key to ensuring peace and stability in society. States use taxes to pay social services, non-profit organizations, and social enterprise firms to engage in economic development. These governments, particularly those advocating gender equality, should hire Banker Ladies as part of their development work. In June 2021, I spoke to two feminist gender equality experts, both white women, who were willing to learn more but were not sure into what pigeon-hole they could fit the Banker Ladies.[1] That experts have never heard of ROSCAs is part of the problem, demonstrating the need for cultural diversification among managers working on gender. The global development sector, the World Bank, USAID, UNDP, and Global Affairs Canada should also be thinking about hiring Banker Ladies to consult and advise on inclusive finance, especially in microfinance programs.

Building Up Civil Society

Women who organize ROSCAs are fostering unity among Black Canadian women. When I started preliminary interviews in Toronto, Canada, in 2013, I noticed that ROSCAs were tightly organized by culture. Jamaicans had their Partner, Somalis had Hagbad, and Nigerians had their Ajo. Only a few years later, this situation has changed. Now it is not uncommon to find a Sudanese woman join a Jamaican Partner or a Nigerian in a Trini-managed

---

1 Meeting with managers Suzanne Cooper and Gillian Moore of Women and Gender Equality (WAGES) at the Canadian federal government, 8 June 2021.

Susu. In Montreal, a woman called "Susan" shared that, at a hospital where she worked, a group of orderlies organized a Susu with a diverse membership, including white Canadians, Haitians, various Caribbeans, Africans, and Filipinas (focus group, 2016). Somali women told me that they join ROSCAs based on who can lead the group well and not based on religion or cultural identity (focus group, 2017). Black women are bringing Canadian women together through mutual aid and self-help. This work needs to be paid and recognized as a social benefit.

ROSCAs in the Americas have brought goodness to humanity. The Banker Ladies are making social finance reach those who are hard to reach. They can shift the mindset against ROSCAs among scholars and the public towards an understanding of the inner workings of ROSCAs as legitimate co-operatives rooted in self-help and mutual aid. African people have influenced the development of ROSCAs in the Caribbean and Canada because they have drawn on traditions to help one another. Black women in the social and solidarity economy turn to systems of self-help to uplift themselves and their communities.

Even as people decide to migrate from Africa and the Caribbean, they are thinking about remaking business. Black immigrants to Canada have brought ROSCA systems to myriad parts of the country as they resettled there. They have created special dynamics for welcoming and integrating others to join in these peer-to-peer lending systems. African-inspired socially conscious forms of mutual aid have long-dominated the lives of persons of African descent throughout the world. Often this work has been done out of necessity and has served as a form of comfort.

The Banker Ladies give excluded Afro-Caribbean people a safe place to lodge their savings. There is little dispute that identity and partisan politics trouble the region, and these interfere in business and society. Overcoming the negative aspects of partisanship and clientelism requires socially conscious activism. ROSCAs provide an alternative to an oppressive system. These banks contribute to strengthening civil society and people's voices. Policymakers should be concerned about the rights of ROSCA users, and how these systems bring value to the Canadian social economy.[2] This act of helping and caring – a two-way street and reciprocal in nature – is key to why the Banker Ladies are able to sustain the trust of ROSCA users. In a very deliberate and pragmatic way, by grouping themselves together, the women find a sure way to stifle the racism and bias they experience in business and society. Their way of using economic activity is quietly politicizing people to take notice of what is really going on.

Members of the African diaspora have ancestors who were used in brutal ways during the slave trade and to advance European capitalist development. As a result, they respond in deeply personal ways to any intent towards commercialization and profit, regardless of the stakes. African peoples, whether in Africa or in the diaspora, have found ways to cope and to co-opt the banking system, particularly through co-operation. This type of organizing has always been important to African (Mayoukou 1994) and Indigenous Peoples (Betasamosake Simpson 2020) – a system of mutual aid that puts people first. I carried out this study knowing that persons concerned about inequality among Black people need to scrutinize the people engaged in the social and solidarity economy who are claiming to help Black lives. The social and solidarity economy, and the motives of individuals who make a living within the third sector, are seldom questioned. The rhetoric coming out of the social and solidarity economy and the microfinance industry seems to come from good people; however, there is a need for them to check their privilege and have them own up to it.

5. Seeing Economic Difference to Mitigate Civil Forfeitures

In the Caribbean context, ROSCAs are clearly a champion of solidarity economics. This status is undisputed by elites and ordinary people alike. Caribbean ROSCAs are celebrated as impressive forms of self-help by most people in the region. They are neither hidden

---

2   It was Naila Kabeer's (2002) *The Power to Choose* which made me think about the need to consider the rights of the very women that elites want to help through labour standards. However, to get this right they need to consult the workers themselves, or these standards can actually hurt the women.

nor carried out in secret. The Caribbean Banker Ladies do not shy away from what they do. They talk freely about the many ways that ROSCAs help them live. This is not the story in Canada. Black people in Canada choose to perform mutual aid quietly (Hossein 2016d, 2017c). Seeking refuge in a ROSCA is a way of protecting themselves from those who denigrate them. As a result, there is no consensus among the Banker Ladies in Toronto and Montreal about whether or not to share what they do with the wider public. People fear the repercussions. In many cases, I was permitted access only if I promised to keep what they do private and not reveal "real names."

What the Banker Ladies in Canada want is to stop the confiscation of their financial goods, and they want to educate the public about ROSCAs and the value of economic solidarity and co-operatives. Making change and following J.K. Gibson-Graham's (1996, 2006) ideas on "economic difference" is really about helping each other through co-operation and gifting people you care about. In Ontario, sharing monies among each other is hard to do because of laws. For example, the *Civil Remedies Act* (Ontario 2001), a draconian set of laws that gives authorities the legal power to seize funds that are deemed to be earned in questionable ways. Toronto lawyer Justin Safayeni (2018) argues that this law on forfeiture is long overdue to be repealed by the legislature because of the harms it causes to some groups. Education and speaking about mutual aid financing are ways to limit the harms of this act.

In 2022, the Banker Ladies Council emerged as a group of ROSCA system users looking to stand up as engaged citizens to speak about the value of ROSCAs in Canadian society. This helped to advocate for a money pooling and gift system by people who know and trust each other, limiting the power of the *Civil Remedies Act* in some ways. The point of the Banker Ladies Council is to serve as an advocate and show that ROSCAs are about leading social and economic justice. If the society in which they live were to recognize the ROSCAs that they organize as beneficial to humankind, then they would not be demeaned for this work. Detractors who disregard their labour, or label ROSCA users as engaged in illegal and illicit activities, would have no basis for these claims.

Another point of the Council is for policymakers to value the Banker Ladies for their labours in community development, efforts that are reaching excluded people and building up civic life. These women should be paid for their economic development work. A doctoral student at the University of Toronto, hailing from the village of Nalerigu in northern Ghana, observed the first meeting of the Banker Ladies Council and published a short piece on the harms and lived experiences of these women, and why Susu (ROSCAs) help them cope and build bonds (Mutaru 2022).[3] Many of the Banker Ladies who depend on ROSCAs come as newcomers and live modestly. While they encounter financial inequalities, they also use the ROSCA system to repair the harms of gender and racial discrimination. If ROSCAs were to be seriously acknowledged, state leaders and those active in the non-profit and co-operative sectors would need to revise their own development programs to budget for funds to hire Banker Ladies to train staff in community-based banking.

The Banker Ladies of the African diaspora hold close their unique historical experiences of migration, enslavement, and colonialism. Their lived experience has shaped the way that low-income Black women organize financial goods. These women take the time – time away from their own families – to set up ROSCAs because they feel they must. They want business to be done co-operatively, humanely, and ethically. Their kind of engagement is brave given the environments in which they live, and the pressures imposed to individualize business. Through their practice of collectivity, the Banker Ladies are also assisting in writing new scripts for theory making in the field of feminist political economy – that is, Black and feminist, and mounted on the value of the co-operators themselves. It takes "collective courage" to do business this way, particularly in contexts where Black women are ignored and made to feel inferior. Despite all the traumas they bear, the Banker Ladies are activist co-operators who educate the public. They show us that the informal institutions have a place in our world worthy of studying. They have long known that reaching excluded people involves unsettling regularized, corporatized systems in favour of economic co-operation, something which can benefit all of humanity.

---

3 See the open-access story in the Grassroots Economic Organizing newsletter (Mutaru 2022).

Afterword

V. EUDINE BARRITEAU
Professor Emerita of Gender and Public Policy, University of the West Indies at Cave Hill, Barbados

As I read Caroline Shenaz Hossein's singular study of African and African-descended women in Canada and the Caribbean – combatting racism, generating financial resilience and constructing knowledge, reclaiming ancestral ways of knowing, and deploying these mutual aid, community-building practices to subvert social and economic exclusion – Audre Lorde's timeless theorizing on the power of the erotic comes foremost to mind. Lorde's epistemic construct of the erotic identified the life affirming character of women's activities when animated by a recognition and acceptance of the creative force within women which encompasses all dimensions of our existence: "When I speak of the erotic, then I speak of it as an assertion of the lifeforce of women; of that creative energy empowered, the knowledge and use of which we are now reclaiming in our language, our history, our dancing, our loving, our work, our lives" (1978, 55).

Hossein's path-breaking, painstaking, rigorous research constitutes a labour of love. It emanates from a profound respect for these exceptional women, these Banker Ladies who defied and rejected misconceived societal expectations and their attendant dismissals. Most of all, Hossein's sweeping interrogation of the literature on informal financial institutions, the distinctions between social and solidarity economy, the exposure of racist practices against Black women, the lacuna on Black feminist political economy, the stultified theorizing of economic development and its limitations in grasping the economic behaviour of Black women engineering social and economic well-being offers a brilliant example of scrupulous, thorough scholarship distilled, but not diluted, to reach an audience beyond the academy. Hossein speaks fearlessly to policymakers in state bureaucracies in Canada and development experts mining the "fields" of practice in the Global South, even as they built "great houses" of abstract theory while ignoring the situated knowledge of the women and groups they declare ostensibly that they are seeking to help.

In her research, motivated and sustained over a period of 15 years, Hossein states she is invested in achieving citational justice on behalf of the academic contributions by Black feminist political theorists that have been ignored. However, *The Banker Ladies* achieves and exceeds that goal. Ultimately Hossein's study initiates an expansive project of gender, racial, and epistemological justice in the academy and wider society. She demands a re-centring of Black women acting with agency to economically empower and socially care for each other in the face of multiple adversities, including overt racism, who continue to "engage in other activities in the name of joy" (9). She rejects the misconception of self-help as a coping mechanism, and with the Banker Ladies' own words, demonstrates that self-help is a liberating practice. Still, while Hossein prioritizes the experiences of Black or African-descended women in the Caribbean and Canada, she does not essentialize or deny the experiences and existence of other groups: "Ideas of the cooperation are long-standing and not unique to members of the African diaspora" (24).

Hossein is determined to harness the "life force" of the Banker Ladies even as she is careful not to glorify their creative energies in sustaining Rotating Savings and Credit Associations (ROSCAs) in Canada and the Caribbean. By juxtaposing her extensive experience with development work in Africa, Asia, and the Caribbean with statements from commercial and government bureaucrats – and most critically, the voices of the women initiating and successfully managing community-based informal banking networks – Hossein generates critical insights that neither policymakers, nor commercial bankers, nor theorists should ignore. She proves that economic actions and economic decisions are lived experiences. They are not abstract assumptions divorced from the multiple, competing, complex realities of daily life in often racist or economically hostile communities.

One of the telling contributions of Hossein's analysis is prioritizing and delineating the stark differences between the experiences of the Banker Ladies in Africa and the Caribbean, on one hand, and that of the Banker Ladies in Canada. In the Global South, the Banker Ladies can speak freely about their economic and social activities in and to promote ROSCAs. In Canada, they cannot and do not, "because they fear reprisals" (53). Hossein exposes the sharp contrast and demarcation between the public recognition the Banker Ladies in the Caribbean enjoy even without access to any form of state resources, and the public denigration, fear, and anti-Black racism and sexism experienced by their Canadian counterparts. This fear and hostility are compounded further for Black or African-descended Muslim women in Canada. The main criterion for the difference in the Global North and the Global South is cultural. Whether in state institutions or the formal commercial banking sector, in Africa and the Caribbean, senior state officials and commercial banking executives know the nation-building role historically and contemporaneously played by ROSCAs in their societies. Across the globe, these indomitable women are leading informal community-based banking networks on their own terms and creating social and economic well-being individually and communally. The conditions by which they are able to do so may differ, but as Audre Lorde has theorized, and Caroline Hossein has extensively documented, they refuse to accept powerlessness in their lives.

The Banker Ladies provides ground-breaking knowledge about a category of informal financial institutions that build bonds of social and financial solidarity for women – and their families and communities – located at the periphery of classist or racist social structures. The vital work these women undertake provides individuals with much needed financial capital, alleviates economic deprivation, and builds social cohesion in communities. I agree with the four recommendations Hossein provides and expect this monumental work to lead to a re-evaluation towards a full *valuing* of the worth of informal banking networks in Canada and other countries of the Global North.

At the conclusion of this remarkable and valuable study, it is evident that Caroline Shenaz Hossein is engaged with a far more extensive epistemological project. She is forcing a rethinking of how we conceptualize the creation of knowledge, who can be knowers, and validating ways of knowing that do not fit Euro-centric theoretical concerns. In Hossein's theorizing, the Banker Ladies' narrative becomes an epistemic vehicle for questioning and debunking how knowledge claims are made and what knowledge can be created when theorists respect and value the vantage point of indigeneity. Hossein centres and valorizes Indigenous systems of knowing and meaning making. She cautions development experts, commercial bankers, and policymakers to question what they think they know about the lives and livelihood of Black women with whom they have not conversed, and about the women's economic behaviour which they have not taken the time to investigate. This is very consequential work and worth the wait to have this knowledge added to university courses, academic literature, and policymaking frameworks. These fields for public and academic discourse span women and entrepreneurship, management studies, economic development studies, Black feminist theory, anti-racism in business and social practices, and feminist epistemology. Caroline Shenaz Hossein and the Banker Ladies network, whether they realize it or not, have listened to Audre Lorde – Black, feminist, lesbian, poet, activist, and theorist. They are in touch with Lorde's life-affirming definition of the erotic and are therefore less willing to accept powerlessness, "or those other supplied states of being which are not native to [them], such as resignation, despair, self-effacement, depression, self-denial" (1978, 55). As Hossein proclaims, besides the life-affirming economic contributions the Banker Ladies make, they are engaging in activities in the name of joy.

References

Field Work

Caribbean

Grenada

Interviews. 2013.

Guyana

Interviews. 2008. Georgetown, Guyana.
Interviews. 2010. Georgetown, Guyana.

Haiti

Focus groups. 9 October 2010. Bon Repos in Port-au-Prince.
Interviews. 2008.
Interview, local businessman. 2 October 2010. Port-au-Prince, Haiti.
Interviews. 2011.
Interviews. 2012.
Interviews. 2013.
Interviews. 2015.

Jamaica

Interviews. 2009.

Canada

Ontario

Banker Ladies Council, The. 2022. Bathurst Manor, Toronto.
Banker Ladies Council, The, meeting notes. 2022 and 2023.
Focus Group. 2015. Firgrove, Toronto.
Focus Group, 26 March 2015. Scarborough, Toronto.
Focus Group. 2015. Warden Woods, Toronto.
Focus Group. July 2017. Warden Woods, Toronto.
Focus Group and Meeting. 2017. Toronto.
Focus Group and Meeting. 2018. East End Toronto.
Focus Group with Somali women. 2016.
Focus Group with Somali women. 2017.
Focus Group with Somali women. June 2018. Toronto.
Interview, senior expert on debt. 15 February 2015.
Interview, Bryan Prince. 2016. Buxton National Historical Site and Museum,
    Buxton, Ontario.
Interviews. 2016. Rexdale, Toronto.
Interview, Munira Abukar, 3 November 2017.
Interview. November 2017.
Interviews. 2018. Rexdale, Toronto.

Quebec

Focus Group. 18 June 2016. Montreal.
Focus Groups. 2016. Little Burgundy and Côte-des-Neiges, Montreal.
Focus Group. 2017. Papineau and Saint-Michel, Montreal.
Focus Group. 16 June 2018.
Focus Groups and Interviews. 2016. Montreal.
Focus Groups and Interviews. 2017. Montreal.
Focus Groups and Interviews. 2018. Montreal.
Interview, community banking executive. 2016. Montreal
Interview, senior manager. August 2017. Chantier, Montreal.
Interview, businesswoman. 6 June 2018. Beaubien, Montreal.
RA (Research Assistant) Notes. August 2016.

Ethiopia

Focus Groups. October 2018. Bahir Dar.
Focus Group, male bajaj drivers. 27 October 2018.

Ghana

Focus Group. July 2017. Accra.
Focus Groups. 2017. Tema, Kumasi and Cape Coast.

India

Interviews and Meetings. 29 November 2018. Christabell, Trivandrum.
Interviews and Meetings. November 2018–January 2019. Kolkata and Kerala.

Publications, Media, Films, and Television

Actuniger (online paper, Niger). 2018. "Reki Djermakoye : DG Asusu S.A. : « Je reste et demeure la directrice générale malgré les chantages et menaces »." 19 March 2018. https://www.actuniger.com/societe/13909-reki-djermakoye-dg-asusu-s-a-je-reste-et-demeure-la-directrice-generale-malgre-les-chantages-et-menaces.html.

Agarwal, Bina. 2020. "A Tale of Two Experiments: Institutional Innovations in Women's Group Farming." *Canadian Journal of Development Studies* 41, no. 2 (April): 169–92. https://doi.org/10.1080/02255189.2020.1779673.

Agnew, Vijay. 1996. *Resisting Discrimination: Women from Asia, Africa, and the Caribbean and the Women's Movements in Canada.* Toronto: University of Toronto Press.

AGO (Art Gallery of Ontario). 2017. *Free Black North.* Exhibit, 22 September 2017, Toronto.

Alamenciak, Tim. 2014. "Banking While Black." *Toronto Star*, 10 December 2014. https://www.thestar.com/news/gta/banking-while-black-toronto-man-accuses-scotiabank-of-racial-profiling/article_ed047b23-d7fc-5add-b820-cb2880bdd982.html.

Alami, Ilias, and Vincent Guermond. 2023. "The Color of Money at the Financial Frontier." *Review of International Political Economy* 30, no. 3 (May): 1073–97. https://doi.org/10.1080/09692290.2022.2078857.

Alexander, Anne. 1997. *The Antigonish Movement: Moses Coady and Adult Education Today.* Toronto: Thompson Educational.

Aliber, Michael. 2002. *Informal Finance in the Informal Economy: Promoting Decent Work among the Working Poor.* Working Paper on the Informal Economy. Geneva: ILO.

Amin, Ash. 2009. *The Social Economy: International Perspectives on Economic Solidarity.* London: Zed Books.

Andaiye. 2020. *The Point Is to Change the World: Selected Writings of Andaiye.* Edited by Alissa D. Trotz. London: Pluto Press.

Annisette, Marcia. 2006. "People and Periods Untouched by Accounting History: Ancient Yoruba Practice." *Accounting History* 11, no. 4 (November): 399–417. https://doi.org/10.1177/1032373206068704.

Antrobus, Peggy. 2004. *The Global Women's Movement: Origins, Issues and Strategies.* London: Zed Books.

Appleby, Timothy, Josh Wingrove, and Kim Mackrael. 2012. "Somali-Canadian Shot Dead in Toronto Had Ties to Alberta Drug Trade." *Globe and Mail*, 25 June 2012. https://www.theglobeandmail.com/news/toronto/somali -canadian-shot-dead-in-toronto-had-ties-to-alberta-drug-trade /article4368785/.

Ardener, Shirley. 1964. "The Comparative Study of Rotating Credit Associations." *Journal of the Royal Anthropological Institute of Great Britain and Ireland* 94, no. 2 (July–December): 201–29. https://doi.org/10.2307 /2844382.

Ardener, Shirley, and Sandra Burman, eds. 1996. *Money-Go-Rounds: The Importance of Rotating Savings and Credit Associations for Women.* Oxford: Berg.

Aredo, Dejene. 2004. "Rotating Savings and Credit Associations: Characterization with Particular Reference to the Ethiopian Iqqub." *Savings and Development* 28, no. 2 (January): 179–200.

Aryeetey, Ernest, and Fritz Gockel. 1991. "Mobilizing Domestic Resources for Capital Formation in Ghana: The Role of Informal Financial Markets." AERC Research Paper no. 3, August. Nairobi: Initiative Publishers.

Asante, Molefi Kete. 1980. *Afrocentricity: The Theory of Social Change.* Buffalo: Amulefi.

– 2007. *An Afrocentric Manifesto: Toward an African Rennaissance.* Cambridge: Polity Press.

Ashe, Jeffrey. 2023. "Yunus Was Wrong: Savings, Not Credit, Is a Human Right." *Nextbillion*, 14 August 2023. https://nextbillion.net/yunus-was -wrong-savings-human-right-financial-inclusion-shift-focus/.

Ashe, Jeffrey, with Kyla Jagger Neilan. 2014. *In Their Own Hands: How Savings Groups Are Revolutionizing Development.* San Francisco: Berrett Koehler Publishing.

– n.d. *In Their Own Hands: How Savings Groups Are Revolutionizing Development* (website). Archived 23 August 2018 at the Wayback Machine. https://web .archive.org/web/20180823021126/https://intheirownhands.com/.

Astor, Maggie, Christina Caron, and Daniel Victor. 2017. "A Guide to the Charlottesville Aftermath." *New York Times*, 13 August 2017. https://

www.nytimes.com/2017/08/13/us/charlottesville-virginia-overview
.html?mcubz=0.

Aulakh, Raveena. 2012. "Toronto Somali Community's Cry: 'Our Kids Are Dying.'" *Toronto Star*, 21 September 2012. https://www.thestar.com /news/crime/toronto-somali-community-s-cry-our-kids-are-dying /article_1c316e46-c996-5adc-a73a-95f584acb1a9.html.

Austin, David. 2013. *Fear of a Nation: Race, Sex and Security in Sixties Montreal.* Toronto: Between the Lines.

Banks, Nina. 2005. "Black Women and Racial Advancement: The Economics of Sadie Tanner Mossell Alexander." *Review of Black Political Economy* 33, no. 1 (June): 9–24. https://doi.org/10.1007/s12114-005-1028-4.

– 2008. "The Black Worker, Economic Justice, and the Speeches of Sadie T.M. Alexander." *Review of Social Economy* 66, no. 2 (June): 139–61. https://doi .org/10.1080/00346760701335707.

– 2019. "Intersecting Inequalities: Race and the Invisibility of Black Women's Work." Opening Plenary Address, "Solidarities and Challenges at the Intersection of Inequalities," at the 28th International Feminist Economics Association (IAFFE) Annual Conference, Glasgow, Scotland, 27–29 June 2019.

– 2020. "Black Women in the United States and Unpaid Collective Work: Theorizing the Community as a Site of Production." *Review of Black Political Economy* 47, no. 4 (December): 343–62. https://doi.org/10.1177 /0034644620962811.

– 2021. *Democracy, Race, and Justice: The Speeches and Writing of Sadie T.M. Alexander.* New Haven, CT: Yale University Press.

Banks, Nicola, David Hulme, and Michael Edwards. 2015. "NGOs, States, and Donors Revisited: Still Too Close for Comfort?" *World Development* 66 (February): 707–18. https://doi.org/10.1016/j.worlddev.2014.09.028.

Baradaran, Mehrsa. 2015. *How the Other Half Banks: Exclusion, Exploitation, and the Threat to Democracy.* Cambridge, MA: Harvard University Press.

Barclay, Akira, Valaida Fullwood, and Tracey Webb. 2019. "The Sweetness of Giving Circles." *Nonprofit Quarterly*, 29 March 2019. https://www .nonprofitquarterly.org/the-sweetness-of-circles/.

Barker, Drucilla K., Suzanne Bergeron, and Susan Feiner. 2021. *Liberating Economics: Feminist Perspectives on Families, Work, and Globalization.* 2nd ed. Ann Arbor, MI: Michigan University Press.

Barrett, Paul. 2015. *Blackening Canada: Diaspora, Race, Multiculturalism.* Toronto: University of Toronto Press.

Barriteau, Eudine. 2003. "Theorizing the Shift from 'Woman' to 'Gender' in Caribbean Feminist Discourse: The Power Relations of Creating

Knowledge." In *Confronting Power, Theorizing Gender: Interdisciplinary Perspectives in the Caribbean*, edited by Eudine Barriteau, 27–45. Kingston: University of the West Indies Press.

Barton, Dominic, Dezso Horvath, and Matthias Kipping. 2016. *Re-imagining Capitalism: Building a Responsible Long-Term Model*. Toronto: Oxford University Press.

Barton, Paul Alfred. 2000. *Susu Economics: The History of Pan-African Trade, Commerce, Money and Wealth*. Part 1. First Book Library, self-published.

Baruah, Bipasha. 2010. "NGOs in Microfinance: Learning from the Past, Accepting Limitations, and Moving Forward." *Geography Compass* 2, no. 8 (August): 1–14. https://doi.org/10.1111/j.1749-8198.2010.00362.x.

Bascom, William R. 1952. "The Esusu: A Credit Institution of Yoruba." *Journal of the Royal Anthropological Institute of Great Britain and Ireland* 82, no. 1 (January–June): 63–9. https://doi.org/10.2307/2844040.

Basu, Amrita, ed. 2010. *Women's Movements in the Global Era: The Power of Local Feminisms*. Boulder: Westview.

Bateman, Milford. 2011. *Confronting Microfinance: Undermining Sustainable Development*. Sterling: Kumarian Press.

Begashaw, Girma. 1978. "The Economic Role of Traditional Savings and Credit Institutions in Ethiopia." *Savings and Development* 2, no. 4: 249–64.

Bekerie, Ayele. 2003. "Iquib and Idir: Socio-Economic Traditions of Ethiopians." *Tadias Online*. http://www.tadias.com/v1n6/OP_2_2003-1.html.

Benjamin, Akua L. 2003. "The Black/Jamaican Criminal: The Making of Ideology." PhD diss., University of Toronto, no. 305258209.

Bergan, Renée, and Mark Schuller, dirs. 2009. *Poto Mitan: Haitian Women, Pillars of the Global Economy*. New York: Tet Ansanm. Film, 50 min. http://www.potomitan.net/.

Berns-McGowan, Rima. 1999. *Muslims in the Diaspora: The Somali Communities of London and Toronto*. Toronto: University of Toronto Press.

Besson, Jean. 1996. "Women's Use of ROSCAs in the Caribbean: Reassessing the Literature." In Ardener and Burman 1996, 263–89.

Besteman, Catherine. 1999. *Unravelling Somalia: Race, Class, and the Legacy of Slavery*. Philadelphia: University of Pennsylvania Press.

Betasamosake Simpson, Leanne. 2020. *As We Have Always Done: Indigenous Freedom through Radical Resistance*. Minneapolis: University of Minnesota Press.

Bhatt, Ela. 2005. *We Are Poor but So Many: The Story of Self-Employed Women in India*. Oxford: Oxford University Press.

Birch, Kean, Mark Peacock, Richard Wellen, Caroline Shenaz Hossein, Sonya Scott, and Alberto Salazar. 2017. *Business and Society: A Critical Introduction*. London: Zed Books.

Black Social Economy. 2022. Produced by Kindea Lab. Posted 28 April 2022. YouTube video, 1:56. https://www.youtube.com/watch?v=8e2NRfEnoos.

Blackman, Margot. 2016. "Remembering Ms. Daisy Tonge: A True Community Woman." *Montreal Community Contact*. No issue number.

Blackman, Margot, and Stanley Brooks. 2002. "Su-su Anyone." *Montreal Community Contact*. No issue number.

Blaisdel, Bob, ed. 2004. *Selected Writings and Speeches of Marcus Garvey*. New York: Dover Books.

Bohn, Simone, and Patricia Kreiger Grossi. 2018. "The Quilombolas' Refuge in Brazil: The Social Economy, Communal Space and Shared Identity." In Hossein 2018b, 161–86.

Bollier, David. 2014. *Think Like a Commoner: A Short Introduction to the Life of the Commons*. Gabriola Island: New Society Publishers.

Bortei-Doku Aryeetey, Ellen, and Ernest Aryeetey. 1996. "Mobilizing Cash for Business: Women in Rotating Susu Savings Clubs in Ghana." In Ardener and Burman 1996, 77–94.

Bouchard, Marie J., ed. 2013. *Innvoation and the Social Economy: The Quebec Experience*. Toronto: University of Toronto Press.

Bouchard, Marie J., Paulo Cruz Filho, and Zerdani Tassadit. 2015. "Social Enterprise in Quebec: Understanding their 'Institutional Footprint.'" *Canadian Journal of Nonprofit and Social Economy Research* 6, no. 1 (Spring): 42–62. https://doi.org/10.22230/cjnser.2015v6n1a198.

Bouman, Frits J.A. 1977. "Indigenous Savings and Credit Societies in the Third World." *Savings and Development* 1, no. 4: 181–219. https://www.jstor.org/stable/25829637.

– 1995. "Rotating and Accumulating Savings and Credit Associations: A Development Perspective." *World Development* 23, no. 3 (March): 371–84. https://doi.org/10.1016/0305-750X(94)00141-K.

Boyce Davies, Carol. 2008. *Left of Marx: The Political Life of Communist Claudia Jones*. Durham: Duke University Press.

Brennan, Richard J. 2015. "Ontario to Invest $4M in Businesses with Social Conscience." *Toronto Star*, 19 February 2015. https://www.thestar.com/news/canada/ontario-to-invest-4m-in-businesses-with-social-conscience/article_f027596b-b17e-5fdb-aa01-1a3b73fdaa97.html.

Bridge, Simon, Brendan Murtagh, and Ken O'Neil. 2009. *Understanding the Social Economy and the Third Sector*. London: Palgrave Macmillan.

Brohman, John. 1995. "Universalism, Eurocentrism, and Ideological Bias in Development Studies: From Modernisation to Neoliberalism." *Third World Quarterly* 16, no. 1 (March): 121–40. https://doi.org/10.1080/713700447.

Buckland, Jerry. 2012. *Hard Choices: Financial Exclusion, Fringe Banks, and Poverty in Urban Canada*. Toronto: University of Toronto Press.

Buckland, Jerry, Chris Robinson, and Brenda Spotton-Visano. 2018. *Payday Lending in Canada in a Global Context: A Mature Industry with Chronic Challenges*. New York: Palgrave.

Bundles, A'Lelia. 2001. *On Her Own Ground: The Life and Times of Madam C.J. Walker*. New York: Washington Square Press.

Bykova, Alina. 2017. "Man Shot Dead in Etobicoke Days after Fatal Shooting in the Same Area." *Toronto Star*, 9 October 2017. https://www.thestar .com/news/crime/man-shot-dead-in-etobicoke-days-after-fatal-shooting -in-the-same-area/article_c9625921-82e7-5181-aa17-ecafb9e56eb2.html.

Campos Medina, Patricia, Erika Nava, and Sol Aramendi. 2023. "Tandas and Co-operativas: Understanding the Social Economy of Indigenous Mexican Immigrants Settled in Perth Amboy, New Jersey, and Staten Island, New York." In Hossein, Wright Austin, and Edmonds 2023, 90–107.

Canada. 2022. "Canada's *Emergency Act*." Justice Laws Website. Last modified 22 February 2022. https://www.canada.ca/en/department -justice/news/2022/02/canadas-emergencies-act.html.

Carruthers, Errlee. 1995. "Prosecuting Women for Welfare Fraud in Ontario: Implications for Equality." *Journal of Law & Society Policy* 11, no. 10 (January): 241–62. https://doi.org/10.60082/0829-3929.1102.

CBC News. 2017. "Father of Young Dixon Shooting Victim Says He Was Shot at Just Hours before Son's Funeral." *CBC News*, 13 October 2017. https:// www.cbc.ca/news/canada/toronto/dixon-zakariye-ali-family-shot -father-1.4354681.

Chantier de l'économie sociale. n.d. Home Page (website). Accessed 12 January 2024. https://chantier.qc.ca/.

Chazan, Naomi. 1994. "Engaging the State: Associational Life in Sub-Saharan Africa." In *State Power and Social Forces*, edited by Migdal, Joel Samuel, Atul Kohli, and Vivienne Shue, 255–92. Cambridge: Cambridge University Press.

Cherry, Myisha. 2021. *The Case for Rage: Why Anger Is Essential to Anti-Racist Struggle*. New York: Oxford University Press.

Cheru, Fantu. 2016. "Developing Countries and the Right to Development: A Retrospective and Prospective African View." *Third World Quarterly* 37, no. 7 (July): 1268–83. https://doi.org/10.1080/01436597.2016.1154439.

Chin, Falice. 2020. "Banking Barriers: How the Canadian Financial Sector Excludes Black Entrepreneurs, Stifling Innovation." *CBC Radio*, 31 October 2020. https://www.cbc.ca/radio/costofliving/banking-while -black-1.5780927.

Chiteji, Ngina S. 2002. "Promises Kept: Enforcement and the Role of Rotating Savings and Credit Associations in an Economy." *Journal of International Development* 14, no. 4 (May): 393–411. https://doi.org/10.1002/jid.847.

Christabell P.J. 2009. *Women Empowerment through Capacity Building: The Role of Microfinance.* New Delhi: Concept Publishing.

– 2013. "Social Innovation for Women Empowerment: *Kudumbashree* in Kerala." *Innovation and Development* 3, no. 1 (April): 139–40. https://doi.org/10.1080/2157930X.2013.764630.

– 2016. *Inclusive Growth through Social Capital Formation: Is Microfinance an Effective Tool for Targeting Women?* New Delhi: Concept Publishing.

Chua, Amy. 2003. *World on Fire: How Exporting Free Market Democracy Breeds Economic Hatred and Global Instability.* New York: Random House.

City of Toronto. n.d. "Toronto at a Glance." Population (July 2022) and 2016 Census. Accessed 22 February 2024. https://www.toronto.ca/city-government/data-research-maps/toronto-at-a-glance/.

Clealand, Danielle Pilar. 2017. *The Power of Race in Cuba: Racial Ideology and Black Consciousness during the Revolution.* New York: Oxford University Press.

Coates, Ta-Nehisi. 2015. *Between the World and Me.* New York: Random House.

Cohen, Jennifer. 2018. "What's 'Radical' about [Feminist] Radical Political Economy?" *Review of Radical Political Economies* 50, no. 4 (December): 716–26. https://doi.org/10.1177/0486613418789704.

Coleman, Nancy. 2020. "Why We're Capitalizing B." *New York Times*, 5 July 2020. https://www.nytimes.com/2020/07/05/insider/capitalized-black.html.

Collet, Bruce A. 2007. "Islam, National Identity and Public Secondary Education: Perspectives from the Somali Diaspora in Toronto, Canada." *Race Ethnicity and Education* 10, no. 2 (July): 131–53. https://doi.org/10.1080/13613320701330668.

Collier, Paul. 2000. *Economic Causes of Civil Conflict and Their Implications for Policy.* Washington, DC: World Bank.

Collins, Daryl, Jonathan Morduch, Stuart Rutherford, and Orlanda Ruthven. 2009. *Portfolios of the Poor: How the World's Poor Live on $2 a Day.* Princeton, NJ: Princeton University Press.

Colloque sur la Microfinance. 2010. Ministère de la Économie. Port-au-Prince, Haiti, 28–29 September 2010.

Combahee River Collective. 1977. "The Combahee River Collective Statement." https://www.blackpast.org/african-american-history/combahee-river-collective-statement-1977/.

Community Economies Collective. 2014. "Diverse Economies Iceberg." https://www.communityeconomies.org/resources/diverse-economies -iceberg.

"Cooperative, Mutual Aid and Solidarity Economies." 2021. Web conference, University of Kerala, 18 January 2021.

Conrad, Earl. 1943. Harriet Tubman. Mumbai: Associated Publishers Limited.

Copestake, James, Martin Greeley, Susan Johnson, Naila Kabeer, and Anton Simanowitz. 2005. *Money with a Mission: Microfinance and Poverty Reduction*. Vol. 1. Bradford: ITDG Publishing.

Cotter, Adam. 2022. "Experiences of Discrimination among the Black and Indigenous Populations in Canada, 2019." *Juristat*, 16 February 2022. Statistics Canada catalogue no. 85-002-X. https://www150.statcan.gc.ca /n1/pub/85-002-x/2022001/article/00002-eng.htm.

Cox, Oliver Cromwell. 1948. *Race, Caste, and Class*. New York: Monthly Review Press.

– 1959. *The Foundations of Capitalism*. New York: Philosophical Library.

– 1964. *Capitalism as a System*. New York: Monthly Review Press.

Curl, John. 2012. *For All the People: Uncovering the Hidden History of Co-operation, Co-operative Movements, and Communalism in America*. 2nd ed. Oakland: PM Press.

Das Gupta, Tania. 2007. "Immigrant Women's Activism: The Last Thirty Years." In *Race, Racialization, and Antiracism in Canada and Beyond*, edited by Genevieve Fuji Johnson and Randy Enomoto, 105–16. Toronto: University of Toronto Press.

Datta, Rekha. 2000. "On Their Own: Development Strategies of the Self- Employment Women's Association (SEWA) in India." *Development* 43, no. 4 (December): 51–5. https://doi.org/10.1057/palgrave.development .1110196.

Davies, Thomas. 2018. "Historical Development of NGOs." In *The Handbook on Research on NGOs*, edited by Aynsley Kellow and Hannah Murphy-Gregory, 15–34. Cheltenham, UK: Edwards Elgar.

Davis, Angela. 1983. *Women, Race, and Class*. New York: Vintage.

Davis, Joshua Clarke. 2017. *From Head Shops to Whole Foods: The Rise and Fall of Activist Entrepreneurs*. New York: Columbia University Press.

DeClerq, Katherine. 2014b. "Toronto Council Candidate's Election Sign Defaced with Words 'Go Back Home.'" *Toronto Star*, 12 October 2014. https://www.thestar.com/news/gta/city-hall/toronto-council -candidates-election-sign-defaced-with-words-go-back-home/article _e3229ff1-3537-5d24-9821-38e57f2f5d3f.html.

Develtere, Patrick. 1993. "Cooperative Movements in the Developing Countries. Old and New Orientations." *Annals of Public and Cooperative*

Economics 64, no. 2 (April): 179–208. https://doi.org/10.1111/j.1467-8292 .1993.tb01389.x.

Devika, J. 2016. "The 'Kudumbashree Woman and the Kerala Model Woman: Women and Politics in Contemporary Kerala." *Indian Journal of Gender Studies* 23, no. 3 (October): 393–414. https://doi.org/10.1177/0971521516656077.

Devika, J., and BinithaV. Thampi. 2007. "Between 'Empowerment' and 'Liberation': The Kudumbashree Initiative in Kerala." *Indian Journal of Gender Studies* 14, no. 1 (January): 33–60. https://doi.org/10.1177 /097152150601400103.

Dieng, Rama Salla, and Lyn Ossome. Forthcoming. "Feminist Political Economy, Land, and Decolonisation in Africa and the Global South." Chap. 5 in *Decolonize, Humanize*, edited by Kathyrn Toure, Roopal Thaker, and Rama Salla Dieng. Bamenda: Langaa.

Diop, Anta Cheikh. 1974. *The African Origin of Civilization: Myth or Reality.* New York: Lawrence Hill.

DISE Collective (The Diverse Solidarity Economies Collective). n.d. "The Diverse Solidarity Economies Collective." Accessed 12 January 2024. https://africanaeconomics.com/.

Dombroski, Kelly, and Stephen Healy. 2018. "Surviving Well Together." *Tui Motu* 223: 4–5. https://hail.to/tui-motu-interislands-magazine/article/643RuCs.

Drew, Benjamin. 1856. *The Refugee: or the Narratives of Fugitive Slaves in Canada.* Toronto: Ryerson University. https://pressbooks.library .torontomu.ca/therefugee/.

Du Bois, W.E.B. 1903. *The Souls of Black Folk.* Repr. Minneapolis: Filiquarian Publishing.

– 1907. *Economic Co-operation among Negro Americans.* Atlanta: Atlanta University Press.

– 1973. *The Education of Black People: Ten Critiques, 1906–1960,* edited by Herbert Aptheker. New York: Monthly Review Press, 1973.

Dunford, Christopher. 2009. "Credit Unions and Rural Banks Reaching Down and Out to the Rural Poor through Group-based Microfinance." *Enterprise Development and Microfinance* 20, no. 2 (June): 108–24. https:// doi.org/10.3362/1755-1986.2009.012.

Economist. 2016. "Most-Failed State: Twenty-Five Years of Chaos in the Horn of Africa." 10 September 2016. https://www.economist.com/news/middle-east -and-africa/21706522-twenty-five-years-chaos-horn-africa-most-failed-state.

Eikenberry, Angela M. 2009. *Giving Circles: Philanthropy, Voluntary Association, and Democracy.* Bloomington: Indiana University Press.

Elson, Diane. 1995. "Male Bias in Macro-economics: The Case of Structural Adjustment." In *Male Bias in the Development Process* , 2nd ed., edited by Diane Elson, 164–90. Manchester: Manchester University Press.

Elson, Peter R., Andres Gouldsborough, and Robert Jones. 2009. *Building Capital, Building Community: A Comparative Analysis of Access to Capital for Social Enterprises and Nonprofits in Ontario and Quebec*. Toronto: Social Economy Centre, University of Toronto.

Eltis, David, and David Richardson. 2010. *Atlas of the Transatlantic Slave Trade*. New Haven, CT: Yale University Press.

Emory University. n.d. *Slave Voyages*. Accessed 29 April 2021. https://www .slavevoyages.org/.

Escobar, Arturo. (1995) 2012. *Encountering Development: The Making and Unmaking of the Third World*. Princeton, NJ: Princeton University Press.

– 2020. *Pluriversal Politics: The Real and the Possible*. Durham: Duke University Press.

Fairbairn, Brett. 1994. *The Meaning of Rochdale: The Rochdale Pioneers and the Co-operative Principles*. Centre for the Study of Co-operatives. Regina: University of Saskatchewan.

Falola, Toyin. 1995. "Money and Informal Credit Institutions in Colonial Western Nigeria." In *Money Matters: Instability Values and Social Payments in the Modern History of West African Communities*, edited by Jane I. Guyer, 162–87. Portsmouth: Heinemann.

Farrakhan, Louis. 2019. *Back Where We Belong: Selected Speeches by Minister Louis Farrakhan*, edited by Yusuf Jah. Los Angeles: KingDo Media.

Fatton, Robert. 2002. *Haiti's Predatory Republic: The Unending Transition to Democracy*. Boulder, CO: Lynne Rienner.

– 2007. *The Roots of Haitian Despotism*. Boulder, CO: Lynne Rienner.

Federici, Silvia. 2019. *Re-enchanting the World: Feminism and the Politics of the Commons*. Oakland: PM Press.

Figart, Deborah M. 2014. "Underbanked and Overcharged: Creating Alternatives to Alternative Financial Service Providers." *Dollars & Sense*, 9–11.

Fontan, Jean-Marc, Pierre Hamel, Richard Morin, and Eric Shragge. 2009. "Community Organizations and Local Governance in a Metropolitan Region." *Urban Affairs Review* 44, no. 6 (July): 832–57. https://doi.org /10.1177/1078087408326901.

Forstater, Mathew. 2007. "From Civil Rights to Economic Security: Bayard Rustin and the African American Struggle for Full Employment, 1945–1978." *International Journal of Political Economy* 36, no. 3 (September): 63–74. https://doi.org/10.2753/IJP0891-1916360304.

Friedline, Terri. 2021. *Banking on a Revolution: Why Financial Technology Won't Save a Broken System*. New York: Oxford University Press.

Galabuzi, Grace-Edward. 2006. *Canada's Economic Apartheid: The Social Exclusion of Racialized Groups in the New Century*. Toronto: Canadian Scholars Press.

Gates, Henry Louis, Jr. 2017. *Africa's Great Civilization*. Directed by Virginia Quinn and Mark Bates. Television series, PBS, February 2017.

Geertz, Clifford. 1962. "The Rotating Credit Association: A Middle Rung in Development." *Economic Development and Cultural Change* 10, no. 3 (April): 241–63. https://doi.org/10.1086/449960.

Gentle, Eileen. 1989. *Before the Sunset*. Sainte-Anne-de-Bellevue, QC: Shoreline.

Ghebreslassie, Makda. 2017. "'We Bury a Lot of Youth': Somali-Canadian Community Cries Out for Action fter 2 Fatal Shootings." *CBC News*, 12 October 2017. https://www.cbc.ca/news/canada/toronto/shootings -dixon-islington-1.4351462.

Ghumman, Sonia, and Ann Marie Ryan. 2013. "Not Welcome Here: Discrimination towards Women Who Wear the Muslim Headscarf." *Human Relations* 66, no. 5 (May): 671–98. https://doi.org/10.1177 /0018726712469540.

Gibson-Graham, J.K. 1996. *The End of Capitalism (as We Knew It): A Feminist Critique of Political Economy*. Oxford: Blackwell Publishers.

– 2003. "Enabling Ethical Economies: Cooperativism and Class." *Critical Sociology* 29, no. 2 (March): 123–61. https://doi.org/10.1163/156916303769155788.

– 2006. *A Postcapitalist Politics*. Minneapolis: University of Minnesota Press.

Gibson-Graham, J.K., Jenny Cameron, and Stephen Healy. 2013. *Take Back the Economy: An Ethical Guide for Transforming Our Communities*. Minneapolis: University of Minnesota Press.

Gibson-Graham, J.K., and Kelly Dombroski, eds. 2020. *The Handbook of Diverse Economies*. Cheltenham, UK: Edward Elgar Press.

Gilmore, Scott. 2015. "Canada's Race Problem? It's Even Worse than America's." *Maclean's*, 22 January 2015. https://www.macleans.ca/news /canada/out-of-sight-out-of-mind-2.

Global News. 2017. "Somali Community Makes Public Plea for Help in Wake of Deadly Shooting in City's West-End." *Global News*, 12 October 2017. Video, 2:08. https://globalnews.ca/video/3799468/somali-community -makes-public-plea-for-help-in-wake-of-deadly-shooting-in-citys-west-end.

Global Tapestry of Alternatives. n.d. "Main Page: GTA." Accessed 13 January 2024. https://globaltapestryofalternatives.org/.

Gordon Nembhard, Jessica. 2014a. *Collective Courage: A History of African American Cooperative Economic Thought and Practice*. University Park: Penn State University Press.

– 2014b. "Cooperative Economics and Civil Rights." *The Laura Flanders Show*, 8 April 2014. YouTube video, 15:29. https://youtu.be/_TVIghQMkBg.

– 2020. "Racial Equity in Co-ops: 6 Key Challenges and How to Meet Them." *Nonprofit Quarterly*, 17 May 2022. https://nonprofitquarterly.org /racial-equity-in-co-ops-6-key-challenges-and-how-to-meet-them/.

– 2023. "Black Political Economy, Solidarity Economics, and Liberation: Toward an Economy of Caring and Abundance." *Review of Radical Political Economics* 55, no. 4 (December): 525–38. https://doi.org/10.1177/04866134231163216.

Grant, William, and Hugh Allen. 2002. "CARE's Mata Masu Dubara (Women on the Move) Program in Niger: Successful Financial Intermediation in the Rural Sahel." *Journal of Microfinance* 4, no. 2 (Fall): 189–216.

Gray, Obika. 2004. *Demeaned but Empowered: The Social Power of the Urban Poor in Jamaica*. Kingston: University of the West Indies Press.

Greaves, Elaine. n.d. "Board of Director." London Capital Credit Union. Accessed 14 January 2024. https://credit-union.coop/governance/.

Guinnane, Timothy W. 2001. "Cooperatives as Information Machines: German Rural Credit Cooperatives, 1883–1914." *Journal of Economic History* 61, no. 2 (June): 366–89. https://doi.org/10.1017/S0022050701028042.

Haiti. 1987. *Haitian Constitution*. https://pdba.georgetown.edu/Constitutions/Haiti/constitution1987en.pdf.

Hall, Marlie. 2011. "'Sou-sou': Black Immigrants Bring Savings Club Stateside." *The Grio*, 20 May 2011. https://thegrio.com/2011/05/20/sou-sou-black-immigrants-bring-savings-club-stateside/.

Hall, Stuart. 1992. "The West and the Rest: Discourse and Power." In *Formations of Modernity*, edited by Stuart Hall and Bram Gieben, 275–331. Cambridge: Polity Press.

Hall, Peter A., and David Soskice. 2001. *Varieties of Capitalism: The Institutional Foundations of Comparative Advantage*. Oxford: Oxford University Press.

Handa, Sudhanshu, and Kirton Claremont. 1999. "The Economies of Rotating Savings and Credit Associations: Evidence from the Jamaican 'Partner.'" *Journal of Development Economics* 60, no. 1 (October): 173–94. https://doi.org/10.1016/S0304-3878(99)00040-1.

Harewood, Cheryl. 2023. "Angela Alleyne's Meeting Turn with Food." *Nation News Barbados*, 5 March 2023.

Haritaworn, Jin, Ghaida Moussa, and Syrus Marcus Ware. 2018. *Marvellous Grounds*. Toronto: Between the Lines.

Haro, Lia, and Romand Coles. 2019. "Reimagining Fugitive Democracy and Transformative Sanctuary with Black Frontline Communities in the Underground Railroad." *Political Theory* 47, no. 5 (October): 646–73. https://doi.org/10.1177/0090591719828725.

Harriot, Michael. 2017. "For White People Who Compare Black Lives Matter to White Supremacy." *The Root*, 23 August 2017. https://www.theroot.com/for-white-people-who-compare-black-lives-matter-to-whit-1798349198.

Harrison, Faye V. 1988. "Women in Jamaica's Informal Economy: Insights from a Kingston Slum." *New West Indian Guide* 62, nos. 3–4: 103–28. https://doi.org/10.1163/13822373-90002040.

– 2008. *Outsider Within: Reworking Anthropology in the Global Age*. Urbana: University of Illinois Press.

Harriss, John. 2002. *Depoliticizing Development: The World Bank and Social Capital*. London: Anthem.

Hart, Keith, Jean-Louis Laville, and Antonio David Cattani. 2010. *The Human Economy*. Cambridge: Polity Press.

Harvey, David. 2007. "Neoliberalism as Creative Destruction." *The Annals of the American Academy of Political and Social Sciences* 610, no. 1 (March): 21–44. https://doi.org/10.1177/0002716206296780.

Haynes, Curtis, Jr. 2018. "From Philanthropic Black Capitalism to Socialism: Cooperativism in Du Bois's Economic Thought." *Socialism and Democracy* 32, no. 3 (September): 125–45. https://doi.org/10.1080/08854300.2018.15 62824.

Haynes, Curtis, Jr., and Jessica Gordon Nembhard. 1999. "Cooperative Economics: A Community Revitalization Strategy." *Review of Black Political Economy* 27, no. 1 (June): 47–71. https://doi.org/10.1007/s12114 -999-1004-5.

Heinel, Robert Debs, and Nancy Gordon Heinel. 2005. *Written in Blood: The Story of the Haitian People 1492–1995*. Expanded version by Michael Heinl. Laham: University Press of America.

Hembree, Michael F. 1991. "The Question of Begging: Fugitive Slave Relief in Canada, 1830-1865." *Civil War History* 37, no. 4 (December): 314–27. https://doi.org/10.1353/cwh.1991.0022.

Herskovits, Melville Jean, and Frances Shapiro Herskovits. 1947. *Trinidad Village*. New York: Knopf.

Hill, Robert A., and Barbara Bair. 1987. *Marcus Garvey: Life and Lessons*. A Centennial Companion to the Marcus Garvey and the Universal Negro Improvement Association Papers. Berkeley: University of California Press.

Hill Collins, Patricia. 2000a. *Black Feminist Thought: Knowledge, Consciousness, and the Politics of Empowerment*. 2nd ed. New York: Routledge.

– 2000b. "Gender, Black feminism and Black Political Economy." *Annals of the American Academy of Political and Social Science* 568, no. 1 (March): 41–53. https://doi.org/10.1177/000271620056800105.

Hooker, Juliet. 2009. *Race and the Politics of Solidarity*. New York: Oxford University Press.

hooks, bell. (1981) 2015. *Ain't I a Woman: Black Women and Feminism*. Repr. New York: Routledge.

– 1999. *All about Love: New visions*. New York: HarperCollins.

Hopkins, Gail. 2006. "Somali Community Organizations in London and Toronto: Collaboration and Effectiveness." *Journal of Refugee Studies* 19, no. 3 (September): 361–80. https://doi.org/10.1093/jrs/fel013.

Hossein, Caroline Shenaz. 2013. "The Black Social Economy: Perseverance of Banker Ladies in the Slums." *Annals of Public and Cooperative Economics* 84, no. 4 (December): 423–42. https://doi.org/10.1111/apce.12022.

– 2014a. "The Exclusion of Afro-Guyanese in Micro-Banking." *The European Review of Latin America and Caribbean Studies*, no. 96 (April): 75–98. https://doi.org/10.18352/erlacs.9468.

– 2014b. "Haiti's *caisses populaires*: Home-Grown Solutions to Bring Economic Democracy." *International Journal of Social Economics* 41, no. 1: 42–59. https://doi.org/10.1108/IJSE-10-2012-0165.

– 2014c. "The Politics of Resistance: Informal Banks in the Caribbean." *Review of Black Political Economy* 41, no. 1 (January): 85–100. https://doi.org/10.1007/s12114-013-9171-9.

– 2015. "Government-Owned Micro-Banking and Financial Exclusion: A Case Study of Small Business People in East Port of Spain, Trinidad and Tobago." *Canadian Journal for Latin American and Caribbean Studies* 40, no. 3 (September): 394–410. https://doi.org/10.1080/08263663.2015.1090707.

– 2016a. "'Big Man' Politics in the Social Economy: A Case Study of Microfinance in Kingston, Jamaica." *Review of Social Economy* 74, no. 2 (April): 148–71. https://doi.org/10.1080/00346764.2015.1067754.

– 2016b. "Money Pools in the Americas: The African Diaspora's Legacy in the Social Economy." *The Forum for Social Economics* 45, no. 4 (October): 309–28. https://doi.org/10.1080/07360932.2015.1114005.

– 2016c. *Politicized Microfinance: Money, Power, and Violence in the Black Americas*. Toronto: University of Toronto Press.

– 2016d. "A Trusted Ancient African Tradition of Savings." *Montreal Community Contact*, 25 July 2016. https://mtlcommunitycontact.com/a-trusted-ancient-african-tradition-of-savings/.

– 2017a. "A Black Perspective on Canada's Third Sector: Case Studies on Women Leaders in the Social Economy." *Journal of Canadian Studies* 51, no. 3 (Fall): 749–81. https://doi.org/10.3138/jcs.2017-0040.r2.

– 2017b. "A Case Study of the Influence of Garveyism on the African Diaspora." *Social Economic Studies Journal* 66, nos. 3–4 (September–December): 151–74.

– 2017c. "Fringe Banking in Canada: A Preliminary Study of the 'Banker Ladies' and Economic Collectives in Toronto's Inner Suburbs." *Canadian Journal of Nonprofit and Social Economy Research* 8, no. 1 (Spring): 32–43.

- 2018a. "Banking While Black: The Business of Exclusion." *The Conversation*, 7 May 2018. https://theconversation.com/banking-while-black-the -business-of-exclusion-94892.
-, ed. 2018b. *The Black Social Economy in the Americas: Exploring Diverse Community-Based Alternative Markets*. New York: Palgrave Macmillan.
- 2019. "A Black Epistemology for the Social and Solidarity Economy: The Black Social Economy." *Review of Black Political Economy* 46, no. 3 (September): 209–29. https://doi.org/10.1177/0034644619865266.
- 2020. "Rotating Savings and Credit Associations (ROSCAs): Mutual Aid Financing." Chap. 39 in Part V Finance in Gibson-Graham and Dombroski 2020, 354–61.
- 2021a. "Canada's Hidden Cooperative System: The Legacy of the Black Banker Ladies." Big Thinking Lecture by the Federation for the Humanities and the Social Sciences. *Federation HSS*, 9 March 2021. YouTube video, 1:00:05. https://www.youtube.com/watch?v=77fWTxqPORI.
- 2021b. "Much Gratitude to the Caribbean for Boxhand, Susu and Partner: We Now Have Humane Systems of Economic Cooperation." *Stabroek News*, 25 October 2021, within the column *In the Diaspora*, edited by Alissa D. Trotz. https://www.stabroeknews.com/2021/10/25/features /in-the-diaspora/much-gratitude-to-the-caribbean-for-boxhand-susu -and-partner-we-now-have-humane-systems-of-economic -cooperation/.
Hossein, Caroline Shenaz, and Kadasi Ceres. 2022. "Acknowledging Marxist Economist C.Y. Thomas's Legacy in Canada's Economic Development Sector." *Canadian Journal of Nonprofit and Social Economy Research* 13, no. 1 (September): 27–43. https://doi.org/10.29173/cjnser384.
Hossein, Caroline Shenaz, and Christabell P.J. 2022. *Community Economies in the Global South: Case Studies of Rotating Savings, Credit Associations, and Economic Cooperation*. Oxford: Oxford University Press.
Hossein, Caroline Shenaz, and Megan Pearson. 2023. "Black Feminists on the Third Sector: Here Is Why We Choose the Solidarity Economy." *Review of Black Political Economy* 50, no. 2 (June): 222–48. https://doi.org/10.1177 /00346446221132319.
Hossein, Caroline Shenaz, and Samuel Kwaku Bonsu. 2023. "Situating the Ancient West African Practice of Collectivity: A Study of Susu Institutions in Ghana's Cities." *Rethinking Marxism* 35, no. 1 (January): 108–34. https://doi.org/10.1080/08935696.2022.2159744.
Hossein, Caroline Shenaz, Sharon Wright Austin, and Kevin Edmonds, eds. 2023. *Beyond Racial Capitalism: Co-operatives in the African Diaspora*. Oxford: Oxford University Press.

Hudson, Peter J. 2017. *Bankers and Empire: How Wall Street Colonized the Caribbean*. Chicago: University of Chicago Press.

Hunter, Herbert. 2000. *The Sociology of Oliver C. Cox: New Perspectives*. Bingley: Emerald.

INCITE! 2017. *The Revolution Will Not be Funded! Beyond the Nonprofit Industrial Complex*. Durham: Duke University Press.

Izumida, Yoichi. 1992. "The Kou in Japan: A Precursor to Modern Finance." In *Informal Finance in Low-Income Countries*, edited by Dale W. Adams and Robert E. Hunter, 165–80. Boulder, CO: Westview Press.

Jain, L.C. 1929. *Indigenous Banking in India*. London: Macmillan.

James, Carl E., and Andrea Davis, ed. 2012. *Jamaica in the Canadian Experience: A Multiculturizing Presence*. Halifax: Fernwood.

James, Carl, David Este, Wanda Thomas Bernard, Akua Benjamin, Bethan Lloyd, and Tana Turner. 2010. *Race and Well-Being: The Lives, Hopes and Activism of African Canadians*. Halifax: Fernwood.

James, C.L.R. 1989. *The Black Jacobins: Toussaint L'Ouverture and the San Domingo Revolution*. 2nd ed. Rev. New York: Vintage.

Jeter, Clay, dir. 2023. *Live to 100: Secrets of the Blue Zones*. Television series, Netflix.

John, Tamanisha J. 2020. "Racialized Financial Exclusion in the Anglophone Caribbean." *Social Economic Studies* 69, nos. 3–4 (September–December): 225–51.

Jolly, Jasper. 2022. "Bank of England Owned 599 Slaves in 1770s, New Exhibit Reveals." *Guardian*, 15 April 2015. https://www.theguardian.com/world/2022/apr/15/bank-of-england-owned-599-slaves-in-1770s-new-exhibition-reveals.

Jones, Rupert. 2014. "Is Peer-to-Peer Lending Too Good to Be True?" *Guardian*, 15 February 2014. https://www.theguardian.com/money/2014/feb/15/peer-to-peer-lending-nicola-horlick.

Kabeer, Naila. 1994. *Reversed Realities: Gender Hierarchies in Development Thought*. London: Verso.

– 2002. *The Power to Choose: Bangladeshi Women and Labour Market Decisions in London and Dhaka*. London: Verso.

Kabeer, Naila, Ratna Sudarshan, and Kirsty Milward. 2013. *Organizing Women Workers in the Informal Economy: Beyond the Weapons of the Weak*. London: Zed Books.

K'adamwe, K'nife, Allan Bernard, and Edward Dixon. 2011."Marcus Garvey the Entrepreneur? Insights for Stimulating Entrepreneurship in Developing Nations." *76 King Street: Journal of Liberty Hall* 2: 37–59.

Karenga, Maulana. 1972. "Overturning Ourselves: From Mystification to Meaningful Struggle." *Black Scholar* 4, no. 2 (October): 6–14. https://doi.org/10.1080/00064246.1972.11431268.

- 1975. "In Love and Struggle: Toward a Greater Togetherness," *Black Scholar* 6, no. 6 (March): 16–28. https://doi.org/10.1080/00064246.1975.11431491.
- 1993. *Introduction to Black Studies*. 2nd ed. Los Angeles: University of Sankore Press.
- 1997. *Kawaida: A Communitarian African Philosophy*. Los Angeles: University of Sankore Press.

Katzin, Margaret Fisher. 1959. "The Jamaican Country Higgler." *Social and Economic Studies* 8, no. 4 (December): 421–40.

Keith, Nelson W., and Novella Z. Keith. 1992. *The Social Origins of Democratic Socialism in Jamaica*. Philadelphia: Temple University Press.

Kelley, Robin D.G. 2002. *Freedom Dreams: The Black Radical Imagination*. Boston: Beacon Press.

Kendi, Ibram X., and Keisha Blain, eds. 2021. *Four Hundred Souls*. New York: One World, an imprint of Random House.

Kerala (Government of India). n.d. "Kudumbashree." Accessed 19 January 2019. https://www.kudumbashree.org.

Kinyanjui, Mary Njeri. 2012. *Vyama: Institutions of Hope – Ordinary People's Market Coordination and Society Organizations*. Nairobi, Kenya: Nsemia.
- 2019. *African Markets and the Utu-Ubuntu Business Model: A Perspective on Economic Informality in Nairobi*. Cape Town: African Minds Publishers.

Klak, Thomas H., and Jeanne K. Hey. 1992. "Gender and State Bias in Jamaican Housing Programs." *World Development* 20, no. 2 (February): 213–27. https://doi.org/10.1016/0305-750X(92)90100-A.

Kleist, Nauja, and Masud S.I. Abdi. 2022. *Global Connections: Somali Diaspora Practices and their Effects*. n.p.: Rift Valley Institute. https://reliefweb.int /report/somalia/global-connections-somali-diaspora-practices-and -their-effects.

Koenane, Mojalefa Lehlohonolo. 2019. Economic Development in Africa through the Stokvel System: "Our" Indigenous Way or 'Theirs.'" *Filosofia Theoretica: Journal of African Philosophy, Culture and Religions* 8, no. 1 (May): 109–24. https://doi.org/10.4314/ft.v8i1.8.

Korstenbroek, Timo, and Peer Smets. 2019. "Developing the Potential for Change: Challenging Power through Social Entrepreneurship in the Netherlands." *Voluntas* 30, no. 3 (June): 475–86. https://doi.org/10.1007/s11266-019-00107-6.

Kovach, Margaret. 2005. "Emerging from the Margins: Indigenous Methodologies." In *Research as Resistance: Critical, Indigenous, and Anti-oppressive Approaches*, edited by Leslie Brown and Susan Strega, 19–37. Toronto: Canadian Scholars Press.

Krishna, Anirudh. 2002. *Active Social Capital: Tracing the Roots of Development and Democracy*. New York: Columbia University Press.

Kropotkin, Peter. (1902) 1976. *Mutual Aid: A Factor of Evolution*. Repr. Manchester: Extending Horizons Books.

Kusow, Abdi M. 1998. *Migration and Identity Processes among Somali Immigrants in Canada*. Detroit: Wayne State University Press.

– 2004. "Contesting Stigma: On Goffman's Assumptions of Normative Order." *Symbolic Interaction* 27, no. 2 (May): 179–97. https://doi.org/10.1525/si.2004.27.2.179.

Laforest, Rachel. 2009. *The New Federal Agenda and the Voluntary Sector*. Montreal: McGill-Queen's University Press.

Lehmann, Julie-Marthe, and Peer Smets. 2019. "An Innovative Resilience Approach: Financial Self-Help Groups in Contemporary Financial Landscapes in the Netherlands." *Economy and Space* 52, no. 5 (August): 898–915. https://doi.org/10.1177/0308518X19882946.

Lemmons, Kasi, dir. 2020. *Self-Made: Inspired by the Life of Madam C.J. Walker*. Produced by LeBron James, Maverick Carter, Janine Sherman Barrois, and Kasi Lemmons. Television mini-series, Netflix.

Lévesque, Benoît. 2013. "How the Social Economy Won Recognition in Quebec at the End of the Twentieth Century." In Bouchard 2013, 24–70.

Levin, Daniel. 1975. "Susu." *Caribbean Review* 7, no. 1 (January–March): 19–23.

Lewis, Ioan Myrddin. 2003. *A Modern History of the Somali: Nation and State in the Horn of Africa*. Athens: Ohio University Press.

Lewis, Rupert. 1987. *Marcus Garvey: Anti-colonial Champion*. Kent: Karia Press.

Light, Ivan. 1984. Immigrant and Ethnic Enterprise in North America. *Ethnic and Racial Studies* 7, no. 2 (April): 195–216. https://doi.org/10.1080/01419870.1984.9993441.

Lorde, Audre. 1984. *Sister Outsider*. New York: Crossing Press.

Low, Alaine. 1995. *A Bibliographic Survey of Rotating Savings and Credit Associations*. Oxford: Oxfam.

Loxley, John. 2008. *Doing Community Economic Development*. Halifax: Fernwood.

Luxton, Meg. 1980. *More than a Labour of Love: Three Generations of Women's Work in the Home*. Toronto: Women's Press.

Madibbo, Amal I. 2012. *Minority within a Minority: Black Francophone Immigrants and the Dynamics of Power and Resistance*. 1st ed. London: Routledge.

Maiorano, John, Laurie Mook, and Jack Quarter. 2017. "Is There a Credit Union Difference? Comparing Canadian Credit Union and Bank Branch Locations." *Canadian Journal of Nonprofit and Social Economy Research* 7, no. 2 (January): 40–56. https://doi.org/10.22230/cjnser.2016v7n2a236.

Maguire, Robert. 1997. "From Outsiders to Insiders: Grassroots Leadership and Political Change." In *Haiti Renewed: Political and Economic Prospects*, edited by Robert Maguire, 154–66. Washington: Brookings Institution.

Mama, Amina. 2005. "Feminism: Africa and African Diaspora." In *New Dictionary of the History of Ideas*, edited by Maryanne Cline Horowitz, vol. 2, 810–15. New York: Scribner.

Marable, Manning. (1983) 2015. *How Capitalism Underdeveloped Black America: Problems in Race, Political Economy, and Society*. Repr. Chicago: Haymarket Books.

Marano, Carla. 2010. "Rising Strongly and Rapidly: The Universal Negro Improvement Association in Canada, 1919–1940." *Canadian Historical Review* 91, no. 4 (June): 233–59. https://doi.org/10.3138/chr.91.2.233.

Martin, Tony. 1983. *Marcus Garvey, Hero: A First Biography*. Dover, MA: Majority.

Massaquoi, Notisha, and Njoki N. Wane. 2007. *Theorizing Empowerment: Canadian Perspectives on Black Feminist Thought*. Toronto: Inanna.

Maxwell, Joseph A. 2012. *Qualitative Research Design: An Interactive Approach*. New York: Sage.

Maynard, Edward S. 1996. "The Translocation of a West African Banking System: The Yoruba ESUSU Rotating Credit Association in the Anglophone Caribbean." *Dialectical Anthropology* 21, no. 1 (March): 99–107. https://doi.org/10.1007/BF00244379.

Mayoukou, Celestin. 1994. *Le systeme des Tontines en Afrique : Un systeme bancaire informel. Le case du Congo*. Paris: L'Harmattan.

Mbembe, Achille. 2001. *On the Postcolony*. Berkeley: University of California Press.

Mbembe, Achille. 2017. *Critique of Black Reason*. Durham: Duke University Press.

McInnis, Allen. 2016. "Quebec Must Do More to Fight Discrimination against Immigrants in Workplace: FTQ." *Montreal Gazette*, 28 January 2016. https://montrealgazette.com/news/quebec/quebec-must-do-more-to -fight-discrimination-against-immigrants-in-workplace-ftq.

McIsaac, Elizabeth, Lynne Toupin, and Stella Park. 2013. *Shaping the Future: Leadership in Ontario's Labour Force*. Toronto: Ontario Nonprofit Network and Mowat Centre for Policy Innovation. https://theonn.ca/wp-content /uploads/2011/06/ONN-Mowat-Shaping-the-Future-Final-Report .October2013.pdf.

McKittrick, Katherine. 2006. *Demonic Grounds Black Women and the Cartographies of Struggle*. Minneapolis: University of Minnesota Press.

McKnight, John, and Peter Block. 2012. *The Abundant Community: Awakening the Power of Families and Neighborhoods*. San Francisco: Berett-Koehler

McMurtry, J.J. 2010. *Living Economics: Canadian Perspectives on the Social Economy, Co-operatives, and Community Economic Development*. Toronto: Emond Montgomery.

Meeks, Brian. 2001. *Caribbean Revolutions and Revolutionary Theory: An Assessment of Cuba, Nicaragua, and Grenada*. Kingston: University of the West Indies Press.

Meier, August. 1975. "Toward a Reinterpretation of Booker T. Washington." *Journal of Southern History* 23, no. 2 (May): 220–7. https://doi.org/10.2307/2955315.

Mendell, Marguerite. 2009. "The Three Pillars of the Social Economy in Quebec." In *The Social Economy: Alternative Ways of Thinking about Capitalism and Welfare*, edited by Ash Amin, 176–209. London: Zed Books.

Mendell, Marguerite, and Beatrice Alain. 2015. "Enabling the Social and Solidarity Economy through the Co-construction of Public Policy." In Utting 2010, 166–82.

Mensah, Joseph. 2010. *Black Canadians: History, Experience, Social Conditions*. 2nd ed. Halifax: Fernwood.

Mensah, Joseph, and Chris J. Williams. 2015. "Seeing/Being Double: How African Immigrants in Canada Balance Their Ethno-racial and National Identities." *African and Black Diaspora: An International Journal* 8, no. 1 (January): 1–16. https://doi.org/10.1080/17528631.2014.986024.

Mequanent, Getachew. 1996. "The Role of Informal Organizations in Resettlement Adjustment Process: A Case Study of *Iqubs*, *Idirs*, and *Mahabers* in the Ethiopian Community in Toronto." *Refuge: Canada's Journal on Refugees* 15, no. 3 (April): 30–40. https://doi.org/10.25071/1920-7336.21195.

Michie, Jonathan, Joseph R. Blasi, and Carlo Borzaga. 2017. *The Oxford Handbook of Mutual, Co-operative and Co-owned Business*. Oxford: Oxford University Press.

Midgley, James. 1981. *Professional Imperialism: Social Work in the Third World*. London: Heinemann Educational Books.

Miller, Ethan. 2010. "Solidarity Economy: Key Concepts and Issues." In *Solidarity Economy I: Building Alternatives for People and Planet*, edited by Emily Kawano, Thomas Neal Masterson, and Jonathan Teller-Ellsberg, 25–41. Amherst, MA: Center for Popular Economics.

Mills, Sean. 2016. *A Place in the Sun: Haiti, Haitians and the Remaking of Quebec*. Montreal: McGill-Queen's University Press.

Mintz, Sidney. 1955. "The Jamaican Internal Marketing Pattern: Some Notes and Hypotheses." *Social and Economic Studies* 4, no. 1 (March): 95–103.

– 2010. *Three Ancient Colonies: Caribbean Themes and Variations*. Cambridge, MA: Harvard University Press.

Mitchell-Walthour, Gladys L. 2023. *The Politics of Survival: Black Women Social Welfare Beneficiaries in Brazil and the United States*. New York: Columbia University Press.

Mohamed, Farah. 2014. *Queen Araweelo*. Alexandria: Somalia Media Network.

Molefe, Motsamai. 2019. *An African Philosophy of Personhood, Morality, and Politics*. London: Palgrave Macmillan.

Mohanty, Chandra Talpade. 1991. "Under Western Eyes: Feminist Scholarship and Colonial Discourses." In *Third World Women and the Politics of Feminism*, edited by Chandra Talpade Mohanty, Ann Russo, and Lourdes Torres, 51–80. Bloomington: Indiana University Press.

Mondesir, Esery, dir. 2021. *The Banker Ladies*. Produced by Diverse Solidarities Economies Collective and Caroline Shenaz Hossein. Lawrence, KS: Films for Action. Film, 50 min. https://www.filmsforaction.org/watch/the-banker-ladies/.

Montasse, Emmanuel. 1983. *La gestion strategique dans le cadre du développement d'Haiti au moyen de la coopérative, caisse d'epargne et de credit*. Port-au-Prince: IAGHEI, UEH.

Monture, Patricia. 2010. "Race, Gender, and the University: Strategies for Survival." In *States of Race: Critical Race Feminism for the 21st Century*, edited by Sherene Razack, Malinda Smith, and Sunera Thobani, 23–37. Toronto: Between the Lines.

Morgan, Anthony. 2016. "Why Canada Needs Black Lives Matter." *Toronto Star*, 25 July 2016. https://www.thestar.com/opinion/contributors/why-canada-needs-black-lives-matter/article_8f20069a-d541-5e48-ba1a-2c21f3c826dc.html.

Mullings, Beverley. 2021. "Caliban, Social Reproduction and Our Future Yet to Come." *Geoforum* 118 (January): 150–8. https://doi.org/10.1016/j.geoforum.2020.11.007.

Munshani, Kalyani. 2005. *The Impact of Global International Informal Banking on Canada*. Toronto: Nathanson Centre for the Study of Organized Crime and Corruption.

Murphy, Peter, prod. 2009. *You Can Do It: The Story of the Antigonish Movement*. Antigonish, NS: Seabright Productions. Film, 72 min.

Mutaru, Amidu. 2022. "The Banker Ladies of Canada Organize Coops to Combat Exclusion." *Grassroots Economic Organizing Newsletter*, 22 August 2022. https://geo.coop/articles/how-ghana-susu-system-helps-african-diaspora.

Nasser, Shanifa. 2016. "Black and 'Scared': Torontonians Mourn, Call for Action after Somali Man's Death in Ottawa," *CBC News*, 6 August 2016. https://www.cbc.ca/news/canada/toronto/black-and-scared-torontonians-mourn-call-for-action-after-somali-man-s-death-in-ottawa-1.3710065.

The National. 2021. "Banking While Black." *CBC Television*, 29 April 2021.

Niamey Soir. 2019. "Madam Rekia Djermakoye toujours en ordre de bataille !" 19 June 2019. Archived 24 March 2023 at the Wayback Machine. https://

web.archive.org/web/20230324005244/https://www.niameysoir
.com/mme-rekia-djermakoye-toujours-en-ordre-de-bataille/.

Niger-Thomas, Margaret. 1996. "Women's Access to and the Control of Credit in Cameroon: The Mamfe Case." In Ardener and Burman 1996, 95–111.

Njie, Haddy. 2022. "Community Building and Ubuntu: Using Osusu in the Kangbeng-Kafoo Women's Group in The Gambia." In *Community Economies in the Global South: Case Studies of Rotating Savings, Credit Associations, and Economic Cooperation*, edited by Caroline Shenaz Hossein and Christabell P.J., 125–44. Oxford: Oxford University Press.

North, Peter. 2016. "Money Reform and the Eurozone Crisis: Panacea, Utopia or Grassroots Alternative?" *Cambridge Journal of Economics* 40, no. 5 (September): 1–5. https://doi.org/10.1093/cje/bew022.

Nussbaum, Barbara. 2003. "Ubuntu: Reflections of a South African on Our Common Humanity." *Reflections: the Society for Organizational Learning and the Massachusetts Institute of Technology* 4, no. 4 (February): 21–6.

Nyerere, Julius K. 1968. *Ujamaa: Essays on Socialism*. Oxford: Oxford University Press.

N'Zengou-Tayo, Marie-José. 1998. "Fanm Se Poto Mitan: Haitian Woman, the Pillar of Society." *Feminist Review: Rethinking Caribbean Difference* 59 (Summer): 118–42. https://doi.org/10.1080/014177898339497.

Obenga, Theophile. 1992. *Ancient Egypt and Black Africa*. London: Karnak House.

Obeng-Odoom, Franklin. 2020. *The Commons in an Age of Uncertainty: Decolonizing Nature, Economy, and Society*. Toronto: University of Toronto Press.

OCASI (Ontario Council of Agencies Serving Immigrants). 2016. *Somali Refugee Resettlement in Canada*. https://ocasi.org/sites/default/files /OCASI_Presentation_Somali_Resettlement_Metropolis_2016.pdf.

O'Connell, Sean. 2009. *Credit and Community: Working-Class Debt in the UK since 1880*. Oxford: Oxford University Press.

OECD. n.d. "Social Economy." Accessed 22 February 2022. https://www .oecd.org/employment/leed/social-economy.htm.

Ofari, Earl. 1970. *The Myth of Black Progress*. Cambridge: Cambridge University Press.

Ojo, Tokunbo. 2006. "Ethnic Print Media in the Multicultural Nation of Canada: A Case Study of the Black Newspaper in Montreal." *Journalism* 7, no. 3 (August): 343–61. https://doi.org/10.1177/1464884906065517.

Olson, Mancur. 1965. *The Logic of Collective Action*. Cambridge: Cambridge University Press.

Ontario. 2001. *Civil Remedies Act.* S.O. 2001, c. 28. https://www.ontario.ca /laws/statute/01r28.

Orr, Marion. 1999. *Black Social Capital: The Politics of School Reform in Baltimore, 1986–1998.* Lawrence: University Press of Kansas.

Ostrom, Elinor. 2009. *Governing the Commons: The Evolution of Institutions.* Cambridge: Cambridge University Press.

– 2012. "The Future of the Commons: Beyond Market Failure and Government Regulation." Memorial Lecture hosted by the Institute of Economic Affairs, 29 March 2012.

Oyěwùmí, Oyèrónkẹ́. 1997. *The Invention of Women Making an African Sense of Western Gender Discourses.* Minneapolis: University of Minnesota Press.

Pagliaro, Jennifer. 2014. "Toronto Community Grants Not Targeting the Most Challenged Areas." *Toronto Star,* 12 December 2014. https://www.thestar .com/news/gta/city-hall/toronto-community-grants-not-targeting-the -most-challenged-areas/article_faff3669-1c88-555f-bda4-a6459f268bf2.html.

Paradkar, Shree. 2020. "This Egyptian-Canadian Woman Went to Withdraw Her Own Money at RBC. What Happened Next Is the Subject of a Lawsuit against the Bank and Peel Police." *Toronto Star,* 6 February 2020. https:// www.thestar.com/news/gta/this-egyptian-canadian-woman-went-to -withdraw-her-own-money-at-rbc-what-happened-next/article_823aaf11 -f7c7-5ae2-a23b-ab2a05c08651.html.

Peck, Raoul. 2017. *I Am Not Your Negro: A Companion Edition to the Documentary Film Directed by Raoul.* New York: Vintage.

Peesker, Saira. 2018. "Feeling Excluded from Traditional Incubators, Entrepreneurs Create Their Own." *Globe and Mail,* 17 June 2018. https:// www.theglobeandmail.com/business/small-business/startups/article -feeling-excluded-from-traditional-incubators-entrepreneurs-create/#c -image-0.

Polanyi, Karl. 1944. *The Great Transformation: The Political and Economic Origins of Our Time.* Boston: Beacon Press.

"Politicized Microfinance." 2022. Produced by Kindea. Posted 28 April 2022. YouTube video, 1:50. https://www.youtube.com/watch?v=-wKcchQuhrM.

powell, john a. 2021. "Bridging or Breaking? The Stories We Tell Will Create the Future We Inhabit." *Nonprofit Quarterly,* 15 February 2021. https:// nonprofitquarterly.org/bridging-or-breaking-the-stories-we-tell-will -create-the-future-we-inhabit/.

Power, Marilyn. 2004. "Social Provisioning as a Starting Point for Feminist Economics." *Feminist Economics* 10, no. 3 (November): 3–19. https://doi .org/10.1080/1354570042000267608.

Prieto, Leon, Simone Phipps, Lilia Giugni, and Neil Stott. 2021. "Teaching (Cooperative) Business: The 'Bluefield Experiment' and the Future of Black Business Schools." *Academy of Management Learning & Education* 20, no. 3 (September): 320–41. https://doi.org/10.5465/amle.2020.0127.

Prince, Bryan. 2004. *I Came as a Stranger: The Underground Railroad*. Toronto: Tundra Books.

Quarter, Jack. 1992. *Canada's Social Economy: Co-operatives, Non-Profits, and Other Community Enterprises*. Toronto: James Lorimer.

– 2000. *Beyond the Bottom Line: Socially Innovative Business Owners*. West Port: Quorum Books.

Quarter, Jack, and Laurie Mook. 2010. "An Interactive View of the Social Economy." *Canadian Journal of Nonprofit and Social Economy Research* 1, no. 1 (December): 8–22. https://doi.org/10.22230/cjnser.2010v1n1a4.

Quarter, Jack, Laurie Mook, and Ann Armstrong. 2009. *Understanding the Social Economy: A Canadian Perspective*. Toronto: University of Toronto Press.

– 2018. *Understanding the Social Economy: A Canadian Perspective*. 2nd ed. Toronto: University of Toronto Press.

Quarter, Jack, Sherida Ryan, and Andrea Chan, eds. 2015. *Social Purpose Enterprises: Case Studies for Social Change*. Toronto: University of Toronto Press.

Radio-Canada. 2016. "Aussant revient au Québec pour diriger le Chantier de l'économie sociale." *Radio-Canada Info*, 14 July 2016. https://ici.radio-canada.ca/nouvelle/729740/aussant-chantier-economie-sociale-jean-martin.

Rankin, Katherine. 2001. "Governing Development: Neoliberalism, Microcredit and Rational Economic Women." *Economy and Society* 30, no. 1 (January): 18–37. https://doi.org/10.1080/03085140020019070.

Rapley, John. 2006. "The New Middle Ages." *Foreign Affairs* 85, no. 3 (May–June): 95–103. https://doi.org/10.2307/20031970.

Rebel Sky Media. 2018. *The Inclusive Economy: Stories of CED in Manitoba*. Produced by the Canadian Centre for Policy Alternatives Manitoba, Canadian Community Economic Development (CED) Network, and Manitoba Research Council. Directed by Brad Leitch. Documentary, 27:02. Available from the Canadian CED Network. 2018. *The Inclusive Economy: Stories of CED in Manitoba*. Facebook, 30 January 2018. https://www.facebook.com/CCEDNet/videos/the-inclusive-economy-stories-of-ced-in-manitoba/1943163802379950/.

Reddock, Rhoda. 1985. "Freedom Denied: Indian Women and Indentureship in Trinidad and Tobago, 1845–1917." *Political Weekly* 20, no. 43 (26 October): 79–87.

– 2006. "Reflections: Peggy Antrobus." *Development and Change* 37, no. 6 (November): 1365–77. https://doi.org/10.1111/j.1467-7660.2006.00532.x.

– 2007. "Gender Equality, Pan-Africanism and the Diaspora." *International Journal of African Renaissance Studies* 2, no. 2 (November): 255–67. https://doi.org/10.1080/18186870701751749.

– 2021. "Welcome to Paradise: Neoliberalism, Violence and the Social and Gender Crisis in the Caribbean." In *Decolonial Perspectives on Entangled Inequalities: Europe and the Caribbean*, edited by Encarnación Gutiérrez Rodríguez and Rhoda Reddock, 55–76. London: Anthem.

Reynolds, Graham. 2016. *Viola Desmond's Canada: A History of Blacks and Racial Segregation in the Promised Land*. Toronto: Fernwood.

Robinson, Cedric J. (1980) 2016. *The Terms of Order: Political Science and the Myth of Leadership*. Repr., with a foreword by Erica Edwards. Chapel Hill: University of North Carolina Press.

– 1983. *Black Marxism: The Making of the Black Radical Tradition*. 2nd ed. London: Zed Press.

Rodney, Walter. 1982. *How Europe Underdeveloped Africa*. Washington, DC: Howard University Press.

– 1996. *The Groundings with My Brothers*. London: Bogle L'Ouverture.

Rodríguez, Clelia O. 2018. *Decolonizing Academia: Poverty, Oppression and Pain*. Halifax: Fernwood.

Roelvink, Gerda, Kevin St. Martin, and J.K. Gibson-Graham. 2015. *Making Other Worlds Possible: Performing Diverse Economies*. Minneapolis: University of Minnesota Press.

Rothschild, Joyce. 2009. "Workers' Cooperatives and Social Enterprise: A Forgotten Route to Social Equity and Democracy." *American Behavoralist* 52, no. 7 (March): 1023–41. https://doi.org/10.1177/0002764208327673.

Roy, Ananya. 2010. *Poverty Capital: Microfinance and the Making of Development*. New York: Routledge.

Rutherford, Stuart. 2000. *The Poor and Their Money*. New Delhi: Oxford University Press.

Rumney, Emma. 2021. "Focus: Big Banks Target South Africa's Informal Saving Clubs' Cash." *Reuters*, 7 October 2021. https://www.reuters.com/world/africa/big-banks-target-south-africas-informal-saving-clubs-cash-2021-10-07/.

Ryan, Selwyn, and Lou Anne Barclay. 1992. *Sharks and Sardines: Blacks in Business in Trinidad and Tobago*. Culture and Entrepreneurship in the Caribbean. St. Augustine, Trinidad: Institute of Social Economic Research.

Safayeni, Justin. 2018. "Civil Forfeiture, an Uncivil Remedy: Ontario's Civil Remedies Act Is an Extraordinary and Draconian Piece of Legislation." *Law Times*, 12 February 2018. https://www.lawtimesnews.com/archive/civil-forfeiture-an-uncivil-remedy/262917.

Sandbrook, Richard, Marc Edelman, Patrick Heller, and Judith A. Teichman. 2007. *Social Democracy in the Global Periphery: Origins, Challenges, Prospects.* Cambridge: Cambridge University Press.

Sandford, Gregory, and Richard Vigilante. 1984. *Grenada: The Untold Story.* New York: Madison Books.

Schatz. Edward. 2009. *Political Ethnography: What Immersion Contributes to the Study of Power.* Chicago: University of Chicago Press.

Schumacher, E.F. 1973. *Small Is Beautiful: Economics as If People Mattered.* New York: Harper and Row.

Sen, Amartya K. 1999. *Development as Freedom.* New York: Knopf.

Sengupta, Rajdeep, and Craig P. Aubuchon. 2008. "The Microfinance Revolution: An Overview." *Federal Reserve Bank of St. Louis Review* 90, no. 1 (January–February): 9–30. https://doi.org/10.20955/r.90.9-30.

Sethi, Raj Mohini. 1996. "Women's ROSCAs in Contemporary Indian Society." In Ardener and Burman 1996, 163–79.

Sherwood, Harriet. 2023. "Windrush 'Pardner Hand' Savings Scheme Celebrated at the Bank of England Museum." *Guardian*, 16 June 2023. https://www.theguardian.com/uk-news/2023/jun/16/windrush-pardner-hand-saving-scheme-celebrated-at-bank-of-england-museum.

Shragge, Eric, and Jean-Marc Fontan. 2000. *Social Economy: International Debates and Perspectives.* Montreal: Black Rose Books.

Silva, Silvane. 2023. "A Site of Contestation for Black Life: The Study of Quilombolas in the State of São Paulo, Brazil." In Hossein, Wright Austin, and Edmonds 2013, 154–68.

Sives, Amanda. 2010. *Elections, Violence and the Democratic Process in Jamaica: 1994–2007.* Kingston: Ian Randle.

Smets, Peer. 2000. ROSCAs as a Source of Housing Finance for the Urban Poor: An Analysis of Self-Help Practices from Hyderabad, India. *Community Development Journal* 35, no. 1 (January): 16–30. https://doi.org/10.1093/cdj/35.1.16.

Smith, Christen Anne. 2016. "Towards a Black Feminist Model of Black Atlantic Liberation: Remembering Beatriz Nascimento." *Meridians: Feminisms, Race, Transnationalism* 14, no. 2 (September): 71–87. https://doi.org/10.2979/meridians.14.2.06.

Smith, Miriam. 2005. *Civil Society? Collective Actors in Canadians Political Life.* Peterborough, ON: Broadview Press.

Smith-Omomo, Julia. 2019. *African Indigenous Financial Institutions: The Case of Congo and Liberia.* New York: Palgrave.

Somali Canadian Association. n.d. "About Us." Accessed 14 January 2024. https://somalicanadian.com/about-us/.

Spade, Dean. 2020a. *Mutual Aid: Building Solidarity during this Crisis (and the Next)*. New York: Verso Books.

– 2020b. "Solidarity Not Charity: Mutual Aid for Mobilization and Survival." *Social Text* 38, no. 1 (142, March): 131–51. https://doi.org/10.1215/01642472 -7971139.

St. Pierre, Maurice. 1999. *Anatomy of Resistance: Anti-colonialism in Guyana 1823–1966*. London: Macmillan.

Statistics Canada. 2022a. "Census Profile, 2021 Census of Population." Released 9 February 2022; updated 15 November 2023. https://www12 .statcan.gc.ca/census-recensement/2021/dp-pd/prof/index.cfm?Lang=E.

Statistics Canada. 2022b. "More Than Half of Canada's Black Population Calls Ontario Home." 28 February 2022. https://www.statcan.gc.ca/o1 /en/plus/441-more-half-canadas-black-population-calls-ontario-home.

Steel, William F., and Ernest Aryeetey. 1994. "Informal Savings Collectors in Ghana: Can They Intermediate?" *Finance and Development* 31, no. 1 (March): 36–7.

Steele, Beverley. 2003. *Grenada: A History of Its People*. London: Macmillan.

Sterritt, Angela. 2020. "Indigenous Grandfather and 12-Year-Old Handcuffed in Front of a Vancouver Bank after Trying to Open a Bank Account." *CBC News*, 9 January 2020. https://www.cbc.ca/news/canada/british -columbia/indigenous-girl-grandfather-handcuffed-bank-1.5419519.

Stewart, Dianne M. 2007. "Collecting on Their Investments, One Woman at a Time: Economic Partnerships among Caribbean Immigrant Women in the United States." *International Journal of African Renaissance Studies* 2, no. 1 (July): 35–57. https://doi.org/10.1080/18186870701384244.

Stewart, James. 1984. "Building a Cooperative Economy: Lessons from the Black Experience." *Review of Social Economy* 42, no. 3 (December): 360–8. https://doi.org/10.1080/00346768400000031.

Stone, Carl. 1980. *Democracy and Clientelism in Jamaica*. New Brunswick, NJ: Transaction.

– 1986. *Class, State, and Democracy in Jamaica*. New York: Praeger.

Sullivan, Leon. 1969. *Build, Brother, Build: From Poverty to Economic Power*. Philadelphia: Macrae Smith.

Tadesse, Michael Emru. 2020. "The Black Social Economy in Germany: A Study of ROSCAs by Ethiopian Immigrants." Master's thesis, School of Social Work at Alice Salomon University of Applied Sciences, Berlin, Germany.

Tadesse, Michael Emru, and Esra Erdem. 2023. "Postcapitalist Imaginaries of Finance: A Diverse-Economies Perspective on Equubs within the Ethiopian Diaspora in Germany." *Rethinking Marxism* 35, no. 2 (April): 265–84. https://doi.org/10.1080/08935696.2023.2183694.

Tafari-Ama, Imani. 2006. *Blood, Bullets and Bodies: Sexual Politics below Jamaica's Poverty Line*. New York: Multi-Media Communications.

Táíwò, Olúfẹ́mi O. 2020a. "Being-in-the-Room Privilege: Elite Capture and Epistemic Deference." *The Philosopher* 108, no. 4. https://www.thephilosopher1923.org/essay-taiwo.

– 2020b. "Identity, Power, and Speech with Olúfẹ́mi Táíwò." Hosted by Daniel Denvir. *The Dig*, 5 December 2020. Podcast, audio, 1:47:31. https://www.thedigradio.com/podcast/identity-power-and-speech-with-olufemi-taiwo/.

Táíwò, Olúfẹ́mi, and Achille Mbembe. 2021. "Becoming Black: Coercive Power, the State, and Racism in a Time of Crisis." https://longreads.tni.org/stateofpower/becoming-black-coercive-power-the-state-and-racism-in-a-time-of-crisis.

Taylor, Keeanga-Yamahtta. 2016. *From #BlackLivesMatter to Black Liberation*. Chicago: Haymarket Books.

Tettey, Wisdom J., and Korbla P. Puplampu. 2005. *The African Diaspora in Canada: Negotiating Identity and Belonging*. Calgary: University of Calgary Press.

Thériault, Luc. 2012. "The Foundations of the Social Economy: Co-operatives, Non-profits and Other Social Enterprises." In *Social Economy: Communities, Economies and Solidarity in Atlantic Canada*, edited by Sonja Novkovic and Leslie Brown, 22–38. Cape Breton: Cape Breton University Press.

Thomas, Clive Y. 1974. *Dependency and Transformation: The Economics of the Transition to Socialism*. New York: Monthly Review Press.

– 1988. *The Poor and the Powerless: Economic Policy and Change in the Caribbean*. New York: New York University Press.

Tirfe, Mamo. 1999. *The Paradox of Africa's Poverty: The Role of Indigenous Knowledge, Traditional Practices and Local Institutions*. Lawrenceville: Red Sea Press.

Tilley, Lisa, and Robbie Shilliam. 2018. "Raced Markets: An Introduction." *New Political Economy* 23, no. 5 (September): 534–43. https://doi.org/10.1080/13563467.2017.1417366.

Trouillot, Michel-Rolph. (1995) 2015. *Silencing the Past: Power and the Production of History*. Repr. Boston: Beacon Press.

Ulysse, Gina A. 2007. *Downtown Ladies: Informal Commercial Importers, a Haitian Anthropologist and Self-Making in Jamaica*. Chicago: University of Chicago Press.

United Nations. 2011. "International Year for People of African Descent." https://www.un.org/en/events/iypad2011/.

Uttig, Peter, ed. 2010. *Social and Solidarity Economy: Beyond the Fringe?* London: Zed Press.

Van Dam, Andrew. 2023. "Paper Checks Are Dead. Cash Is Dying. Who
    Still Uses Them?" *Washington Post*, 18 September 2023. https://www
    .washingtonpost.com/business/2023/09/15/paper-checks-who-uses/.
Van den Brink, Rogier, and Jean-Paul Chavas. 1997. "The Microeconomics
    of an Indigenous African Institution: The Rotating Savings and Credit
    Association." *Economic Development and Cultural Change* 45, no. 4 (July):
    745–72. https://doi.org/10.1086/452306.
Van Staveren, Irene. 2015. *Economics after the Crisis: An Introduction to
    Economics from a Pluralist and Global Perspective.* New York: Routledge.
Vélez-Ibáñez, Carlos G. 1983. *Bonds of Mutual Trust: The Cultural Systems
    of Rotating Credit Associations among Urban Mexicans and Chicanos.* New
    Brunswick: Rutgers University Press.
Wahid, Wahid A.N. 1994. "The Grameen Bank and Poverty Alleviation
    in Bangladesh: Theory, Evidence and Limitations." *American Journal of
    Economics and Sociology* 53, no. 1 (January): 1–15. https://doi.org
    /10.1111/j.1536-7150.1994.tb02666.x.
Walcott, Rinaldo and Idil Abdillahi. 2019. *BlackLife: Post-BLM and the Struggle
    for Freedom.* Winnipeg: ARP Books.
Walker, Barrington. 2012. "Jamaicans: The Making of Modern Canada." In
    James and Davis 2012, 23–34.
Wall Kimmerer, Robin. 2015. *Braiding Sweetgrass: Indigenous Wisdom, Scientific
    Knowledge and Teachings of Plants.* Minneapolis: Milkweed Editions.
Wallerstein, Immanuel. 2000. "Oliver C. Cox as World Systems Analyst." In
    The Sociology of Oliver C. Cox: New Perspectives, edited by Herbert Hunter,
    173–83. Bingley: Emerald.
Washington, Booker T. (1901) 2013. *Up from Slavery: An Autobiography.*
    Reprint. New Delhi: Ratna Sagar Press.
Waters, William. 1988. "Social Economics: A Solidarist Perspective," *Review
    of Social Economy* 46, no. 2 (October): 113–43. https://doi.org/10.1080
    /00346768800000024.
Whitehead, Colson. 2016. *The Underground Railroad.* New York: Doubleday.
Wicks, Judy. 2015. "What Is an Activist Entrepreneur? An Interview with
    Judy Wicks." *The Laura Flanders Show*, 17 February 2015. Video, 25:40.
    https://www.geo.coop/story/what-activist-entrepreneur.
Wilkerson, Isabel. 2011. *The Warmth of Other Suns: The Epic Story of America's
    Great Migration.* New York: Vintage Books.
Williams, Eric. (1944) 2004. *Capitalism & Slavery.* Repr. Chapel Hill:
    University of North Carolina Press.
Williams, Richard C. 2007. *The Cooperative Movement: Globalization from Below.*
    Hampshire: Ashgate.

Willms, Luke, dir. 2023. *"Unbankable –* Official Teaser." Posted 23 November 2023. YouTube video, 1:39. https://www.youtube.com/watch?v=FFo5gJJuM6E.

Willoughby-Herard, Tiffany. 2015. *Waste of a White Skin: The Carnegie Corporation and the Racial Logic of White Vulnerability.* Oakland: University of California Press.

Wilson, Kalpana. 2012. *Race, Racism and Development: Interrogating History, Discourse and Practice.* London: Routledge.

Wilson, Kim. 2002. "The New Microfinance: An Essay on the Self-Help Group Movement in India." *Journal of Microfinance* 4, no. 2 (Fall): 217–45.

Winfield Fretz, Joseph. (1947) 2020. *Christian Mutual Aid: A Handbook of Brotherhood Economics.* Repr. Eugene: Wipf and Stock.

Wingrove, Josh, and Kim Mackrael. 2012. "Why So Many Somali-Canadians Who Go West End Up Dead." *Globe and Mail,* 22 June 2012. https://www.theglobeandmail.com/news/national/why-so-many-somali-canadians-who-go-west-end-up-dead/article4365992/.

Winks, Robin. 1997. *The Blacks in Canada: A History.* Montreal: McGill-Queen's University Press.

Witter, Michael. 1989. "Higglering/Sidewalk Vending Informal Commercial Trading in Jamaican Economy." Department of Economics occasional paper series no. 4 (June). UWI-Mona.

Wong, David C. 1996. "A Theory of Petty Trading: The Jamaican Higgler." *Economic Journal* 106, no. 435 (March): 507–18. https://doi.org/10.2307/2235264.

The World Bank. 2021. "The Global Findex Database 2021: Financial Inclusion, Digital Payments, and Resilience in the Age of COVID-19." https://www.worldbank.org/en/publication/globalfindex.

Wright Austin, Sharon D. 2007. *The Transformation of Plantation Politics: Black Politics, Concentrated Poverty, and Social Capital in the Mississippi Delta.* Albany: State University of New York Press.

– 2018. *The Caribbeanization of Black Politics: Race, Group Consciousness and Political Participation in America.* Albany: State University of New York Press.

– 2023. "The Black Social Economy and the Social and Solidarity Economy." *Encyclopedia of the Social and Solidarity Economy: A Collective Work of the United Nations Inter-Agency Task Force on SSE (UNTFSSE),* edited by Ilcheong Yi, with Peter Utting, Jean-Louis Laville, Barbara Sak, Caroline Shenaz Hossein, Sifa Chiyoge, Cecilia Navarra, Denison Jayasooria, Fernanda Wanderley, Jacques Defourny, and Rocio Nogales-Muriel, 92–6. Cheltenham, UK: Edward Elgar in partnership with United Nations

Institute for Social Development (UNISD). https://www.e-elgar.com
/shop/gbp/encyclopedia-of-the-social-and-solidarity
-economy-9781803920917.html.

Yee, Shirley J. 1994. "Gender Ideology and Black Women as Community-
Builders in Ontario, 1850–70." *Canadian Historical Review* 75, no. 1
(March): 53–73. https://doi.org/10.3138/CHR-075-01-03.

Yunus, Muhammad. 2007. *Banker to the Poor: Micro-Lending and the Battle
against World Poverty*. New York: Public Affairs.

– 2010. *Building Social Businesses: The New Kind of Capitalism That Serves
Humanity's Most Pressing Needs*. New York: Public Affairs.

Zimonjic, Peter. 2022. "Most Bank Accounts Frozen under the Emergencies
Act Are Being Released, Committee Hears." *CBC News*, 22 February 2022.
https://www.cbc.ca/news/politics/emergency-bank-measures-finance
-committee-1.6360769.

Index

Notes: The letter *f* following a page number denotes a figure and the letter *t*, a table.

About the Author

Photo by Wade Hudson, 2022.

Dr. Caroline Shenaz Hossein is Associate Professor of Global Development and Political Economy at the University of Toronto Scarborough with a cross-appointment to the graduate programme of Political Science. She holds a Canada Research Chair of Africana Development and Feminist Political Economy (Tier 2) and holds an Ontario Early Researcher Award (2018–25). She is author of the multi-prize winning *Politicized Microfinance: Money, Power, and Violence in the Black Americas* (University of Toronto Press, 2016), co-author of *Business and Society: A Critical Introduction* (Zed Books, 2017), editor of *The Black Social Economy in the Americas: Exploring Diverse Community-Based Alternative Markets* (Palgrave Macmillan, 2018), and co-editor of both *Community Economies in the Global South* (Oxford University Press, 2022) and *Beyond Racial Capitalism: Co-operatives in the African Diaspora* (Oxford University Press, 2023). Her work has been funded by the Social Sciences and Humanities Research Council of Canada (2017–20). Prior to becoming an academic, she worked for nine years with several global non-profits and spent eight years as a self-employed consultant. She holds a PhD in Political Science (University of Toronto), an MPA (Cornell University), LL.B (University of Kent at Canterbury) and BA (Saint Mary's University, Halifax). She has held Visiting Professorships at the University of West Indies-Mona, Jamaica (Fulbright), Institute of Development Studies at the University of Guyana, Polanyi Institute for Political Economy, Concordia University, Bahir Dar University, Ethiopia and Jadavpur University, India and a Fellowship with the Post-growth Institute. Her passion is her work in the Diverse Solidarity Economies (DISE) Collective at https://africanaeconomics.com and Twitter @carolinehossein.